A TIME FOR CHOOSING

A TIME FOR CHOOSING
THE SPEECHES OF
RONALD REAGAN
1961—1982

Regnery Gateway
Chicago
In cooperation with
Americans for the Reagan Agenda

Americans for the Reagan Agenda is a national grass-roots organization that supports the main themes of the Reagan Presidency.

Published by Regnery Gateway, Inc.
360 West Superior Street
Chicago, IL 60610-0890

Cataloging in Publication Data
(will be supplied later)

ISBN: 0-89526-622-9

Manufactured in the United States of America.

1. United States — Politics and government — 1945- — Addresses, essays, lectures. 2. Conservatism — United States — Addresses, essays, lectures. 3. California — Politics and government — 1951- — Addresses, essays, lectures. I. Baltizer, Alfred A. 1941- . II. Bonetto, Gerald M., 1943- . III. Title.
E838.5.R435 1983 973.92 83-42905
ISBN 0-89526-622-9

For almost two centuries we have proved man's capacity for self-government, but today we are told we must choose between left and right, or, as others suggest, a third alternative, a kind of safe middle ground.

I suggest to you there is no left or right, only an up or down. Up to the maximum of individual freedom consistent with law and order, or down to the ant heap of totalitarianism, and regardless of their humanitarian purpose, those who would sacrifice freedom for security have, whether they know it or not, chosen this downward path. . . .

Ronald Reagan
A Time for Choosing
October 27, 1964

CONTENTS

ACKNOWLEDGMENTS

I wish to thank Dr. Gerald M. Bonetto who worked diligently at the Hoover Institute and elsewhere combing through the thousands of pages that comprise the President's speeches and in easing my task. The selection of speeches, however, are mine alone, and does not reflect the choice of either the President or anyone else in the Administration. In addition, Dr. Bonetto and I have exercised limited editorial review, principally providing punctuation for purposes of clarity in reading. We have also provided titles for untitled speeches and a subtitle for each speech to indicate its specific subject matter.

I should like to thank Mrs. Molly Sturgis Tuthill, Reagan archivist at the Hoover Institute, who skillfully guided Dr. Bonetto through the many volumes of Mr. Reagan's gubernatorial papers. Thanks also go to Mr. Robert Walker of Adolph Coors Company who, initially, suggested to me the need for a volume of the President's speeches, and, then, introduced me to Mr. Douglas Hofmeister, Vice President and publisher of Regnery Gateway Press. Mr. Hoffmeister, in turn, has been extremely helpful at all stages of the production of this book; I owe him special thanks.

A separate work must be said about Mr. Donald F. Sammis, Chairman of Americans for the Reagan Agenda. As an entrepreneur and private citizen, he has indefatigably thrown himself into support of the Reagan Agenda. His personal commitment to political and economic freedom and to the twin ethics of self-reliance and voluntary community service has served as the inspiration for this volume and for the overall objectives of Americans for the Reagan Agenda. In a broader sense, his commitment to the Reagan Agenda challenges those who come into contact with him to support personal initiative, and to exercise the freedom from which this initiative is born, to meet the needs of the American people.

A word is also needed to thank the staff of Americans for the Reagan Agenda. They were greatly responsible for the publication of this book. Gary Van Buskirk was in charge of the creative production, and Daniel Addison, Daniel Cathcart, and Benjamin Waldman contributed many useful suggestions.

Finally, I owe special thanks to the following individuals: Houston M. Burnside, Jr., Priscilla Damon Fawcett, Larry Field, Marcia Wilson Hobbs, Jaquelin H. Hume, William Lowenberg, Dr. Stanley Margulies, Henry Miller, Jerry Oren, John Pritzlaff, Edward Ray, Frank and Martha Stella, W. Clement Stone, J.A. Sullivan, Julian Virtue, Dean A. Watkins, Frank Whetstone, and The Republican National Committee. Without their generous support, this project would not have been possible.

Alfred Balitzer
Americans for the Reagan
Agenda

PREFACE

Ever since Ronald Reagan entered upon the stage of American politics, he has been a source of both inspiration and controversy. His detractors frequently refer to him as ultra-conservative, right-wing, ideological, or extremist. The American people, however, seem not to view him in this way. They have elected him to every office he has sought. Moreover, public opinion has steadily moved in the direction of Mr. Reagan's political philosophy—a movement that has much to do with his own public rhetoric. He has not had to sell the American people on the principles for which he stands. They already subscribed to them. What he has done is to articulate what they "feel in their bones." Like them, he is concerned with personal freedom and a better life, and with recovering the fundamental principles upon which these rights are founded. Thus, contrary to his critics' charges, the President's political philosophy rests near the center of American public opinion.

Mr. Reagan's political philosophy is not reactionary. It is based on principle that has been tempered by the experience of governing. Accordingly, he has been consistently innovative in his approach to social and political problems. For example, he is often said to be on the wrong side of women's issues. But, as Governor of California, long before there was a strong women's movement in the United States, he spearheaded reforms that provided rights for women that did not exist in other states. He initiated or supported fifteen major changes for greater equality for women in such areas as employment, credit and insurance eligibility, property rights, security purchases, divorce settlements, job security during pregnancy, and rape victims' rights. He also made California a model of environmental concern with the Clear Water (1969) and Clean Air (1970) Acts long before there was an environmental movement. As with so many other movements in our time, the reforms Mr. Reagan brought about in California spread eastward, influencing the rest of the nation.

Mr. Reagan's early advocacy of women's rights and environmental legislation was an attempt to restore a balance to areas of our life where fundamental principles and rights have been disregarded. He realizes that the statesman must reconcile competing interests and perspectives within a framework of shared principles. He identifies these principles as "conservative" or the principles of the American people. By contrast, ideology and ideological purists undermine the delicate balance of interests in democratic society, distorting the grounds of genuine political principle and practice. In a speech to the American Conservative Union Banquet, February, 1977, Mr. Reagan said:

> I have always been puzzled by the inability of some political and media types to understand exactly what is meant by adherence to political principle. All too often in the press and the television evening news it is treated as a call for "ideological purity." Whatever ideology may mean—and it seems to mean a variety of things, depending upon who is using it—it always conjures up in my mind a picture of a rigid, irrational clinging to abstract theory in the face of reality. We have to recognize that in this country "ideology" is a scare-word. And, for good reason. Marxist-Leninism is, to give but one example, an ideology. All the facts of the real world have to be fitted to the Procrustean bed of Marx and Lenin. If the facts don't happen to fit the ideology, the facts are chopped off and discarded.

Let us lay to rest, once and for all, the myth of a small group of ideological purists trying to capture a majority. Replace it with the reality of a majority trying to assert its rights against the tyranny of powerful academics, fashionable left-revolutionaries, some economic illiterates who happen to hold elective office, and the social engineers who dominate the dialogue and set the format in political affairs. If there is any ideological fanaticism in American political life, it is to be found among the enemies of freedom on the left and right—those who would sacrifice principle to theory, those who worship only the god of political, social, and economic abstractions, ignoring the realities of everyday life. . . .

Our first job is to get this message across to those who share most of our principles. If we allow ourselves to be portrayed as ideological shock troops without correcting this error we are doing ourselves and our cause a disservice.

This statement shows the importance of having access to Mr. Reagan's own words. He is a leader whose essential thought and approach to the political world is moderated by political experience. This is why he disavows being on the extreme right, and why the extreme right occasionally attacks him. It is also the reason why he is continually challenged by the left; they are the principal cause of the imbalance in American society today.

Mr. Reagan's arrival on the American political scene in 1964 has great symbolic value. He provided a voice for the "silent majority," making it the electoral majority of 1980. In 1964, the New Deal coalition was still intact, endorsed by both Democratic and Republican Administrations. Only a few years later, however, the Great Society of Lyndon Johnson—with its promises and its failures—reminded Americans that they had lost certain basic values in electing Administrations that sought to provide for the total welfare of the citizens. This paved the way for the timely message of Ronald Reagan. His public rhetoric inspired his followers and was politically effective: it twice enabled him to be elected governor of California, and positioned him as a leading Republican candidate for the Presidency throughout the 1970s.

Ronald Reagan's Presidential victory is not a political accident of a failed Carter Presidency—as some political personalities argue. The fact is that few American politicians have kept themselves so prominent and visible in the national eye for so long a time. This is due largely to his public rhetoric, an ability that has led political commentators to refer to him as the "Great Communicator." Strangely, however, no volume of Mr. Reagan's speeches has been published for general distribution since the printing of *The Creative Society* in 1968. *A Time for Choosing: The Selected Speeches of Ronald Reagan, 1961-1982* fills this void. In it the President speaks for himself.

The title of the book is carefully chosen. It is taken from the famous 1964 Goldwater television talks, now known simply as *The Speech,* which marks Mr. Reagan's debut as a national political figure. This address, along with the others in the book, represents the best of the President's public rhetoric and delineates the constant theme of his political career—the distinction between freedom and tyranny. Morever, these speeches reveal that no other post-World War II American leader has been so consistent in understanding and articulating the crisis of our time. In fact, the only other Western leader in recent memory who has made this theme the focal point of his political career is Winston S. Churchill.

Mr. Reagan emphasizes that at the core of humanity

is the freedom of the ordinary man, and that the role of government is to secure the rights of the citizen. "We believe," he says, "that liberty can be measured by how much freedom Americans have to make their own decisions—even their own mistakes. Government must step in when one's liberties impinge on one's neighbors. Government must protect constitutional rights, deal with other governments, protect citizens from aggressors, assure equal opportunity, and be compassionate in caring for those citizens who are unable to care for themselves." If freedom is the possession of the ordinary man, it is also the ordinary man, through the ballot, who can endanger a free, democratic society by asking of government more than it can or should provide. Mr. Reagan continually reminds us of this fact—in particular, of the gradual accumulation of centralized power in Washington. Thus, his speeches have a didactic function. They are intended to educate the ordinary man to the conditions of his freedom as well as to the perils of a reckless attitude toward government.

The President thus opposes any program, such as regulation in housing, health, farming, commerce, or education that simply, without necessity, increases the power and activity of government. "Because no government ever voluntarily reduced itself in size, government programs once launched never go out of existence." Government cannot do, and should not attempt to do, everything for its citizens. Mr. Reagan is adamant on this point. He knows that a government that attempts to provide for every desire of its citizens results in tyrannical rule. Such rule degrades man. It stifles individual excellence and personal freedom. The ability and willingness of government to rob each of us of the faculties to think, feel, and act for ourselves is the permanent threat to a free society to which the President continually speaks.

The threat to freedom is equally perilous in the international arena. Nowhere has individual freedom and human dignity suffered more than under the deadening footsteps of the Soviet Union. "Only now and then do we in the West hear a voice from out of the darkness. Then there is silence—the silence of human slavery. There is no more terrifying sound in human experience. . . . The very heart of the darkness is the Soviet Union and from that heart comes a different sound. It is the whirling sound of machinery and the whisper of the computer technology we ourselves have sold them. It is the sound of building, building of the strongest military machinery ever devised by man." According to Mr. Reagan, the tyranny of the Soviet Union is total. It suppresses its own citizens, exports world-wide revolution, builds the mightiest military machine in human history, openly condemns Western values, and abuses the goodwill of Western democracies in their search for peaceful intercourse. The Russian military giant, the President stresses, believes that the competition between Marxist and Western liberal ideas is permanent and irreconcilable. He cautions us not to be fooled by Soviet propaganda. The West must be alert to Soviet conduct and policies and not be led into the foolish ways of the democracies that prevailed before the beginning of the Second World War. Above all, the President understands that the ground for exporting Soviet ideology is the advance of Soviet arms. Only strength of arms and a renewed commitment to democratic ideals is capable of resisting Soviet expansion.

Peace is possible, but only through strength. Strength of arms. however, can only be maintained through self-confidence in and a commitment to the basic values underlying our way of life. The President calls upon us to restore America as the "shining city upon a hill"—as a model worthy of universal imitation. His belief in the tenets of freedom, in universal ideas and not cultural relativism, has made him an aggressive advocate for renewing the moral ascendancy of Western civilization by taking the offensive against the tyrannical communist world.

Alfred Balitzer
February 6, 1983

1961

ENCROACHING CONTROL

(The Peril of Ever-Expanding Government)

Speaking at the annual meeting of the Phoenix (Arizona) Chamber of Commerce, March 30th

1.

It must seem presumptuous to some of you for a member of my profession to stand here and attempt to talk on problems of the nation. We in Hollywood are not unaware of the concept many of our fellow citizens have of us and our industry. We realize that our merchandise is made up of tinsel, colored lights, and a large measure of make-believe. It is also true that our business methods and practices have reflected this footlight glamour more than the very real side of our very real business.

However, a few years ago "a funny thing happened to us on the way to the theatre." Ugly reality came to our town on direct orders of the Kremlin. Hard-core party organizers infiltrated our business. They created cells, organized Communist fronts, and, for a time, deceived numbers of our people, who with the best of intentions, joined these fronts while still ignorant of their true purpose. The aim was to gain economic control of our industry and then subvert our screen to the dissemination of Communist propaganda.

Whatever the shortcomings, Hollywood had achieved a great deal. In the finest traditions of free enterprise, 70 percent of the playing time of all the screens of the world had been captured by the output of the American film capital. You may disagree sometimes with our "boy meets girl" plot, but all over the world our pictures were a window through which less fortunate humans had a glimpse of freedom and of our material comforts as well. The men in the Kremlin wanted this propaganda medium for their own destructive purposes.

Confident of their power, the Reds in our midst made one mistake in judgment. They mistook their ability to deceive for success in conversion. Under the guise of a jurisdictional strike, they made an open effort to destroy the guilds and unions which remained free from their control. Ultimately, they hoped for one vertical union of motion picture people under the umbrella of Harry Bridges' maritime union. After the first shock, the people of the movie colony rallied quickly—we lived through scenes that heretofore had been only make-believe. Thousands of massed pickets overturned cars, homes were bombed, and threats of acid in the face were directed at performers. Months later their power was broken. The studios had remained open thanks to the refusal of management and the majority of our people to be intimidated.

We now know of course that we only won an isolated battle. In the "spirit of Camp David" the Communist Party has ordered once again the infiltration of the picture business as well as the theatre and television. They are crawling out from under the rocks; and memories being as short as they are, there are plenty of well-meaning but misguided people willing to give them a hand.

We don't mean to present ourselves as "being able to run the circus now that we've seen the monkey," but it is possible we have an awareness not shared by many of our fellow citizens.

Most people agree that the ideological struggle with Russia is the number one problem in the world. Millions of words are used almost daily to record the fluctuating temperature of the Cold War. And yet, many men in high places in government and many who mold opinion in the press and on the airwaves subscribe to a theory that we are at peace, and we must make no overt move which might endanger that peace. "Men cry peace, but there is no peace." The inescapable truth is that we are at war, and we are losing that war simply because we don't, or won't realize that we are in it.

True, it is a strange war fought with unusual weapons, but we cannot yell foul, because it is a declared war. Karl Marx established the cardinal principle that communism and capitalism cannot coexist in the world together. Our way of life, our system, must be totally destroyed; then the world Communist state will be erected on the ruins. In interpreting Marx, Lenin said, "It is inconceivable that the Soviet Republic should continue to exist for a long period side by side with imperialistic states. Ultimately, one or the other must conquer."

Last November, the Communist parties of eighty-one countries held a convention in Moscow; and on December 6, reaffirmed this principle of war to the death. In a 20,000-word manifesto, they called on Communists in countries where there were non-Communist governments to be traitors and work for the destruction of their own governments by subversion and treason.

Only in that phase of the war which causes our greatest fear are we ahead—the use of armed force. Thanks to the dedicated patriotism and realistic thinking of our men in uniform, we would win a shooting war. But, this isn't a decisive factor in the Communist campaign. They never really intended to conquer us by force unless we yielded to a massive peace campaign and disarmed. Then the Russians would resort to armed conflict if it could shortcut their timetable with no great risk to themselves.

In 1923, Lenin said that they would take Europe, next organize the hordes of Asia, then surround the United States, and, he predicted, ". . . that last bastion of Capitalism will not have to be taken. It will fall in our outstretched hands like overripe fruit."

Eastern Europe has been taken, and Communists are organizing the hordes of Asia around the red colossus of China. Even now, it would appear we are preparing to drink the bitter cup of capitulation in Laos, only partly diluted by face-saving devices. Cuba is a Soviet beachhead ninety miles offshore, and more than 250,000 Communist organizers are spread up and down Latin America.

Meanwhile, other Communist tactics are also working on schedule. Bulganin said, "The American working man is too well fed; we cannot appeal to him, but when through inflation America has priced herself out of the world market and unemployment follows—then we will settle our debt with the United States."

American apathy is due at least in part to our belief that the small number of American Communists is evidence of weakness and a lack of threat. But history makes no secret of the fact that Lenin became the leader of the world conspiracy on just that issue—that the Communist Party would remain a small, dedicated, highly-trained cadre which would use and manipulate the masses when necessary. Lenin termed us the "willing idiots." In our lifetime, this dedicated handful has enslaved one-third of the world's people on one-fourth of the earth's land surface.

The Communists are supremely confident of victory. They believe that you and I, under the constant pressure of the Cold War, will give up, one by one, our democratic customs and traditions. We'll adopt emergency "temporary" totalitarian measures, until one day we'll awaken to find we have grown so much like the enemy that we no longer have any cause for conflict.

Three months before his last visit to this country, Nikita Khrushchev said, "We can't expect the American people to jump from capitalism to communism, but we can assist their elected leaders in giving them small doses of socialism, until they awaken one day to find they have communism." This is not a new thought. In 1788 James Madison told the Virginia convention, "Since the general civilization of mankind, I believe there are more instances of the abridgment of the freedom of the people by gradual and silent encroachment of those in power than by violent and sudden usurpations."

Others much more recently have counted on this with no realization they would one day be furthering the Soviet cause. A socialist clergyman, writing in the *New Leader,* the socialist magazine of 1927, called for a new strategy. He said socialists should place themselves in government jobs and work for government ownership of power, and control of railroads, banking, and key industries. He called his program "encroaching control."

Appealing not to the worst, but to the best in our natures, those of the liberal persuasion have used our sense of fair play—our willingness to compromise—and have perfected a technique of "foot in the door" legislation. Get any part of a proposed program accepted, then with the principle of governmental participation in that field established, work for expansion, always aiming at the ultimate goal—a government that will someday be a big brother to us all.

Traditionally, one of the easiest first steps in imposing statism on a people has been government paid medicine.

It is the easiest to present as a humanitarian project. No one wants to oppose care for the sick. Today, we have the costliest governmental medical program in the world in our Veterans Administration hospitals. All of us are agreed that a man wounded in the service of his country is entitled to the finest in medical and hospital care. However, today three out of four Veterans Administration beds are filled with patients suffering diseases or injuries neither originated by nor aggravated by military service. There are only 40,000 service-connected disabilities in the United States, yet every year the federal budget contains millions of dollars for additional Veterans Administration hospital building and expansion. Counting the twenty-three million of us who are veterans plus other governmental programs, one of four citizens are entitled to some form of government-paid medical or hospital care.

It is now proposed that all people of social security age be given government paid medical and hospital care. Once again, emergency is invoked, and we are given a picture of millions of senior citizens desperately needing medical care and unable to finance it. In all the emotional presentation, the leaders of this program seem strangely reluctant to face the facts. In the last ten years, 127 million Americans have come under the protection of some form of medical and hospital insurance. This includes more than one-third of those of social security age and more than 70 percent of all citizens. If the present rate of increase continues, by 1970 some 90 percent of the population will be so insured. As nearly as can be determined, less than 10 percent of our senior citizens require aid in meeting their medical needs.

The last session of Congress adopted a measure known as the Kerr-Mills bill to provide money for state-administered aid to these people. However, without even waiting to see if this meets the problem, a revised version of the once defeated Forand bill is advocated to force all people into a compulsory government health insurance program, regardless of need. Why? Well, ex-Congressman Forand provides the answer. He says, "If we can only break through and get our foot in the door, then we can expand the program after that." Walter Reuther has said his group makes no secret of the fact that they want nationalized health service for all. *New American,* a socialist magazine writes, "The Forand bill will not be paid on the insurance principle according to factors of estimated risk. It will be paid for through the tax mechanisms of Social Security. . . . Once the bill is passed, this nation will be provided with a mechanism for socialized medicine."

In 1935, Social Security started with 3 percent contribution of $3,000 of income. Now it is 6 percent of $4,800 and if the proposed expansions plus the medical program are adopted, by 1969 it will be 11 percent of $5,000. It is no secret that pressure is being exerted to remove even the $5,000 ceiling and base Social Security payments on total gross income.

Social Security was never intended to replace private savings, pensions, or insurance. It was to provide a basis for savings so that outright distribution would not follow unemployment by reason of death, disability, or old age. In that light, the actuarial benefit payments would total $1.2 billion per year, but the temptation to politicians to vote people a raise, particularly in election years, was too great. In 1957, the total outgo was more than $7 billion and in 1959, outgo began exceeding income. The recipients of Social Security benefits today will collect $65 billion more than they paid in. You and I, who are paying into this program, are unfunded to an amount between $300 and $600 billion.

The average citizen has been led to believe he and his employer are contributing to a fund and that some day he will call upon this, his own money, to carry him over his non-earning years. But this isn't what Social Security representatives said before the United States Supreme Court. They stated that Social Security was not an insurance program and was not based on any actuarial standard. They stated that Social Security dues are a tax for the general use of the government, and the payment of that tax does not automatically entitle anyone to benefits. Benefit payments are a welfare program which can be curtailed or cancelled anytime Congress should so decide.

And what of our sons—the young man joining the work force in the next few years? He will be taxed to try and catch up on that mounting deficit. If he would have his Social Security tax to invest in private insurance, it would provide for almost double the benefits provided by Social Security. This is not the only price we are paying in individual freedom.

The press recently told of a group whose religious belief forbade their participation in any government welfare program. Their property was seized and their cattle sold at auction to enforce their payment of Social Security taxes.

In education, the foot in the door was the $900 million National Education Act of 1958. The excuse was, as usual, the Cold War. Russia had put a Sputnik into orbit; obviously, our educational system must be at fault. Now one of the largest spending lobbies in Washington is promoting a $2.5 billion program to alleviate allegedly crowded schools, underpaid teachers, and bankrupt school districts.

Again, the facts seem strangely at variance. Ninety-nine and one-half percent of the nation's school districts have not even approached their bonded limit of indebtedness. A 35 percent increase in students over the last decade has been matched by a 134 percent increase in spending by the local communities. An increase of 10 million students has seen classrooms built for 15 million. Five hundred colleges, as of this moment, can take an additional 200,000 students without adding so much as a desk or chair. We are told we must build 60,000 classrooms a year for the next ten years, but they forget to tell us we've been building 68,000 a year for the last five years and that continuation of this rate will give us a surplus of classrooms by 1970.

Of course, we want teachers to be paid adequately; and we are doing something about it. Their average pay has risen in the last few years from $3100 to $5300 annually. The truth is, not one shred of evidence has been presented that federal aid of any kind is required. Could we possibly believe that three-fourths of one billion dollars a year in federal aid could solve any great emergency when we are spending nearly twenty billion dollars a year at the local level?

Federal aid is the foot in the door to federal control. In spite of their denials, their own words betray them. The Director of Public Education of the State of Washington tells of the two-year struggle of his state to meet the rigid requirements of the National Director of Education under the present act. He says, "This is federal control by indirection—all the more dangerous because it poses as a federal handout."

A former president of the National Education Association states publicly, "We might have to have temporary federal control to bring about integration in the South."

A former chairman of the President's youth fitness program says, "We can no longer afford local management of the schools. We must have a national school system to compete on equal terms with Russia."

The Department of Health, Education, and Welfare has quadrupled its staff and admits it is working to create national standards of education and a national curriculum.

In short, federal aid is the first step in a federal school system with teachers and subjects removed from parental control on the theory that a bureau in Washington is better qualified to supervise the upbringing of our youth.

Twenty-seven years ago, our farmers were told that a federal subsidy did not mean federal control. Now we have seen a rancher, Evetts Haley, Jr., fined $4000 for raising wheat on his own land and feeding it to his own cattle. The Supreme Court upheld his conviction with a single-sentence ruling—"Yes, an agency of the federal government has the right to tell an American citizen what he can grow on his own land for his own use."

This nation has tried to *curb* the production of a surplus by making it so financially attractive to *produce* a surplus that we own enough wheat to bake twenty-five loaves of bread for every person alive. In the State of New Mexico, citizens learned they could rent state-owned land for twenty-five cents an acre and immediately apply for and receive $9 an acre from the federal government for not planting the land.

All of the "farm mess" is concerned with the 20 percent of agriculture coming under government regulation and subsidy. Eighty percent of our agricultural economy is out in the free market of supply and demand. It would seem that the answer to the "farm mess" would be to free the other 20 percent of governmental regimentation; but, what is being advocated? We are told that the only solution to the problem is to bring the other 80 percent into the government program. To that end, a plan is advanced that would result in the licensing of every farm in the United States with complete governmental regulation of production and price.

Thomas Jefferson said, "If we let Washington tell us when to sow and when to reap, the Nation shall soon want for bread."

Today, no one denies the American people would resist the nationalization of industry. But, in defiance of this attitude, the federal government owns and operates more than 19,000 enterprises covering forty-seven lines of activity from rum distilling to the manufacture of surgical equipment. The estimated book value of seven hundred governmental activities is $260 billion. Operating tax-free, dividend-free, and rent-free in direct competition with its own citizens, the government loses billions each year in these undertakings.

The next time you are caught in traffic, take satisfaction in the knowledge that one of the government corporations built a six lane highway in Spain. It runs fifteen miles from Madrid to a gambling casino.

All of these things have led to the growth of a collection of internal powers and bureaucratic institutions against which the individual citizen is virtually helpless. We now have a permanent structure of government beyond the reach of Congress and actually capable of dictating policy. This power, under whatever name you choose, is the very essence of totalitarianism.

A year ago, a sub-committee of Congress reported its

findings in the field of federal employees: there are almost two and one-half million. In 1942, there was one top-salaried executive for every eighty-nine employees; today, there is one for every seventeen. The committee further reported it found little evidence that any bureau, agency, or commission created in answer to an emergency ever went out of existence after the emergency disappeared.

Some people attempt to justify government in business on the grounds of greater efficiency due to central control. An example of this efficiency can be found in the Claims Department of the Veterans Administration insurance program. In that department, three government employees take double the time to perform the task normally assigned to one employee in a private insurance company.

Hopeless as it may seem, we can do something about it. We must inform ourselves on the proposals pending in Congress. Look beyond the foot in the door to the ultimate aim. Weigh the price we must pay in individual liberty and whether these programs qualify as things the people can't do for themselves. Then write to your Congressmen and Senators. Also, don't forget to write now and then to say "well done" to your Representative when he has acquitted himself well on the firing line.

A basic point to remember is that none of these extensions of socialism can be effected without money. The fodder upon which our government has fed and grown beyond the consent of the governed is the fruit of the tax system whose only consistency is that a levy once imposed is seldom removed. An excise tax on telephones imposed during the Korean War was to curb telephone use during the emergency and really wasn't intended for revenue.

The war is over, but the tax lingers on—the government has discovered it needs the revenue. This particular tax, plus some of the hundreds of hidden and indirect taxes that burden us, accounts for one-third of your telephone bill. One hundred such taxes account for one-half the price of a loaf of bread, one-fourth the cost of an automobile, one-half your gas and oil.

Once we were told the income tax would never be greater than 2 percent, and that only from the rich. In our lifetime, this law has grown from 31 to more than 440 thousand words. We have received this progressive tax directly from Karl Marx who designed it as the prime essential of a socialist state. In the surtax brackets, the steepest rate of increase occurs through the middle income range where are to be found the bulk of our small businessmen, professional people, and supervisory personnel—the people Marx said should be taxed out of existence. At sixteen- to eighteen-thousand dollars of income, a man reaches the 50 percent rate. From 50 percent on up to the confiscatory 91 percent rate, the government can only justify these brackets on a punitive basis, for the gross revenue derived from all the tax of 50 percent or above is less than three-fourths of $1 billion.

There can be no normal justification of the progressive tax. Perhaps that is why the bureaucrats pretend it is proportionate taxation. Proportionate taxation we would gladly accept on the theory that those better able to pay should remove some of the burden from those least able to pay. The Bible explains this in its instruction on tithing. We are told we should give the Lord one-tenth, and if the Lord prosper us ten times as much, we should give ten times as much. But under our progressive income tax, computing Caesar's share is a little different. If a $5000-a-year man today is prospered 10 times, his income tax increases 53 times as much.

Does this help the little man? A man with a gross income of $3,500, a wife and two children will find when he has finished paying the hidden and indirect taxes, that the tax collector's share of his gross $3,500 is $1,059. Some suggest the answer to his problem is to tax the upper incomes even more—but what leeway is left? If the government confiscated all personal income above $6,000 a year, the increased revenue wouldn't pay the interest on the national debt.

No nation in history has ever survived a tax burden of one-third of its national income. Today, thirty-one cents out of every dollar earned is tax, and of that thirty-one cents, twenty-three cents goes to the federal government; leaving eight cents to be shared by the state, county, and local community. No wonder we are told to ask for federal aid! But wouldn't it make more sense to keep the money here in the first place instead of running it through that puzzle palace on the Potomac only to get it back minus a sizable carrying charge?

Lenin once said, "The way to destroy Capitalism is to debauch the currency and unobservedly confiscate the wealth of its citizens."

Henry VII substituted copper for silver in his coins, and we have been no less deliberate in our inflationary policies. Our dollar has lost more than half its purchasing power in twenty years. Of course, we are told that incomes have kept pace, that we are earning twice as much, so we are still holding our own. This reasoning overlooks the point played by the progressive tax which is based on the number of dollars earned—not their value. The man who earned $5,000 in 1940, must earn $14,000 today to break even and pay his increased surtax. The $10,000-a-year man faces an increase of $12,000 in his tax bill and must now earn $31,000 just to maintain the same purchasing power.

Project these figures ahead just fifteen years, keeping the same annual rate of inflation and the same tax rate, and could anyone even pretend that free enterprise will exist? By 1975, the $5,000-a-year man will have to earn $33,000 and the $10,000-a-year man will have to earn $84,000 just to maintain their 1940 standard of living.

Here is the main battleground! We must reduce the government's supply of money and deny it the right to borrow.

Two years ago, I appeared before the House Ways and Means Committee as a representative of the motion picture industry to urge tax reform. This was an experience similar to going over the Niagara Falls in a barrel—the hard way: upstream. In a month of hearings, representatives of practically every segment of our society appeared before the committee. All of them urged some kind of tax reform. It was obvious that the majority of the committee had little sympathy with our plea, so it was no surprise when, several months later, the committee decided to hold new hearings. This time no volunteers were allowed. A hand-picked group of predominantly campus economists appeared and talked of plugging loopholes to increase the government's tax revenue. Most of these so-called loopholes are the legitimate deductions without which the tax structure would have long since proved unworkable. The suggestions included disallowance of property taxes and interest on loans for income tax purposes and even the elimination of 100 percent deductions of charitable contributions.

The biggest lobby in Washington pushing tax reform

has a bill which will increase the government's tax take about $18 billion. It is no coincidence that they have, on the other hand, recommendations for $18 billion worth of welfare legislation. This measure will actually be presented as tax reduction with some cut in surtax rates.

Those of liberal persuasion say they "reject the notion that the least government is the best government." They claim our citizens are not intelligent enough to spend their money properly. They feel the government should take the money through taxation and then buy the welfare programs for the masses which they are not smart enough to buy for themselves.

When the old-fashioned idea of living within our means and paying something on the national debt is suggested, these same liberals tell us that "only state and local debt is bad." Through some exotic bookkeeping methods, they seem to feel that the federal debt is meaningless. It is—it is incomprehensible.

If I had a four inch stack of thousand dollar bills in my hand, I'd be a millionaire. If we had the national debt of $293 billion before us in thousand dollar bills, the pile would be more than eighteen miles high. Maurice Stans, former budget director, has said that this debt is only the part of the iceberg which shows above the surface. Legislation already enacted into law has obligated our government to more than $750 billion. Add to this the local and state debts plus the private debts of our citizens, and we find that we are mortgaged in an amount more than double the market value of every tangible asset and every foot of real estate in the United States.

When we point out the danger of more deficit spending, we are told, "we are sacrificing our security on the false altar of a balanced budget." This is not so. Our individual freedom and our free enterprise system are the very sources of our strength, and there can be little security any place in the free world if there isn't fiscal stability in the United States.

With no one using the term "socialism" to describe these encroaching controls, we find that today one out of seven of the nation's work force is on the public payroll. In just fifteen years a 50 percent increase in employees has been met with a 170 percent increase in the public payroll. One-fourth of our medicine is socialized. Senator Harry Byrd estimates that forty million Americans receive some form of direct cash payment from government. We have a tax machine that in direct contravention to the Constitution is not designed to solely raise revenue but is used, openly and admittedly, to control and direct the economy and to equalize the earnings of our people.

Do not forsake the other issues; but as Justice Oliver Wendell Holmes said, "Strike for the jugular. Reduce taxes and spending. Keep government poor and remain free." Write to your Congressman as individuals. Fifty letters from a group such as this means more than a resolution or a petition. Demand immediate tax reform which will reduce the percentage of the national income taken by government. There is a bipartisan tax reform bill, the Herlong-Baker bill, now before the House Ways and Means Committee. A five year gradual reduction of rates makes it the best planned tax reform bill introduced in the last hundred years. For every billion saved in government spending, we can have a 2.5 percent reduction of income tax.

If your Congressman should say we must cut costs first and then reduce taxes—don't stand for it. Remind him that no government in history has ever voluntarily reduced itself in size. Governments don't tax to get the money they need. Governments will always find a need for the money they get.

There can only be one end to the war we are in. It won't go away if we simply try to outwait it. Wars end in victory or defeat. One of the foremost authorities on communism in the world today has said we have ten years. Not ten years to make up our minds, but ten years to win or lose—by 1970 the world will be all slave or all free.

In this land occurred the only true revolution in man's history. All other revolutions simply exchanged one set of rulers for another. Here for the first time the Founding Fathers—that little band of men so advanced beyond their time that the world has never seen their like since—evolved a government based on the idea that you and I have the God-given right and ability within ourselves to determine our own destiny. Freedom is never more than one generation away from extinction—we didn't pass it on to our children in the bloodstream. It must be fought for, protected, and handed on for them to do the same, or one day we will spend our sunset years telling our children and our children's children what it was once like in the United States when men were free.

1964

A TIME FOR CHOOSING

(The Speech)

National Television Address, October 27th

2.

I am going to talk of controversial things. I make no apology for this. I have been talking on this subject for ten years, obviously under the administration of both parties. I mention this only because it seems impossible to legitimately debate the issues of the day without being subjected to name-calling and the application of labels. Those who deplore use of the terms "pink" and "leftist" are themselves guilty of branding all who oppose their liberalism as right wing extremists. How long can we afford the luxury of this family fight when we are at war with the most dangerous enemy ever known to man?

If we lose that war, and in so doing lose our freedom, it has been said history will record with the greatest astonishment that those who had the most to lose did the least to prevent its happening. The guns are silent in this war but frontiers fall while those who should be warriors prefer neutrality. Not too long ago two friends of mine were talking to a Cuban refugee. He was a businessman who had escaped from Castro. In the midst of his tale of horrible experiences, one of my friends turned to the other and said, "We don't know how lucky we are." The Cuban stopped and said, "How lucky you are? I had some place to escape to." And in that sentence he told the entire story. If freedom is lost here there is no place to escape to.

It's time we asked ourselves if we still know the freedoms intended for us by the Founding Fathers. James Madison said, "We base all our experiments on the capacity of mankind for self-government." This idea that government was beholden to the people, that it had no other source of power except the sovereign people, is still the newest, most unique idea in all the long history of man's relation to man. For almost two centuries we have proved man's capacity for self-government, but today we are told we must choose between a left and right or, as others suggest, a third alternative, a kind of safe middle ground. I suggest to you there is no left or right, only an up or down. Up to the maximum of individual freedom consistent with law and order, or down to the ant heap of totalitarianism; and regardless of their humanitarian purpose those who would sacrifice freedom for security have, whether they know it or not, chosen this downward path. Plutarch warned, "The real destroyer of the liberties of the people is he who spreads among them bounties, donations, and benefits.

Today there is an increasing number who can't see a fat man standing beside a thin one without automatically coming to the conclusion the fat man got that way by taking advantage of the thin one. So they would seek the answer to all the problems of human need through government. Howard K. Smith of television fame has written, "The profit motive is outmoded. It must be replaced by the incentives of the welfare state." He says, "The distribution of goods must be effected by a planned economy."

Another articulate spokesman for the welfare state defines liberalism as meeting the material needs of the masses through the full power of centralized government. I for one find it disturbing when a representative refers to the free men and women of this country as the masses, but beyond this the full power of centralized government was the very thing the Founding Fathers sought to minimize.

They knew you don't control things; you can't control the economy without controlling *people*. So we have come to a time for choosing. Either we accept the responsibility for our own destiny, or we abandon the American Revolution and confess that an intellectual belief in a far-distant capitol can plan our lives for us better than we can plan them ourselves.

Already the hour is late. Government has laid its hand on health, housing, farming, industry, commerce, education, and, to an ever-increasing degree, interferes with the people's right to know. Government tends to grow; government programs take on weight and momentum, as public servants say, always with the best of intentions, "What greater service we could render if only we had a little more money and a little more power." But the truth is that outside of its legitimate function, government does nothing as well or as economically as the private sector of the economy. What better example do we have of this than government's involvement in the farm economy over the last thirty years. One-fourth of farming has seen a steady decline in the per capita consumption of everything it produces. That one-fourth is regulated and subsidized by government.

In contrast, the three-fourths of farming unregulated and unsubsidized has seen a 21 percent increase in the per capita consumption of all its produce. Since 1955 the cost of the farm program has nearly doubled. Direct payment to farmers is eight times as great as it was nine years ago, but farm income remains unchanged while farm surplus is bigger. In that same period we have seen a decline of five million in the farm population, but an increase in the number of Department of Agriculture employees.

There is now one such employee for every thirty farms in the United States, and still they can't figure how sixty-six shiploads of grain headed for Austria could disappear without a trace, and Billy Sol Estes never left shore. Three years ago the government put into effect a program to curb the over-production of feed grain. Now, $2.5 billion later, the corn crop is one hundred million bushels bigger than before the program started. And the cost of the program prorates out to $43 for every dollar bushel of corn we don't grow. Nor is this the only example of the price we pay for government meddling. Some government programs with the passage of time take on a sacrosanct quality.

One such considered above criticism, sacred as motherhood, is TVA. This program started as a flood control project; the Tennessee Valley was periodically ravaged by destructive floods. The Army Engineers set out to solve this problem. They said that it was possible that once in 500 years there could be a total capacity flood that would inundate some six hundred thousand acres. Well, the engineers fixed that. They made a permanent lake which inundated a million acres. This solved the problem of floods, but the annual interest on the TVA debt is five times as great as the annual flood damage they sought to correct.

Of course, you will point out that TVA gets electric power from the impounded waters, and this is true, but today 85 percent of TVA's electricity is generated in coal-burning steam plants. Now perhaps you'll charge that I'm overlooking the navigable waterway that was created, providing cheap barge traffic, but the bulk of the freight barged on that waterway is coal being shipped to the TVA steam plants, and the cost of maintaining that channel each year would pay for shipping all of the coal by rail, and there would be money left over.

One last argument remains: the prosperity produced by such large programs of government spending. Certainly there are few areas where more spending has taken place. The Labor Department lists 50 percent of the 169 counties in the Tennessee Valley as permanent areas of poverty, distress, and unemployment.

Meanwhile, back in the city, under Urban Renewal, the assault on freedom carries on. Private property rights have become so diluted that public interest is anything a few planners decide it should be. In Cleveland, Ohio, to get a project under way, city officials reclassified eighty-four buildings as substandard in spite of the fact their own inspectors had previously pronounced these buildings sound. The owners stood by and watched 26 million dollars worth of property as it was destroyed by the headache ball. Senate Bill 628 says: "Any property, be it home or commercial structure, can be declared slum or blighted and the owner has no recourse at law. The Law Division of the Library of Congress and the General Accounting Office have said that the Courts will have to rule against the owner."

HOUSING. In one key Eastern city a man owning a blighted area sold his property to Urban Renewal for several million dollars. At the same time, he submitted his own plan for the rebuilding of this area and the government sold him back his own property for 22 percent of what they paid. Now the government announces, "We are going to build subsidized housing in the thousands where we have been building in the hundreds." At the same time FHA and the Veterans Administration reveal they are holding 120 thousand housing units reclaimed from mortgage foreclosure, mostly because the low down payment and the easy terms brought the owners to a point where they realized the unpaid balance on the homes amounted to a sum greater than the homes were worth, so they just walked out the front door, possibly to take up residence in newer subsidized housing, again with little or no down payment and easy terms.

Some of the foreclosed homes have already been bulldozed into the earth, others, it has been announced, will be refurbished and put on sale for down payments as low as $100 and thirty-five years to pay. This will give the bulldozers a second crack. It is in the area of social welfare that government has found its most fertile growing bed. So many of us accept our responsibility for those less fortunate. We are susceptible to humanitarian appeals.

Federal welfare spending is today ten times greater than it was in the dark depths of the Depression. Federal, state, and local welfare combined spend 45 billion dollars a year. Now the government has announced that 20 percent, some 9.3 million families, are poverty-stricken on the basis that they have less than a $3,000 a year income.

If this present welfare spending was prorated equally among these poverty-stricken families, we could give each family more than $4,500 a year. Actually, direct aid to the poor averages less than $600 per family. There must be some administrative overhead somewhere. Now, are we to believe that another billion dollar program added to the half a hundred programs and the 45 billion dollars, will, through some magic, end poverty? For three decades we have tried to solve unemployment by government planning, without success. The more the plans fail, the more the planners plan.

The latest is the Area Redevelopment Agency, and in

two years less than one-half of one percent of the unemployed could attribute new jobs to this agency, and the cost to the taxpayer for each job found was $5,000. But beyond the great bureaucratic waste, what are we doing to the people we seek to help?

Recently a judge told me of an incident in his court. A fairly young woman with six children, pregnant with her seventh, came to him for a divorce. Under his questioning it became apparent her husband did not share this desire. Then the whole story came out. Her husband was a laborer earning $250 a month. By divorcing him she could get an $80 raise. She was eligible for $350 a month from the Aid to Dependent Children Program. She had been talked into the divorce by two friends who had already done this very thing. But any time we question the schemes of the do-gooders, we are denounced as being opposed to their humanitarian goal. It seems impossible to legitimately debate their solutions with the assumption that all of us share the desire to help those less fortunate. They tell us we are always against, never for anything. Well, it isn't so much that liberals are ignorant. It's just that they know so much that isn't so.

We are for a provision that destitution should not follow unemployment by reason of old age. For that reason we have accepted Social Security as a step toward meeting that problem. However, we are against the irresponsibility of those who charge that any criticism or suggested improvement of the program means we want to end payment to those who depend on Social Security for a livelihood.

FISCAL IRRESPONSIBILITY. We have been told in millions of pieces of literature and press releases that Social Security is an insurance program, but the executives of Social Security appeared before the Supreme Court in the case of *Nestor* v. *Fleming* and proved to the Court's satisfaction that it is not insurance but is a welfare program, and Social Security dues are a tax for the general use of the government. Well it can't be both: insurance and welfare. Later, appearing before a Congressional Committee, they admitted that Social Security is today 298 billion dollars in the red. This fiscal irresponsibility has already caught up with us.

Faced with a bankruptcy, we find that today a young man in his early twenties, going to work at less than an average salary, will, with his employer, pay into Social Security an amount which could provide the young man with a retirement insurance policy guaranteeing $220 a month at age 65, and the government promises him $127.

Now, are we so lacking in business sense that we cannot put this program on a sound actuarial basis, so that those who do depend on it won't come to the cupboard and find it bare, and at the same time can't we introduce voluntary features so that those who can make better provision for themselves are allowed to do so? Incidentally, we might also allow participants in Social Security to name their own beneficiaries, which they cannot do in the present program. These are not insurmountable problems.

YOUTH AID PLANS. We have today 30 million workers protected by industrial and union pension funds that are soundly financed by some 70 billion dollars invested in corporate securities and income earning real estate. I think we are for telling our senior citizens that no one in this country should be denied medical care for lack of funds, but we are against forcing all citizens into a compulsory government program regardless of need. Now the government has turned its attention to our young people, and suggests that it can solve the problem of school drop-outs and juvenile delinquency through some kind of revival of the old C.C.C. camps. The suggested plan prorates out to a cost of $4,700 a year for each young person we want to help. We can send them to Harvard for $2,700 a year. Of course, don't get me wrong—I'm not suggesting Harvard as the answer to juvenile delinquency.

We are for an international organization where the nations of the world can legitimately seek peace. We are against subordinating American interests to an organization so structurally unsound that a two-thirds majority can be mustered in the U.N. General Assembly among nations representing less than 10 percent of the world population.

Is there not something of hypocrisy in assailing our allies for so-called vestiges of colonialism while we engage in a conspiracy of silence about the peoples enslaved by the Soviet in the satellite nations? We are for aiding our allies by sharing our material blessings with those nations which share our fundamental beliefs. We are against doling out money, government to government, which ends up financing socialism all over the world.

We set out to help nineteen war-ravaged countries at the end of World War II. We are now helping 107. We have spent 146 billion dollars. Some of that money bought a $2 million yacht for Hailè Selassie. We bought dress suits for Greek undertakers. We bought one thousand TV sets with 23-inch screens for a country where there is no electricity, and some of our foreign aid funds provided extra wives for Kenya government officials. When Congress moved to cut foreign aid they were told that if they cut it one dollar they endangered national security, and then

Senator Harry Byrd revealed that since its inception foreign aid has rarely spent its allotted budget. It has today $21 billion in unexpended funds.

Some time ago Dr. Howard Kershner was speaking to the Prime Minister of Lebanon. The Prime Minister told him proudly that his little country balanced its budget each year. It had no public debt, no inflation, a modest tax rate, and had increased its gold holdings from seventy to 120 million dollars. When he finished, Dr. Kershner said, "Mr. Prime Minister, my country hasn't balanced its budget twenty-eight out of the last forty years. My country's debt is greater than the combined debt of all the nations of the world. We have inflation, we have a tax rate that takes from the private sector a percentage of income greater than any civilized nation has ever taken and survived. We have lost gold at such a rate that the solvency of our currency is in danger. Do you think that my country should continue to give your country millions of dollars each year?" The Prime Minister smiled and said, "No, but if you are foolish enough to do it, we are going to keep on taking the money."

NINE STALLS FOR ONE BULL. And so we built a model stock farm in Lebanon, and we built nine stalls for each bull. I find something peculiarly appropriate in that. We have in our vaults $15 billion in gold. We don't own an ounce. Foreign dollar claims against that gold total $27 billion. In the last six years, fifty-two nations have bought $7 billion worth of our gold and all fifty-two are receiving foreign aid.

Because no government ever voluntarily reduces itself in size, government programs once launched never go out of existence. A government agency is the nearest thing to eternal life we'll ever see on this earth. The United States Manual takes twenty-five pages to list by name every

Congressman and Senator, and all the agencies controlled by Congress. It then lists the agencies coming under the Executive Branch, and this requires 520 pages.

Since the beginning of the century our gross national product has increased by thirty-three times. In the same period the cost of federal government has increased 234 times, and while the work force is only one and one-half times greater, federal employees number nine times as many. There are now two and one-half million federal employees. No one knows what they all do. One Congressman found out what one of them does. This man sits at a desk in Washington. Documents come to him each morning. He reads them, initials them, and passes them on to the proper agency. One day a document arrived he wasn't supposed to read, but he read it, initialled it and passed it on. Twenty-four hours later it arrived back at his desk with a memo attached that said, "You weren't supposed to read this. Erase your initials, and initial the erasure."

While the federal government is the great offender, the idea filters down. During a period in California when our population has increased 90 percent, the cost of state government has gone up 862 percent and the number of employees 500 percent. Governments, state and local, now employ one out of six of the nation's work force. If the rate of increase of the last three years continues, by 1970 one-fourth of the total work force will be employed by government. Already we have a permanent structure so big and complex it is virtually beyond the control of Congress and the comprehension of the people, and tyranny inevitably follows when this permanent structure usurps the policy-making function that belongs to elected officials.

One example of this occurred when Congress was

debating whether to lend the United Nations $100 million. While they debated, the State Department gave the United Nations $217 million and the United Nations used part of that money to pay the delinquent dues of Castro's Cuba.

Under bureaucratic regulations adopted with no regard to the wish of the people, we have lost much of our Constitutional freedom. For example, federal agents can invade a man's property without a warrant, can impose a fine without a formal hearing, let alone a trial by jury, and can seize and sell his property at auction to enforce payment of that fine.

RIGHTS BY DISPENSATION. An Ohio deputy fire marshal sentenced a man to prison after a secret proceeding in which the accused was not allowed to have a lawyer present. The Supreme Court upheld that sentence, ruling that it was an administrative investigation of incidents damaging to the economy. Someplace a perversion has taken place. Our natural unalienable rights are now presumed to be a dispensation of government, divisible by a vote of the majority. The greatest good for the greatest number is a high-sounding phrase but contrary to the very basis of our nation, unless it is accompanied by recognition that we have certain rights which cannot be infringed upon, even if the individual stands outvoted by all of his fellow citizens. Without this recognition, majority rule is nothing more than mob rule.

It is time we realized that socialism can come without overt seizure of property or nationalization of private business. It matters little that you hold the title to your property or business if government can dictate policy and procedure and holds life and death power over your business. The machinery of this power already exists. Lowell

Mason, former anti-trust law enforcer for the Federal Trade Commission, has written "American business is being harassed, bled and even blackjacked under a preposterous crazy quilt system of laws." There are so many that the government literally can find some charge to bring against any concern it chooses to prosecute. Are we safe in our books and records?

The natural gas producers have just been handed a 428-page questionnaire by the Federal Power Commission. It weighs ten pounds. One firm has estimated it will take 70,000 accountant manhours to fill out this questionnaire, and it must be done in quadruplicate. The Power Commission says it must have it to determine whether a proper price is being charged for gas. The National Labor Relations Board ruled that a business firm could not discontinue its shipping department even though it was more efficient and economical to subcontract this work out.

The Supreme Court has ruled the government has the right to tell a citizen what he can grow on his own land for his own use. The Secretary of Agriculture has asked for the right to imprison farmers who violate their planting quotas. One business firm has been informed by the Internal Revenue Service that it cannot take a tax deduction for its institutional advertising because this advertising espoused views not in the public interest.

A child's prayer in a school cafeteria endangers religious freedom, but the people of the Amish religion in the State of Ohio, who cannot participate in Social Security because of their religious beliefs, have had their livestock seized and sold at auction to enforce payment of Social Security dues.

We approach a point of no return when government

becomes so huge and entrenched that we fear the consequences of upheaval and just go along with it. The federal government accounts for one-fifth of the industrial capacity of the nation, one-fourth of all construction, holds or guarantees one-third of all mortgages, owns one-third of the land, and engages in some nineteen thousand businesses covering half a hundred different lines. The Defense Department runs 269 supermarkets. They do a gross business of $730 million a year, and lose $150 million. The government spends $11 million an hour every hour of the twenty-four and pretends we had a tax cut while it pursues a policy of planned inflation that will more than wipe out any benefit with depreciation of our purchasing power.

We need true tax reform that will at least make a start toward restoring for our children the American dream that wealth is denied to no one, that each individual has the right to fly as high as his strength and ability will take him. The economist Sumner Schlicter has said, "If a visitor from Mars looked at our tax policy, he would conclude it had been designed by a Communist spy to make free enterprise unworkable." But we cannot have such reform while our tax policy is engineered by people who view the tax as a means of achieving changes in our social structure. Senator [Joseph S.] Clark (D.-Pa.) says the tax issue is a class issue, and the government must use the tax to redistribute the wealth and earnings downward.

KARL MARX. On January 15th in the White House, the President [Lyndon Johnson] told a group of citizens they were going to take all the money they thought was being unnecessarily spent, "take it from the haves and give it to the have-nots who need it so much." When Karl Marx said this he put it: . . . "from each according to his ability, to each according to his need."

Have we the courage and the will to face up to the immorality and discrimination of the progressive surtax, and demand a return to traditional proportionate taxation? Many decades ago the Scottish economist, John Ramsey McCulloch, said, "The moment you abandon the cardinal principle of exacting from all individuals the same proportion of their income or their property, you are at sea without a rudder or compass and there is no amount of injustice or folly you may not commit."

No nation has survived the tax burden that reached one-third of its national income. Today in our country the tax collector's share is thirty-seven cents of every dollar earned. Freedom has never been so fragile, so close to slipping from our grasp. I wish I could give you some magic formula, but each of us must find his own role. One man in Virginia found what he could do, and dozens of business firms have followed his lead. Concerned because his two hundred employees seemed unworried about government extravagance he conceived the idea of taking all of their withholding out of only the fourth paycheck each month. For three paydays his employees received their full salary. On the fourth payday all withholding was taken. He has one employee who owes him $4.70 each fourth payday. It only took one month to produce two hundred conservatives.

Are you willing to spend time studying the issues, making yourself aware, and then conveying that information to family and friends? Will you resist the temptation to get a government handout for your community? Realize that the doctor's fight against socialized medicine is your fight. We can't socialize the doctors without socializing the patients. Recognize that government invasion of public power is eventually an assault upon your own business. If some among you fear taking a stand because you are afraid of reprisals from customers, clients, or even government, recognize that you are just feeding the crocodile hoping he'll eat you last.

If all of this seems like a great deal of trouble, think what's at stake. We are faced with the most evil enemy mankind has known in his long climb from the swamp to the stars. There can be no security anywhere in the free world if there is not fiscal and economic stability within the United States. Those who ask us to trade our freedom for the soup kitchen of the welfare state are architects of a policy of accommodation. They tell us that by avoiding a direct confrontation with the enemy he will learn to love us and give up his evil ways. All who oppose this idea are blanket indicted as war-mongers. Well, let us set one thing straight, there is no argument with regard to peace and war. It is cheap demagoguery to suggest that anyone would want to send other people's sons to war. The only argument is with regard to the best way to avoid war. There is only one sure way—surrender.

APPEASEMENT OR COURAGE? The spectre our well-meaning liberal friends refuse to face is that their policy of accommodation is appeasement, and appeasement does not give you a choice between peace and war, only between fight and surrender. We are told that the problem is too complex for a simple answer. They are wrong. There is no easy answer, but there is a simple answer. We must have the courage to do what we know is morally right, and this policy of accommodation asks us to accept the greatest possible immorality. We are being asked to buy our safety from the threat of "the bomb" by selling into permanent slavery our fellow human beings enslaved behind the Iron Curtain, to tell them to give up their hope of freedom because we are ready to make a deal with their slave masters.

Alexander Hamilton warned us that a nation which can prefer disgrace to danger is prepared for a master and deserves one. Admittedly there is a risk in any course we follow. Choosing the high road cannot eliminate that risk. Already some of the architects of accommodation have hinted what their decision will be if their plan fails and we are faced with the final ultimatum. The English commentator [Kenneth] Tynan has put it this way: he would rather live on his knees than die on his feet. Some of our own have said "Better Red than dead." If we are to believe that nothing is worth the dying, when did this begin? Should Moses have told the children of Israel to live in slavery rather than dare the wilderness? Should Christ have refused the Cross? Should the patriots at Concord Bridge have refused to fire the shot heard 'round the world? Are we to believe that all the martyrs of history died in vain?

You and I have a rendezvous with destiny. We can preserve for our children this, the last best hope of man on earth, or we can sentence them to take the first step into a thousand years of darkness. If we fail, at least let our children and our children's children say of us we justified our brief moment here. We did all that could be done.

1967

THE CREATIVE SOCIETY

(California and the Problem of Government Growth)

From the first Inaugural Message as Governor of California, January 5th

3.

To a number of us, this is a first and hence a solemn and momentous occasion, and yet, on the broad page of state and national history, what is taking place here is almost commonplace routine. We are participating in the orderly transfer of administrative authority by direction of the people. And this is the simple magic which makes a commonplace routine a near miracle to many of the world's inhabitants: the continuing fact that the people, by democratic process, can delegate this power, yet retain custody of it.

Perhaps you and I have lived with this miracle too long to be properly appreciative. Freedom is a fragile thing and is never more than one generation away from extinction, It is not ours by inheritance; it must be fought for and defended constantly by each generation, for it comes only once to a people. Those who have known freedom and then lost it have never known it again.

Knowing this, it is hard to explain those who even today would question the people's capacity for self-rule. Will they answer this: if no one among us is capable of governing himself, then who among us has the capacity to govern someone else? Using the temporary authority granted by the people, an increasing number lately have sought to control the means of production, as if this could be done without eventually controlling those who produce. Always this is explained as necessary to the people's welfare. But, "The deterioration of every government begins with the decay of the principle upon which it was founded" [Montesquieu]. This is as true today as it was when it was written in 1748.

Government is the people's business, and every man, woman and child becomes a shareholder with the first penny of tax paid. With all the profound wording of the Constitution, probably the most meaningful words are the first three: "We, the People." Those of us here today who have been elected to constitutional office or legislative position are in that three-word phrase. We are of the people, chosen by them to see that no permanent structure of government ever encroaches on freedom or assumes a power beyond that freely granted by the people. We stand between the taxpayer and the taxspender.

It is inconceivable to me that anyone could accept this delegated authority without asking God's help. I pray that we who legislate and administer will be granted wisdom and strength beyond our own limited power; that with Divine guidance we can avoid easy expedients, as we work to build a state where liberty under law and justice can triumph, where compassion can govern, and wherein the people can participate and prosper because of their government and not in spite of it.

The path we will chart is not an easy one. It demands much of those chosen to govern, but also from those who did the choosing. And let there be no mistake about this: We have come to a crossroad—a time of decision—and the path we follow turns away from any idea that government and those who serve it are omnipotent. It is a path impossible to follow unless we have faith in the collective wisdom and genius of the people. Along this path government will lead but not rule, listen but not lecture. It is the path of a Creative Society.

A number of problems were discussed during the campaign, and I see no reason to change the subject now. Campaign oratory on the issues of crime, pollution of air and water, conservation, welfare, and expanded educational facilities does not mean the issues will go away because the campaign has ended. Problems remain to be solved and they challenge all of us. Government will lead, of course, but the answer must come from all of you.

We will make specific proposals and we will solicit other ideas. In the area of crime, where we have double our proportionate share, we will propose legislation to give back to local communities the right to pass and enforce ordinances which will enable the police to more adequately protect these communities. Legislation already drafted will be submitted, calling upon the Legislature clearly to state in the future whether newly-adopted laws are intended to preempt the right of local governments to legislate in the same field. Hopefully, this will free judges from having to guess the intent of those who passed the legislation in the first place.

At the same time, I pledge my support and fullest effort to a plan which will remove from politics, once and for all, the appointment of judges . . . not that I believe I'll be overburdened with making judicial appointments in the immediate future.

Just as we assume a responsibility to guard our young people up to a certain age from the possible harmful effects of alcohol and tobacco, so do I believe we have a right and a responsibility to protect them from the even more harmful effects of exposure to smut and pornography. We can and must frame legislation that will accomplish this purpose without endangering freedom of speech and the press.

When fiscally feasible, we hope to create a California crime technological foundation utilizing both public and private resources in a major effort to employ the most scientific techniques to control crime. At such a time, we should explore the idea of a state police academy to assure that police from even the smallest communities can have the most advanced training. We lead the nation in many things; we are going to stop leading in crime. Californians should be able to walk our streets safely day or night. The law abiding are entitled to at least as much protection as the law-breakers.

While on the subject of crime . . . those with a grievance can seek redress in the courts or legislature, but not in the streets. Lawlessness by the mob, as with the individual, will not be tolerated. We will act firmly and quickly to put down riot or insurrection wherever and whenever the situation requires.

Welfare is another of our major problems. We are a humane and generous people and we accept without reservation our obligation to help the aged, disabled, and those unfortunates who, through no fault of their own, must depend on their fellow man. But we are not going to perpetuate poverty by substituting a permanent dole for a paycheck. There is no humanity or charity in destroying self-reliance, dignity, and self-respect . . . the very substance of moral fiber.

We seek reforms that will, wherever possible, change relief check to paycheck. Spencer Williams, Administrator of Health and Welfare, is assessing the amount of work that could be done in public installations by welfare recipients. This is not being done in any punitive sense, but as a beginning step in rehabilitation to give the individual the self-respect that goes with performing a useful service.

But this is not the ultimate answer. Only private industry in the last analysis can provide jobs with a future. Lieutenant Governor Robert Finch will be liaison between government and the private sector in an all-out program of job training and education leading to real employment.

A truly great citizen of our state and a fine American, Mr. H.C. McClellan, has agreed to institute a statewide program patterned after the one he directed so successfully in the "curfew area" of Los Angeles. There, in the year and a half since the tragic riots, fully half of the unemployed have been channeled into productive jobs in private industry, and more than 2,600 businesses are involved. Mr. McClellan will be serving without pay and the entire statewide program will be privately financed. While it will be directed at all who lack opportunity, it offers hope especially to those minorities who have a disproportionate share of poverty and unemployment.

In the whole area of welfare, everything will be done to reduce administrative overhead, cut red tape, and return control as much as possible to the county level. And the goal will be investment in, and salvage of, human beings.

This Administration will cooperate with the State Superintendent of Public Instruction in his expressed desires to return more control of curriculum and selection of textbooks to local school districts. We will support his efforts to make recruitment of out-of-state teachers less difficult.

On the subject of education . . . hundreds of thousands of young men and women will receive an education in our state colleges and universities. We are proud of our ability to provide this opportunity for our youth and we believe it is no denial of academic freedom to provide this education within a framework of reasonable rules and regulations. Nor is it a violation of individual rights to require obedience to these rules and regulations or to insist that those unwilling to abide by them should get their education elsewhere.

It does not constitute political interference with intellectual freedom for the taxpaying citizens—who support the college and university systems—to ask that, in addition to teaching, they build character on accepted moral and ethical standards.

Just as a man is entitled to a voice in government, so he should certainly have that right in the very personal matter of earning a living. I have always supported the principle of the union shop, even though that includes a certain amount of compulsion with regard to union membership. For that reason it seems to me that government must accept a responsibility for safeguarding each union member's democratic rights within his union. For that reason we will submit legislative proposals to guarantee each union member a secret ballot in his union on policy matters and the use of union dues.

There is also need for a mediation service in labor-management disputes not covered by existing law.

There are improvements to be made in workmen's compensation in death benefits and benefits to the permanently disabled. At the same time, a tightening of procedures is needed to free business from some unjust burdens.

A close liaison with our congressional representatives in Washington, both Democratic and Republican, is needed so that we can help bring about beneficial changes in Social Security, secure less restrictive controls on federal grants, and work for a tax retention plan that will keep some of our federal taxes here for our use with no strings attached. We should strive also to get tax credits for our people to help defray the cost of sending their children to college.

We will support a bipartisan effort to lift the archaic 160-acre limitation imposed by the federal government on irrigated farms. Restrictive labor policies should never again be the cause of crops rotting in the fields for lack of harvesters.

Here in our own Capitol, we will seek solutions to the problems of unrealistic taxes which threaten economic ruin to our biggest industry. We will work with the farmer as we will with business, industry, and labor to provide a better business climate so that they may prosper and we all may prosper.

There are other problems and possible problems facing us. One such is now pending before the United States Supreme Court. I believe it would be inappropriate to discuss that matter now. We will, however, be prepared with remedial legislation we devoutly hope will be satisfactory to all of our citizens if court rulings make this necessary.

This is only a partial accounting of our problems and our dreams for the future. California, with its climate, its resources, and its wealth of young, aggressive, talented people, must never take second place. We can provide jobs for all our people who will work, and we can have honest government at a price we can afford. Indeed, unless we accomplish this, our problems will go unsolved, our dreams unfulfilled and we will know the taste of ashes.

I have put off until last what is by no means least among our problems. Our fiscal situation has a sorry similarity to the situation of a jetliner out over the North Atlantic, Paris-bound. The pilot announced he had news—some good, some bad—and he would give the bad news first. They had lost radio contact; their compass and altimeter were not working; they didn't know their altitude, direction or where they were headed. Then he gave the good news—they had a 100-mile-an-hour tail-wind and they were ahead of schedule.

Our fiscal year began July 1st and will end on the coming June 30th—six months from now. The present budget for this twelve-month period is $4.6 billion, an all-time high for any of the fifty states. When this budget was presented, it was admittedly in excess of the estimated tax revenues for the year. It was adopted with the assurance that a change in bookkeeping procedures would solve this imbalance.

With half the year gone, and faced now with the job of planning next year's budget, we have an estimate provided by the experienced personnel of the Department of Finance. We have also an explanation of how a change in bookkeeping could seemingly balance a budget that called for spending $400 million more than we would take in.

Very simply, it was just another one-time windfall—a gimmick that solved nothing but only postponed the day of reckoning. We are financing the twelve-month spending with fifteen-month income. All the tax revenues for the first quarter of next year—July, August, and September—will be used to finance this year's expenses up to June 30th. And incidentally, even that isn't enough, because we will still have a deficit of some $63 million.

Now, with the budget established at its present level, we are told that it, of course, must be increased next year to meet the added problems of population growth and inflation. But the magic of the changed bookkeeping is all used up. We are back to only twelve months' income for twelve months' spending. Almost automatically we are being advised of all the new and increased taxes which, if adopted, will solve the problem. Curiously enough, another one-time windfall is being urged. If we switch to withholding of personal income tax, we will collect two years' taxes the first year and postpone our moment of truth perhaps until everyone forgets we did not cause the problem—we only inherited it. Or maybe we are to stall, hoping a rich uncle will remember us in his will.

If we accept the present budget as absolutely necessary and add on projected increases plus funding for property tax relief (which I believe is absolutely essential and for which we are preparing a detailed and comprehensive program), our deficit in the coming year would reach three-quarters of a billion dollars.

But Californians are already burdened with combined state and local taxes $113 per capita higher than the national average. Our property tax contributes to a slump in the real estate and building trades industries and makes it well-nigh impossible for many citizens to continue owning their own homes.

For many years now, you and I have been shushed like children and told there are no simple answers to the complex problems which are beyond our comprehension.

Well, the truth is, there are simple answers—they just are not easy ones. The time has come for us to decide whether collectively we can afford everything and anything we think of simply because we think of it. The time has come to run a check to see if all the services government provides were in answer to demands or were just goodies dreamed up for our supposed betterment. The time has come to match outgo to income, instead of always doing it the other way around.

The cost of California's government is too high; it adversely affects our business climate. We have a phenomenal growth with hundreds of thousands of people joining us each year. Of course, the overall cost of government must go up to provide necessary services for these newcomers, but growth should mean increased prosperity and thus a lightening of the load each individual must bear. If this isn't true, then you and I should be planning how we can put up a fence along the Colorado River and seal our borders.

Well, we aren't going to do that. We are going to squeeze and cut and trim until we reduce the cost of government. It won't be easy, nor will it be pleasant, and it will involve every department of government, starting with the Governor's office. I have already informed the legislature of the reorganization we hope to effect with their help in the executive branch and I have asked for their cooperation and support.

The new Director of Finance is in complete agreement that we turn to additional sources of revenue only if it becomes clear that economies alone cannot balance the budget.

Disraeli said: "Man is not a creature of circumstances. Circumstances are the creatures of men." You and I will shape our circumstances to fit our needs.

Let me reaffirm a promise made during the months of campaigning. I believe in your right to know all the facts concerning the people's business. Independent firms are making an audit of state finances. When it is completed, you will have that audit. You will have all the information you need to make the decisions which must be made. This is not just a problem for the administration; it is a problem for all of us to solve together. I know that you can face any prospect and do anything that has to be done as long as you know the truth of what you are up against.

We will put our fiscal house in order. And as we do, we will build those things we need to make our state a better place in which to live and we will enjoy them more, knowing we can afford them and they are paid for.

If, in glancing aloft, some of you were puzzled by the small size of our state flag . . . there is an explanation. That flag was carried into battle in Vietnam by young men of California. Many will not be coming home. One did—Sergeant Robert Howell—grievously wounded. He brought that flag back. I thought we would be proud to have it fly over the Capitol today. It might even serve to put our problems in better perspective. It might remind us of the need to give our sons and daughters a cause to believe in and banners to follow.

If this is a dream, it is a good dream, worthy of our generation and worth passing on to the next.

Let this day mark the beginning.

1967

THE VALUE OF UNDERSTANDING THE PAST

(Eureka College Library Dedication)

Speaking at Eureka College, Eureka, Illinois, September 28th

4.

It must be evident to most of you that only a thin wall of wavering willpower stands between you and an engulfing flood of nostalgia.

Ten years ago, in cap and gown, I stood in this place to receive an honorary degree—a happening which only compounded an already heavy burden of guilt. I had always figured the first degree you gave me was honorary.

That first degree was thirty-five years and a few months ago.

Now, as far as you students are concerned, that makes it definite I am *not* of your generation. There are those with differing political views who would go even further and place me as far back as the Ice Age—some even further to the time of McKinley.

Some here today, however, can bear witness that thirty-five years are like thirty-five minutes, so clear and fresh is memory. No matter how much you students may want to believe this, your imaginations are not quite up to it. You will just have to wait and find out for yourselves. But you will find out.

There is a tendency in today's world to put more than years between us. Somehow, as humans, we have been stratified into a horizontal society instead of vertical. Layers of humanity are separated into age groups from pre-school to those the social thinkers refer to as senior citizens. And somehow we are losing our ability to establish communications between layers. What is even worse, there is a growing hostility between these layers.

It is an unnatural situation. Humanity is vertically structured. The teenager will become the young married or junior executive, and, in turn, the middle-aged and eventually the senior citizen. Each one of us will take his faults and virtues, his pluses and minuses, through the years, being at all times the sum total of all he has experienced.

This separation into horizontal layers makes no sense at all. What of this talk that no one over thirty understands the youth of today? If this is true, then what happens when you reach thirty? Do you suddenly join us and quit understanding those who have not quite reached the magic age?

Each generation is critical of its predecessor. As the day nears when classroom and playing field must give way to the larger arena with its problems of inequality and human misunderstanding, it is easy to look at those in that arena and demand to know why the problems remain unsolved. We who preceded you asked that question of those who preceded us and another younger generation will ask it of you.

I hope there will be less justification for the question when it is your turn to answer. What I am trying to say is that no generation has failed completely, nor will yours succeed completely.

But don't get me wrong. When the generation of which I am a part leaves the stage, history will record that seldom has any generation fought harder or paid a higher price for freedom.

We have known three wars and now a fourth, a cataclysmic worldwide depression that toppled governments and reshaped the map. And, because we could not find the single cure-all for man's inhumanity to man or the answer to human frailty, we have downgraded our performance and confused you as well as ourselves.

It is easy to point to the failures and talk of the mess of our times, and even to promise we will do better. But for the record, since we are the generation that exploded the atomic bomb and brought a permanent terror to the world, we also harnessed the atom for peaceful purposes. And some of those peaceful purposes, in medicine and industrial power, have brought man to the threshold of a fabulous era.

We have defeated polio and tuberculosis and a host of plague diseases that held even more terror for mankind than the threat of the bomb. It is a certainty that your generation and ours will overlap in defeating cancer.

Point an accusing finger and list smog, water pollution, poverty, civil rights, inequality of opportunity. We still seek the answers, and, while many of us disagree as to the solutions, we were the ones who faced up to the problems and charged ourselves with finding the answers. No one in public life fails to treat these problems.

This horizontal stratification has led to lateral communication, and it is highly essential that we restore vertical dialogue, if not an outright recognition of the naturalness and rightness of a vertical structuring of society.

How well do young people understand those whose defect is age thirty-plus? Can you possibly believe your fathers who knew the savagery of World War II or your grandfathers who came of age in the muddy trenches of the Great War could possibly have an affection for war? That we would callously send our sons to war?

Permit me here to build at least a footbridge between the age groups of parent and child, remembering that bridges are open to traffic both ways.

That fellow with the thickening waist and the thinning hair who is sometimes unreasonable about your allowance or letting you have the car . . . his life seems a little dull to you now as he reports for his daily 9 to 5 chores, or looks forward to lowering a golf handicap, or catching a fish no one wants to eat.

I wish you could have known him a few years back on a landing craft at Normandy or Tarawa or on a weekend pass in Peoria. He was quite a guy. Winston Churchill said he was the only man in the world who could laugh and fight at the same time. General [George] Marshall called him our secret weapon. He hated war more than he hated the enemy, but he did what had to be done.

A few years after the end of World War II, I was in a little pub in rural England. The motherly soul who was waiting on trade figured out I was an American (for the life of me, I don't know how). She began to reminisce. "During the war," she said, "some of your chaps were stationed just across the road. They used to come in here and have song-fests. They called me Mom and my husband Pop. It was Christmas Eve and we were here all alone when the door burst open and there they were with presents for us." She paused for a tear or two and then said: "Big strappin' lads they was from a place called 'Ioway'."

I know those over-thirty fellows probably don't tell it very well so that you can see them as they were then, but they all knew what it was like to dream, to say goodbye to a girl and wonder when, if ever, they would see her again. They missed a world that let things like that happen, and swore they would do better when they got back and were running the show.

They came back from war and created an organization to outlaw war, and we have not known a single minute's peace since. The dream was a good dream, no effort was spared and we continue to pour out our treasure to make the dream come true. Proving again our vertical structure, this problem will be yours as well as ours to solve.

It wasn't that we faltered or lacked in willingness. There are organizational difficulties that could not have been foreseen. New and emerging nations with neither power nor responsibility for controlling world forces have a disproportionate voice in world councils. A two-thirds majority can be mustered among a half hundred nations who represent less than 10 percent of the world's population.

Are the problems of urban ghettoes and poverty the result of selfishness on our part or indifference to suffering? No people in all the history of mankind have shared so widely its material resources.

We taxed ourselves more heavily and extended aid at home and abroad. And when the problems grew, we planned more and passed more legislation to add to the scores of programs, until today, they are listed in government catalogues of hundreds of pages. We who are called materialist have tried to solve human problems with material means. We have forgotten man's spiritual heritage; we have placed security above freedom and confused the citizen's responsibility to society with society's responsibility to the individual.

We have to re-study some of our social legislation, legislation that meant well, but has failed in its goals or has created greater problems than the ones it was meant to cure.

We have to re-examine our individual goals and aims.

What do we want for ourselves and our children? Is it enough to have material things? Aren't liberty and morality and integrity and high principles and a sense of responsibility more important?

The world's truly great thinkers have not pointed us toward materialism; they have dealt with the great truths and with the high questions of right and wrong, of morality and of integrity.

They have dealt with the question of man, not the acquisition of things. And when civilizations have disregarded their findings, when they have turned to the things of the flesh, they have disappeared.

You are concerned with us and what seems to be hypocrisy and lack of purpose on our part. And we in turn are concerned about you, seeing a rising spirit of unrest, aimlessness, and drifting, a feeling of rebellion without a real cause that results sometimes in meaningless but violent actions. Now, let me make it plain. I am aware that all of you are unfairly suspect because of a very small percentage of dissidents.

Nevertheless, you do seek a purpose and a meaning to life, and apparently we have failed to give it to you. But, again, our failure was not one of bad intent.

We are the classic example of giving to you what we never had—from TV to wheels and dental care to Little League. But I am afraid we shortchanged you on responsibilities or the right to earn for yourselves.

All too often, because we had to earn, we wanted to give. Our motives have been laudable, but our judgment has been bad. "No" was either a dirty word or dropped from our vocabulary.

Some time ago in Newport, California, a row of luxurious oceanfront homes were threatened by an abnormally high tide and heavy surf. All through the day and night, volunteers worked, piling sandbags, in an effort to save these homes. Local TV stations, aware of the drama, covered the struggle. It was about 2 A.M. when one newscaster grabbed a young fellow in his teens, attired only in wet trunks. He had been working all day and night—one of several hundred of his age group. No, he did not live in one of the homes they were trying to save, and, yes, he was cold and tired. The newscaster inevitably got around to why. The answer was so poignant, such an indictment of so many of us, it should be on a billboard across the nation. He said: "Well, I guess it's the first time we've ever felt like we were needed."

You are needed; we need your courage, your idealism, your new and untried viewpoint. You know more than we did at your age; you are brighter, better informed, even healthier. And because human kind *is* vertically structured, we can take a little credit for that. But, you want a purpose, a cause, a banner to follow, and we owe you that.

A few years ago, a national magazine did a series of articles by prominent people including a president, a vice-president, and distinguished statesmen. Each wrote his idea of what was our national purpose. Somehow, nothing very exciting or profound resulted from these articles. I have always felt it was because they tried to invent something we already have and have had for two hundred years. Our national purpose is to unleash the full talent and genius of the individual, not to create mass movements with the citizenry subjecting themselves to the whims of the state. Here, as nowhere in the world, we are established to provide the ultimate in individual freedom consistent with law and order.

Today, we dedicate this library because Wesley and Clinton Melick have thought not in horizontal lines of just their associates in time. You want a purpose, something to believe in? You might try resolving that you will contribute something to generations unborn—a handhold above your own achievement so that another generation can climb higher and achieve more.

This library is more than a beautiful and functional building. It is first and foremost a repository of knowledge and culture. More facts will be available in this one library than were available in all the libraries of the world a hundred years ago.

That shouldn't surprise you.

Man's knowledge has increased at such a rapid rate since the turn of the century that any book of facts written then would be obsolete now, both in terms of what we know to be true and also what we know to be true no longer.

But a library is more than just a place to go for facts. A library is also a place to go for wisdom. And the purpose of an educational institution is to teach not only knowledge, but also wisdom.

Someone once said that people who want to understand democracy should spend less time in the library with Aristotle and more time on buses and subways.

In a way, that may be true.

But to understand democracy is not necessarily to solve its problems.

And I would venture to say Aristotle, and those others whom you will find not in the buses and subways, but instead in this building here, will give you more answers and more clues to the solutions of our problems than you are likely to find on the buses and subways.

Maybe the best answer is to be found in both, but do not let the library go to waste because you are awaiting the completion of Eureka's first subway.

Now, when I suggest that we turn to books, to the accumulated knowledge of the past, I am not suggesting that we turn back the clock or retreat into some dim yesterday that we remember only with nostalgia, if at all. But we must learn from yesterday to have a better tomorrow.

We are beset by problems in a complex world; we are confused by those who tell us only new and untried ways offer hope. The answers to all the problems of mankind will be found in this building by those who have the desire to find them and perception enough to recognize them.

There will be the knowledge of Aristotle, Plato, and Socrates, and from the vantage point of history, their mistakes. We can look back and see where pure democracy became as dictatorial as a sultan and majority rule without protection for the minority became mob rule.

One of mankind's problems is that we keep repeating the same errors. For every generation some place, two plus two has added up to three, or in another place, five—four seems to elude some of us. This has happened in my generation and I predict, without smugness, it will happen to yours.

But, these two men here today have given something almost beyond comprehension.

Do you doubt the answers can be found here? From the eleventh century, Maimonides, Hebrew philosopher and physician, will give you the eight steps in helping the needy to help themselves.

Can you name one problem that would not be solved if we had simply followed the teachings of the man from Galilee?

We can redirect our nation's course into the paths of freedom and morality and high principle.

And, in so directing it, we can build better lives for ourselves and our children and a better nation for those who come after us, or we can ignore history and go the way of Greece and Rome.

I think that this is the significance of this library. The fact that we can use it to rechart our course, not into the great unknown, but onto paths that are clear and which, if followed, can show us how to cope with the new problems that always confront each generation and can lead us, as a people, on to continued greatness.

There were many who had a hand in this, but they would be the first to say it happened because of you, Wes and Clint Melick. On behalf of all of us who knew Eureka and those still to come, we thank you. Eureka means "We have found a way of life." You have made the search much easier.

1970

OURS IS NOT A SICK SOCIETY

(Accomplishments of the American Free Enterprise System)

Speaking at Sacramento Host Breakfast, Sacramento, California, September 4th

5.

It is a great privilege to address this annual gathering of the leaders of California business and industry. I have long been concerned about the practice of separating our people—pitting group against group—as if the interests of one are totally incompatible with the other. By coincidence, on Monday (Labor Day), I will be speaking to a gathering of rank-and-file members as well as leaders of organized labor. I am sure that my remarks here, and what I say there, would be easily interchangeable. Certainly, there is nothing contradictory about my presence at both of these meetings. For one thing, there is my own background of some twenty-five years as an officer and board member of a union.

But, more important, there is the truism so often expressed by that great labor statesman and patriot—Samuel Gompers, founder of the AFL. Some today would like to have us forget how often he preached that labor and management were partners—equally responsible for the preservation of the American free enterprise system—coequal members of "the establishment."

I am sure Mr. Gompers would have little patience today with those who claim that private enterprise, including labor and management, is engaged in some kind of consortium with government to perpetuate war, poverty, injustice, and prejudice. Nor would Mr. Gompers passively accept the charge that ours is a sick society—beyond repair and incapable of providing answers for the horrendous problems that darken our days and fill our nights with terror.

We hear so much of this these days that I think it is time the establishment—the hard-working, over-taxed men and women of labor and management, the hard-hats and the soft-hats, blue collar and white, housewife and secretary—takes inventory. We have been picked at, sworn at, rioted against, and down-graded until we have a built-in guilt complex.

And this has been compounded by the accusations of our sons and daughters who pride themselves on "telling it like it is." Well, I have news for them—in a thousand social science courses they have been taught "the way it is *not*." They are not informed, they are *mis*-informed, and they know a great many things that are not true. The overwhelming majority of them are fine young people who will turn out just great if we make sure they hear both sides of the story.

(I do not know about the small percentage who "have torch, will travel"—if they can get a free ride. They cannot wait to put on a string of love beads and beat up the Dean . . . in the name of peace. Do not be surprised if the New Left turns out to be the Old Left, in sandals and jeans.)

Let us hope they are bright enough to discover this in time—but they have no chance unless we set the record straight. The world they will take over is less than perfect. Poverty has not been eliminated, bigotry and injustice still exist in too many hearts, and man's greatest stupidity—war—still takes place. But it is a better world than we inherited, which in turn was better than our fathers took over, and so it will be, hopefully, for some generations to come.

As for our generation, I will make no apology. No people in all history paid a higher price for freedom. And no people have done so much to advance the dignity of man. We did not have to make a field trip to the ghetto or the sharecropper's farm to see poverty. We lived it in a great depression. Few of us will ever forget the look in the eyes of men, once able and skilled, who lined up at charity soup kitchens—their pride eaten away by hunger.

Perhaps this is why we have taxed ourselves at a rate higher than any society ever imposed on itself—to give the disadvantaged a second chance at life. We have not been too wise in this effort, and we have failed in achieving our purpose, but not because we lacked compassion. The effort continues.

We fought the grizzliest war in history—and let it be recorded that never have the issues of right and wrong been so clearly defined as they were in that conflict. One wonders how many have given thought to what this world would be like today if our generation had not been willing to bleed its finest young men into the sand at Omaha Beach, the mud of Normandy, and a hundred coral atolls in the Pacific. We knew, and hope our children will learn, that the truly great values upon which civilization is built are those things for which men must be willing to die.

From time to time, a single generation is called upon to preside over a great transition period in man's progress. Ours was such a generation.

The other day a student body president from one of our universities challenged that we could not understand our sons and daughters. He told me that when we were young we did not have jets, nuclear power, instant electronic communications, and computers that could solve in seconds what had previously taken months and years. I agreed: we did not have those things when we were young—we invented them!

I have already lived ten years longer than my life expectancy when I was born. Our children do not even know the names of some of the diseases we knew. Diseases that had maimed and killed for centuries are now almost forgotten because of our efforts, our dollars and our research.

When we were born, two-thirds of us lived in substandard housing; now it is less than ten percent. Ninety percent of all Americans lived below what is considered the poverty line; by the time it was our turn to take over that had been reduced by more than half and in our adult lifetime; we have brought it down to only ten percent. Let those who cry "revolution now" take a second look—for our generation has presided over the greatest social and economic revolution the world has ever seen.

We took on a racial problem no other people had ever tackled before. Granted, we have not erased prejudice from every heart—or will it be erased by militant behavior or parading pickets—but we opened doors that had been locked and barred for a hundred years.

If I may use a personal example again as a measuring point, I began my post-college years as a radio sports announcer broadcasting major league baseball. I had no Willie Mays or Hank Aarons or Maury Wills to describe. The official rule book opened with the line, "Baseball is a game for Caucasian gentlemen." And so it was in most other things—the professions, executive positions, white collar employment, foreman and supervisory jobs, and the skilled crafts. Education for our Negro citizens was barely minimal.

Today, 30 percent of employed Negroes hold what

are classed as high status jobs. In the last decade alone there has been a 50 percent increase in foreman and skilled craftsman jobs held by Negroes. Their median income in the decade of the '60s rose more than 50 percent, and the difference in average years of schooling between Negroes and Whites has virtually disappeared. Probably the most significant figure is that of college opportunity: a higher percentage of our young Negro men and women go to college in America than the percentage of Whites in any other country in the world.

It is true this is still not good enough—much remains to be done, and we are the ones in the forefront saying, "let's get it done." And, if our sons and daughters make the same progress in the next twenty years that we have made in the past twenty, the racial problem will be solved for all time to come.

No, ours is not a sick society; nor is our social and economic system in total disrepair. In the aftermath of World War II, we poured hundreds of billions of dollars into Europe and very possibly prevented a collapse into anarchy. We staved off famine in India and restored our enemies' capacity to produce and to be self-sufficient. Our workers work fewer hours and produce a standard of living kings couldn't afford a short time ago.

For this we are called materialistic. Maybe so. But there are more local symphonies in this country than in all the rest of the world put together, more opera and more amateur theaters, mail order houses advertising original paintings at prices all can afford, golf, boating and equestrian sports—once the special province of the rich—are the weekend pleasure of the working man.

Our materialism has made our children the biggest, tallest, most handsome, and intelligent generation of

Americans yet. They will live longer, with fewer illnesses, learn more, see more of the world, and have more success in realizing their personal dreams and ambitions than any other people in any other period of history—because of our "materialism."

In the meantime, we must see that their evaluation of their heritage is based on fact and not the distortions of some malcontents who suffer mental hyperacidity. One-half of all the economic activity of the human race in its entire history has been conducted under American auspices. In that Marxian Utopia, the Soviet Union must force its workers to labor seven times as long as their American counterparts to earn food, twelve-and-one-half times as long to buy a bar of soap, and fifteen times as many hours to buy a suit of clothes. By diligent effort we, too, could have their kind of Utopia—but we would have to tear down 60 percent of our homes, 65 percent of our railroads, and 90 percent of our phones.

And somehow I think an idealistic generation of young Americans would find the vast bureaucracy of a collectivist state much more lacking in soul than the American businessman they know so little about. More than fifty million Americans are engaged in volunteer work for charities, youth activities, and community projects. More than half of our combined federal, state and local budgets go for health, welfare, and education. On top of this tax burden, our citizens and businesses freely contribute another $14 billion to good causes.

Last year American businessmen found a quarter of a million unemployables who had never in their lifetimes held a steady job. They were trained and put to work in jobs paying more than some had ever dreamed they would have.

Last year these same businessmen spent hundreds of millions of dollars to send kids from the ghettos to college.

You here know something of all this. For three years your State Chamber has joined with labor and government to conduct "Summer Jobs for Youth" campaigns. And the Chamber provided the impetus and the funding for the Athletes for Jobs Program.

Let me interject here on behalf of government my thanks for all that your Chamber, under Ernie Loebbecke and the directors and the staff, is doing in all those fields which have direct bearing on the future of California. Thanks to all of you, we headed off fiscal chaos by defeating Proposition 8 and insuring orderly progress in the financing of schools, veterans homes, recreational development, and the great water project by passing Proposition 7.

Since last we met, the creative partnership between government and business has been greatly expanded and enhanced. Your World Trade Department, dedicated to increasing California's share of the world's export-import market, is in close harmony with our Industry and World Trade Commission which is headed by Bill Roberts at Ampex. You continue to help fund the California bicentennial through the sale of medallions. The list of the Chamber contributions to the California community is great, and so is the list of problems confronting us.

There is the matter of pollution of our environment. Each one of us must help determine what kind of earth future generations will inherit and, in fact, whether future generations will have a habitable earth; for the earth's environment is a closed system and we are close to overtaxing that system.

Free men engaged in free enterprise build better nations with more and better goods and services, higher wages and higher standards of living for more people. But free enterprise is not a hunting license, and it is the hallmark of contemporary management that it recognizes the individual and social responsibilities which go hand-in-hand with freedom.

If we are honest we must accept the fact that the same industrial-technological revolution that has helped raise our standard of living, and has served as a derivative source of income for both the citizen and his government, has also been the cause of a great deal of the effluence which pollutes our environment. We know that we cannot shut down our factories and our plants—we cannot throw hundreds of thousands of our people out of work and destroy our economy. But we can—and we do—expect that business and industry will do everything possible to produce the maximum affluence with the minimum of effluence.

I believe that the vast majority of businessmen are with us on this. They, too, are sick of breathing dirty air and swimming or fishing or boating in dirty water. As a matter of fact, let me commend you on your Advisory Committee on California's Environment which is chaired by Dr. Arnold Beckman. This committee can do great work in helping to improve and protect the quality of life in our state.

But even the work of such a committee will be diminished unless business and industry apply the same inventive genius, the same technological emphasis to the problems of pollution that it used to produce cans that will not rust, plastics that will not decay, and detergents that will not dissolve.

Former Soviet Premier Nikita Krushchev once boasted that he would bury us. He failed—but unless we all get together and solve the problems of pollution, we may bury ourselves—*in garbage.*

At the moment, our minds are concerned with another problem, and those of little faith are already crying "doom" . . . a refrain they chanted after World War II and after Korea. After three straight years of the lowest unemployment we have known in decades, we are in an economic pinch that has (among other things) increased unemployment to almost the level we were accustomed to in the several years prior to 1967. I have no intention of minimizing the hardship of the trained and willing worker who is unable to find a job, but there is no reason to give way to panic.

An effort had to be made to slow inflation—that effort was long overdue; perhaps because those in charge did not have the courage to face the temporary dislocation such a move could bring about. Added to this has been the transition from a war to a peacetime economy. This, too, had to happen and had been ducked. Approximately 800,000 former military personnel and defense workers have entered the labor market nationally. California's share should be about 80,000.

I have little patience with those who question whether we can handle the situation. We have never been more prosperous or more generous with our prosperity, never more truly concerned with the welfare of the less fortunate, with education, and equality of opportunity, never more determined to bring decency and order to the world.

It is time we ended our obsession with what is wrong and realized how much is right, how great is our power, and how little we have to fear.

If California were a nation, we would be one of the

world's great economic giants. The United States would be first in gross national production, and California would rank seventh. The Los Angeles area, alone, produces a gross product exceeded by only nine nations of the world. Only the United States has more automobiles than California, and only the United States and Japan have more telephones.

Except for tiny, oil-rich Kuwait, with its population of 600 thousand, California's 20 million people earn more and spend more than their counterparts in the rest of the world. They are younger—with a median age of thirty; 84 percent of them live in cities of more than 25 thousand population, and still we lead the nation in agricultural wealth.

Half of America's Nobel laureates reside in California, and of the 842 members of the National Academy of Sciences, 110 are on the faculty of the University of California, alone.

If California's problems and California's people were put into a ring together, it would have to be declared a mismatch. There is nothing we cannot do if we put our hearts, minds, and muscle to the job.

If I may paraphrase the late and immortal General George Patton—I pity our poor d--n problems, I surely do.

1972

THE OBLIGATIONS OF LIBERTY

(United States Foreign Affairs)

Speaking to the World Affairs Council, October 12th

6.

I have been abroad in recent months on an errand for the President [Richard Nixon]. I do not pretend that having seen the monkey, I can now run the circus; but I could not make such a trip, meet the heads of state I was privileged to meet, and carry the messages entrusted to me without realizing that America's role in world affairs, the decisions we make, the positions we take in international affairs, will largely determine whether our children live in peace and prosperity.

America's foreign and defense policies in the decade ahead are vital matters that concern every American.

In the past thirty years, we have fought three wars and helped rebuild the countries that were devastated by those wars. We have given more than $150 billion of our national resources to help our friends—and even some of our former enemies—to become economically self-sufficient. We have opened our own markets to imports because we believe in the principle of free trade. We have generously shared our technology. We know that commercial contacts among nations not only help achieve prosperity for all; but they also represent a contribution to peace, because political stability cannot be maintained without financial stability among the major nations of the world.

A few days ago, Denmark joined the European Common Market, the second nation to affiliate with that economic union in the past year. That event, along with

Britain's addition to the Common Market earlier this year, is another signal to us that the future will be very different from what we have known in the past quarter century, an era in which America was largely dominant in the world's commercial affairs.

With Britain's vast trade included, the Common Market Nations now have a greater domestic market potential than our own. The population of the Common Market nations is larger than America's, and their combined exports are twice our total.

The nations we helped to recover following World War II have matured economically. They are making their own products and selling them not only in their home markets, but also in America and elsewhere.

To meet these new conditions will require more than a one-step economic game plan. It should be apparent to any thinking person that the President has a plan that looks far beyond the war in Vietnam that has so bitterly divided our people for a decade. His actions in the past year—the initiatives he has taken diplomatically and economically, the phase-out of the war, and our long-range defense program, all are intertwined in a grand design to achieve a goal we have not known in our lifetimes—a generation of peace and a prosperity based on peace.

Our foreign trade, the world monetary system, and our still-necessary defense alliances are part of this carefully charted path. Each of them is important to achieving the overall objective.

Whether we succeed or not will depend on how America responds to the challenges of the 1970s.

Demagogic talk by the "let's kick business" fraternity will not insure jobs for our skilled and semi-skilled workers. Right now, taxes on business in the United States are proportionately higher than those paid by our competitors in the Common Market and Japan.

One of the decisions we must make involves inflation, because inflation and lagging productivity have been major causes of our trade deficits.

During the build-up for the war in Southeast Asia, America's economic position became distorted. Our country drifted into that conflict without a definite plan for victory or for dealing with the inflation that inevitably accompanies war. And in the late 1960s, America paid the price for that short-sighted attitude. The rate of inflation doubled and then tripled. The value of the dollar eroded, and America found more and more of its products priced out of world markets.

America cannot accept a 6 percent rate of inflation year after year without ultimate economic chaos. Certainly the President knew this, for he acted decisively on a number of fronts. And we are now beginning to see the results.

From mid-1971 to mid-1972, the Consumer Price Index in the United States rose only 2.9 percent. But in a remarkable turnabout, the rate of inflation has been growing to 6 and 7 percent in Europe.

Because America's leaders had the courage to face up to the threat of inflation and do something about it, consumer confidence is being restored; business is expanding; the unemployment rate is dropping.

And after a decade in which our output per man-hour dropped us to last among the fourteen major industrial nations, our productivity rate is now moving ahead.

The President is engaged in negotiations to achieve monetary stability and to lower the high tariffs that discriminate against American goods. At long last America is insisting that other nations pay more than lip service to the principle of free trade. The blunt truth is that while we have given most-favored-nation status to most of our trading partners, they have often responded by making us the least-favored-nation in selling our goods in their markets.

But this is only a part of the challenge America faces in the decade ahead.

The most essential ingredient for America's future prosperity has less to do with productivity and our trade balance than it does with the larger issue of how America sees itself and its role in the world.

We did not seek the role of leadership that has been thrust upon us. But whether we like it or not, the events of our time demand America's participation.

We cannot hide our head in the sand while events swirl about us—events that can determine whether there shall be war or peace—prosperity or economic chaos.

Make no mistake about it. Despite the lessening of tensions and the hopeful signs of great power cooperation in the future, it is America's industrial and economic strength, translated into military potential, that represents the single greatest guarantee of peace for the world.

Now I realize that yours is a non-political organization. But the things that concern you as an organization and as individual citizens are political decisions. In this year of decision we will choose whether to continue fighting with every economic tool we have to reduce inflation or if we want to accept calculated, planned, and programmed inflation that is part of one candidate's economic game plan. We must decide whether America should base its economic prosperity on work, the skills and the productivity of its people; whether we should seek job opportunities for all in the productive private sector; or whether we should put almost half of America's population on a dole—or a make-work public payroll—raising the taxes of those who work in order to redistribute the national income among those who do not.

Most important of all, we will decide whether America is willing to do whatever is necessary to maintain America's freedom against all threats.

We must ask ourselves if we are willing to risk all that we call the American way on the naive hope that our potential enemies have mellowed so much that they no longer have any aggressive designs.

Cutting $30 billion from the defense budget, dismantling great parts of our navy and air force, scaling back the space program, and ignoring technical developments, such as the super sonic transport, are real issues, not subjects for a senior thesis. They are political decisions to be made in the political arena, and they will determine America's fate and possibly the fate of mankind for years to come.

The President wants to end the Cold War era of conflict and to substitute an era of negotiations and peaceful settlements of disputes before they flare into war.

I am sure every American shares that goal. But are we also aware that every nation in history which has sought peace and freedom solely through negotiation has been crushed by conquerors bent on conquest and aggression?

There was a time in the not too distant past when you could have taken all the non-aggression pacts and disarmament treaties with their beribboned seals and signatures, and papered the walls of the League of Nations.

If that is too cynical a view, let me *make it perfectly clear* that along with a willingness to negotiate, America can best protect the peace by maintaining a realistic and credible ability to defend itself, should the need occur.

On my Presidential errands over the past two years, meeting with the heads of state of Asian and European nations, I was made aware of what has to be recognized as a great change in attitude toward the United States. It is my personal opinion that it reflects our departure from decades of trying to buy the world's affection, and our new determination to have the world's respect.

I was in Japan during the time of the President's drastic currency and trade moves, meeting almost daily with the Prime Minister, the Ministers of Trade, Foreign Affairs, etc. The American press quoted many Americans who were fearful of deteriorating relations with our great trading partner. Their opinions were not shared by the Japanese leaders with whom I met. As one of them put it, "Your country and ours have been on a honeymoon during which there have been no disagreements. Now the honeymoon has ripened into a happy marriage, and as in any good marriage, there will be an occasional quarrel."

In Europe this summer, my errand had to do mainly with our NATO headquarters. I discovered that these men who must look at the face of a potential enemy, not across an ocean, but across a border, were convinced that this American President had a realistic understanding of the world situation. What is more, they were aware that he had a plan based on this understanding; that he was going forward with intelligence and calculation; and that his plan offered a real chance for peace based on the world situation as it is, and not on some vague hope that the enemy will decide to become an overnight "goodie two-shoes."

What would be the attitude of the men I met if the United States chose to abandon one ally simply for our own convenience?

There is no way for America to turn inward and embrace isolationism in the world as it is today without jeopardizing all the progress we have made toward peace in this century. For those genuinely concerned with peace and willing to pay the price for it, there is only one path to choose. It is not the easiest; it is the wisest. If we carry the burden of responsibility destiny has placed on our shoulders, we do not become a dropout in world affairs.

1973

HOW OUR SYSTEM WORKS

(Understanding the Competitive Economic System)

Speaking to the American Textile Manufacturers Institute, San Francisco, California, March 29th

7.

Last week Nancy and I were privileged to have as guests in our home some of our returned prisoners of war. It was an unforgettable experience, and one I am happy to say we shall repeat several times until we have hosted all our Californians who endured that long separation from home and loved ones.

Seeing these men and how they have grown even stronger—stronger in their love of country, faith in God, and yes, faith in their fellow Americans—I could not help but wonder: where do we find such men?

The answer, of course, is we found them where we always have, in the small towns, the cities, and the farms of America. We produced them in a society which, with whatever faults it may have, is still the most generous, most just system of human relationships ever devised by man.

But with that answer, another question came to mind: When their almost Rip Van Winkle homecoming loses its newness, when the wonder of new styles and fashions has worn off, will they see other changes they will find harder to get used to?

Have we here at home lost some of the self-reliance which was their very salvation? Is the voice of the demagogue and false prophet a little more strident—able to attract more listeners than in the past? Do we quarrel when we should pull together?

Since World War II, our country has been a benefactor to the world, rebuilding the economies and the industrial plants of those countries which suffered so much damage in war—friends and foe alike.

We have been a generous, even an indulgent trading partner. We have opened our markets to foreign goods and have been more than patient with the tariffs and other trade barriers imposed against our goods. The countries we helped are now our most sophisticated competitors in world trade.

But it is now clear that no economy—even one as strong as ours—can keep on indefinitely shouldering the burdens we have piled on the American economy. Yet voices are continually raised blaming this free way of ours for our troubles. A political and economic mythology which denies the immutable laws of economics has been created.

There is a widespread lack of understanding as to how our system works. Right now, the President is struggling to bring inflation under control. Among other things, he has put a brake on federal spending which has brought charges that somehow he has seized unusual and dangerous powers that threaten our governmental system with dictatorship.

Actually, impoundment has been a prerogative of the chief executive since Jefferson's time. Jefferson refused to spend some $50,000 appropriated by Congress for a gunboat on the Mississippi on the grounds that relations with the Indians had improved sufficiently so that it was not needed.

President Nixon has impounded 3.5 percent of the federal budget, and some Congressmen find this a threat to democracy. Yet in 1961, the late President Kennedy withheld or impounded 7.8 percent of budgeted funds, and the next year 6.1 percent. Lyndon Johnson impounded 6.5 percent of the budget in 1966 and 6.7 percent in 1967. And yet you cannot recall any outraged cries from the Congress. Nor were there any charges that these two Presidents were a threat to our democratic institutions.

But now things are different. Powerful blocs in Congress and in the bureaucracy regard an unspent federal dollar as some sort of mortal sin. They talk of the need for new taxes. Raising taxes to cure inflation is like taking another drink to sober up.

The opposition the President is encountering in his battle against inflation comes from the very people who told us a few years ago that America could afford guns and butter, too—that we could finance a war in Southeast Asia, undertake a massive expansion of government at home, and not disrupt the economy or cause inflation. Indeed, we were told inflation was good for us.

We were asked to accept a dream world that never was and never will be. Inflation doubled and tripled and set our country on an inflationary treadmill that the President is determined to slow down for the simple reason that unless we do, this nation—and that means the world—is headed for the biggest bellyache we have ever known.

We have been riding an economic roller-coaster, an inflated prosperity induced and sustained by war and crisis and financed by borrowing against the future.

And guess what? The future is here. It is now that inevitable morning after, and we find there is a new world we have to adjust to—particularly in this matter of peaceful competition in world trade.

One of our troubles is the shocking decline of productivity in American industry, the needless expense of massive strikes that cripple whole industries and cause American business to lose customers to our competitors.

In the decade of the '60s, Japan's industrial production increased almost five times as much as ours, and the Soviet Union more than doubled our 74 percent gain. Between 1965 and 1970, the amount of goods and services produced per man-hour in America was the lowest of all the fourteen major industrial nations.

Somehow, in these past forty years or so, we have lost sight of just what made America great.

We are still the same creative people. But we have to remember a few of the fundamentals. No one *gave* America its high standard of living. Our people *earned* it—by outproducing every industrial society the world has ever known.

We must demand that other nations pay more than lip service to the principle of free trade. Your industry, I know, is acutely sensitive to this problem.

In 1950, America ranked number one in steel production. Today, the Soviet Union is number one in this vital industry.

Two decades ago, we owned 42 percent of the free world's gold reserves; now we are down to about 8 percent.

As our balance of payments deficit grew bigger, our gold reserves flowed out of America to settle foreign accounts.

The devaluation of the dollar is supposed to help stabilize the world monetary situation, and I am not prepared to argue that it will not. But let us not kid ourselves. To say that it is a solution in itself is like telling the pale fellow leaving the blood bank that he will feel better if he goes back in and gives another quart. The plain truth is the holiday is over, and we have to get back to work. And that means turning off those voices who would have us believe we can sit back and leave everything to government.

For one thing government's record is not all that good. In the 1960s, government declared war on poverty. Poverty won.

When government sets out to solve a problem, the cure may not be worse than the disease. But it is bigger and it costs more. Government does not really solve problems; it subsidizes them. And it does not produce a dime of revenue. It can spend only what it first takes from the pockets of the working men and women of this country.

In the past few years, there has been an increasing assault on the very economic system that built America from a small backward country into the world's strongest. You as businessmen are blamed for many things you have not done, and given little credit for a number of things you have done very well. Under the guise of consumerism, environmental protection, and just the old bromide "Big Business and Big Labor require Big Government"—an assortment of activists for one cause or another are attempting to assume the privileges of management without accepting the responsibilities.

To some people, profit is a six-letter dirty word. Business is viewed with suspicion while government, big government, is hailed as a panacea. There is an appalling lack of understanding of the simple workings of the marketplace and the competitive economic system.

Right now there is concern over the high price of food. But food for the family even at today's prices is only a third of the total cost of government—federal, state, and local. Indeed, the average citizen pays more for government than he pays for food, shelter, and clothing *combined.* He works more than five months of the year just to pay his taxes.

Some weeks ago I asked the National Association of Manufacturers the questions I now ask you: When do you start fighting back? When do you start correcting misconceptions, presenting the facts, because the facts are on your side?

No government agency can match the genius of the private sector in solving problems, in meeting new conditions, in providing services for the people.

Nowhere has the political demagogue had more success than in the area of taxes and the idea that business can be made to pay the costs of government relieving, of course, the citizen of his need to pay.

Only it never works that way. People pay taxes. You can take the demagogues' ammunition away by telling the people, once and for all, the simple truth that business taxes are paid by the consumer in the price of the product.

Just as excessive regulation can stifle creativity, excessive government spending becomes a drag on the economy, a barrier to prosperity.

The critics of free enterprise and American business complain about high prices, but they never mention government's role in high prices.

Why shouldn't business silence the political demagogue once and for all by explaining that business does not pay taxes. Business *collects* taxes for government—the kind of hidden taxes that are so favored by the demagogues.

Yet we are told that if business is just taxed a little more, this would produce more than enough money to finance whatever spending scheme anyone could dream up. Of course the inference is that we can have more goodies from government at no cost to the people.

This has gone on so long that many of you have succumbed to the Karl Marx theory of inevitability. The greatest myth of all is the idea that government is too big to be controlled—that our problems are too complex to be solved, that government spending must keep going up and up, and the people cannot do anything about it.

Permit me to tell you of our experience here in California. Until two years ago, the cost of welfare in California was going up more than three times faster than our state revenues. The whole system was smothered under thousands of loosely written regulations that invited abuses. It was unfair to the taxpayers and to the people who really needed help. And the state was headed for bankruptcy or an every-other-year increase in taxes. So we set out to do what we were told could not be done—reform welfare.

We did not listen to the cries of doom and gloom, and finally, with the people's support, most of the reforms were adopted. When we started, welfare in California was increasing by about 40,000 people a month. Now, just two years later, there are 274,000 fewer people on welfare than when we started. Eligibility standards to eliminate fraud have been instituted. We have been able to give an almost 30 percent increase to the truly needy, plus cost of living adjustments for the senior citizens, the blind and the disabled.

We are implementing a work program for able-bodied adult recipients so they can earn their welfare check or learn a skill that will enable them to become self-supporting.

The total savings is approaching $1 billion in state, local, and federal taxes. And forty-two of California's fifty-eight counties were able to reduce their basic property tax rates in the year after our reforms were enacted.

But we still think government costs too much; the total tax burden is too high. So here we go again. We are proposing a constitutional amendment to limit the amount of taxes the state can take from the people—a lid on state spending.

Some critics call it a visionary concept, a drastic change of course for government. I will not quarrel with that. Our very system of government in America was a visionary concept when it was proposed two hundred years ago.

And it was a drastic change in government. It gave the rule of government to the people. Well, we propose to give our people the opportunity to decide how much of their income state government can take from them in taxes. We believe it is an idea whose time has come. Again the political mythology has kept people from realizing the real cost of government and its rate of increase. Back in 1930, the total cost of government was only about 15 percent of the people's income. By 1950, that had grown to 32 percent. Today, the combined cost of government—federal, state, and local—takes 44.7 cents out of every dollar the people earn. If this rate of increase is allowed to continue—if we do nothing to change it, in fifteen years government's share will be 55 cents and still going up. In our state this means state revenues which are presently $9.8 billion will grow to $47.4 billion in fifteen years. And make no mistake about it, if government is getting $47 billion, government will spend it. We do not believe the people of California can afford that much government.

Under our plan, the state's share of personal income—the amount it could legally take from the people in taxes—would be gradually reduced from what today is 8.75 percent of the personal income to about 7 percent fifteen years from now. There would be no dislocation of present services, and indeed there is ample revenue for growth, inflation and even innovative new programs. But the people's take-home pay would grow faster than the deduction for taxes.

We have made provisions for emergencies. And if the people ever decided they wanted some new program that would push state taxes beyond the allowable tax limit, they could vote for it. But, even with this revenue control program, there would be enough revenue to permit the state budget to double in ten years and to triple—to $27 billion—by 1989. Very simply, we would for fifteen years reduce the percentage of the citizens' earnings taken for taxes by 0.1 percent each year until we reached the 7 percent limit.

This would amount to roughly a 20 percent reduction in total taxes over those fifteen years. In only five years, this could mean a 25 percent reduction of state income taxes.

In ten years, there could be a 60 percent reduction in state income taxes or a two cent cut in the state sales tax. Or any combination of tax reductions could be made, as the legislature determined.

The important thing is this: we will be establishing, once and for all, a maximum amount that state government can take out of the earnings of the people.

We have asked the legislature to put this program before the people. But the philosophy that government should have an unlimited credit card, payable by the taxpayer, is pretty widespread. Because the legislature's majority has said it will refuse to allow the people to vote on this issue, we are launching a petition campaign to gather enough signatures to hold a referendum. We think the people have a right to decide how much of their income government may take.

I should add that when I said this was an idea whose time had come, I had a few facts to substantiate it. Thanks to our welfare reforms and some other economies, we have an $850 million one-time surplus we propose to rebate to the taxpayers, and an ongoing surplus which will permit an across-the-board cut of 7.5 percent in the state income tax.

When an individual spends beyond his income for a long period of time, he ends up bankrupt. When government does it, the extra spending comes out of the pockets of the people through higher taxes. The people are forced to reduce their standard of living to pay for government's excesses.

We must impose some reasonable fiscal restraints. You can lecture your teenagers about spending too much until you are blue in the face, or you can accomplish the same goal by cutting their allowance.

We think it is time to limit government's allowance—to put a limit on the amount of money they can take from the people in taxes. This is the only way we will ever bring government spending under control. And controlling spending is the only way to permanently reduce taxes.

1973

AN IDEA WHOSE TIME HAS COME

(California and Taxation Reform)

Speaking to the California Federation of Women's Clubs, San Francisco, California, May 22nd

8.

Several years ago, when I became Governor, I had a strong belief, a conviction, that in recent years government had strayed from the limitations on what constitutes its real responsibility—that government was indeed seeking not only to protect us from each other—which is and should be government's function—but that government was trying to protect us from ourselves. We cannot possibly afford the government it would take to do that. Even worse, for government to attempt such a thing, government would have to assume powers not granted it by the people, and thus our freedom would be curtailed to a dangerous degree.

The machinery of state government I inherited those several years ago was fast losing the capacity to meet its responsibilities. The twelve-month budget for 1966-67 was to be funded by fifteen-months' revenues. This, of course, meant either drastic cutbacks or a giant tax increase. We had to do both. The tax increase was mandatory because government had spent itself into debt and was continuing to spend a million dollars more each day than it was taking in. But we also started to locate and eliminate what seemed to be useless fat in government.

This brought down on our heads the wrath of all those who believe government has some kind of omnipotence and can solve any problem by throwing money at it. I doubt if anyone here can recall one single instance of criticism in these past six years directed at us for spending.

But every effort we made at economy was attacked as destroying government's effectiveness. When we made changes in hidebound procedures to improve those services which are government's legitimate responsibilities, we were assailed as destroying government on the false altar of penny-pinching. There was no recognition of the fact that the tactic of "cut, squeeze, and trim" applied only to reduction of fat. The muscle fibre necessary to meet the legitimate tasks of government was actually being strengthened.

Almost one thousand highway projects were built with money formerly spent on administrative overhead. The number of full-time government employees, which had increased more than 25 percent in the preceding six years, has remained virtually unchanged. At the same time, we have been able to double the highway patrol and take over policing of the freeways in our metropolitan areas, freeing the police for crime fighting duties. We are virtually the only state with a steadily declining fatality rate on our streets and highways.

We have also added four hundred correctional officers in our prisons because of the higher ratio of violent to non-violent type inmates. Yet, while we have held the overall number of employees level, we have appointed more members of minority groups to policy-making positions than all the previous administrations combined.

In the treatment of the mentally ill, we have been constantly accused of closing hospitals to achieve economy, when in truth we were changing from the old-fashioned concept of lifetime warehousing of mental patients to the newer idea of better treatment in smaller, more personal community health centers aimed at curing and returning them to normal living. The budget for community mental health programs has increased from $18 billion to more than $134 billion. The increases have paid off—we are recognized as a leader in this field throughout the nation.

Charges of false economies in education were made. Yet, the budget for the University of California has gone, from $240 million to $429 million, a 78 percent increase in spending to cover a 38 percent increase in enrollment. There were dire threats that quality would suffer. Well, it has not. In state aid to public schools, K to 12, the six-year increase in dollars has been almost sixteen times greater than the percentage increase in enrollment.

Two years ago, the welfare caseload was increasing 40,000 a month, and 16 percent of the nation's welfare recipients were in California. We proposed a total overhaul and reform of welfare and Medi-Cal. For months the legislative leadership held out against these reforms until public opinion finally persuaded them to concur. Today, there are 263,000 *fewer* people on welfare than there were two years ago. The economies were sizeable, but the truly deserving who depend on us for support had their grants increased 30 percent.

This record of improvement in service to the people is the same throughout the other agencies and departments of government. Parks and recreational facilities have been expanded and improved and any number of services have been speeded up, eliminating tiresome delays.

I have told you these things because right now we have proposed a reform in taxation that we believe will have an even greater effect on life in California than those very successful welfare reforms. But the same complaining voices—the doom criers who have been so consistently wrong—are at it again. They are sure that our tax proposal will put government in a straitjacket and halt progress for all time to come. This we categorically deny.

But let me tell you how we came to propose this program of tax control and limitation. In all our efforts to curb spending these past several years, the clinching argument that curbed the excesses of the big spenders was: "We do not have the money." I am sure you have run up against that line at home now and then—it is sort of unanswerable. And yet it never stopped some from trying. During these last six years, even when the state was virtually insolvent, they would add hundreds of millions of dollars to the budgets with no thought of where and how this spending would be funded. I have vetoed more than a billion dollars out of the legislation returned to me for signature over these past few years. If I had not, the present budget would be a billion dollars higher than it is. But, instead, our constant search for economies plus the reduced costs of welfare and Medi-Cal have at last resulted in a surplus and the prospect of an ongoing surplus which makes possible a tax reduction. By the same token, having a surplus makes holding the line against increased spending more difficult. By June 30, we will have a surplus in the neighborhood of $750 to $850 million. And that is a very nice neighborhood. But spending proposals for that one-time surplus total more than a billion dollars already. And some of these would be for ongoing programs which means that for the second year of the program you would have to have a tax increase. That is the way government got as big as it is.

Knowing we were coming to a day when we could begin to cut back on that tax increase of 1967, we appointed a task force to go to work on the whole subject of taxes and learn how this constant increase in government costs could be controlled. We no longer have the unanswerable argument of "no money."

This task force attracted some of the most distinguished economists in the United States. Dr. Milton Friedman of the University of Chicago; Peter Drucker of Claremont; Roger Freeman of the Hoover Institute, Stanford; Professor C. Lowell Harriss of Columbia University; Professor James Buchanan of Virginia Polytechnic Institute; Professor William Niskanen of the University of California at Berkeley; and Professor Phoebus Dhrymes of U.C.L.A.

These men are of the opinion that government spending in the United States is out of control and that we are at a crossroad. Either we take action—not only to halt the ever-rising cost of government, but to reduce it—or we face economic disaster. It was because of this strongly held belief that they were willing, indeed eager, to help our task force.

Acting on the findings of the task force, we have embarked on a plan to return the one-time surplus to the taxpayers. This has not been received with unrestrained joy by some of the legislative leadership. Suggesting that government return money to the people instead of spending it is a little like getting caught between the hog and the bucket—one gets buffeted about a bit.

But the surplus is the same as an overpayment you might have made on your utility bill. Unable to accurately forecast the savings from the welfare reforms and our other economies, we overcharged you. We took more from you in taxes last year and this year than we needed to pay the ongoing costs of government. This overpayment should be returned to those who paid it. One of those in opposition has called this "an unnecessary expenditure of public funds."

The homeowners and renters property tax relief passed last year was to be funded by a one-cent increase in the sales tax starting June 1. We had hoped the legislature would delay this increase until January 1, thus using some of the surplus to subsidize the property tax relief.

This would in effect be a return to those who contributed to the surplus by way of the sales tax. Most of the surplus, however, can be attributed to the income tax so an amount roughly equal to that sales tax rebate would be returned as a credit of up to 20 percent on this year's income tax.

The second part of our plan has to do with that ongoing surplus I mentioned. We propose an ongoing cut in the income tax of 7.5 percent beginning January 1. For both the one-time rebate and the ongoing tax cut, we would also completely wipe out the income tax for families with incomes of $8,000 or less and individuals below $4,000 a year.

Third, and most important, we propose a long range plan involving an amendment to the State Constitution. The present tax structure of our state takes 8.75 percent out of every income dollar in California. We propose reducing this by 0.1 percent each year for fifteen years until the percentage of the people's total income the state takes in taxes is about 7 percent. This would then become a ceiling beyond which the state could not go without a vote of the people.

Our economic experts pointed out to us that in 1930 governments—federal, state and local combined—only took 15 percent of the people's earnings. By 1950, this had become 32 percent, and today government at all levels is taking 44.7 cents out of every income dollar. Projecting this steady rate of increase forward for fifteen years, government will be taking more than half—54.5 cents from each dollar of income.

Government is an umpire—a policeman if you will. It is not a producer of goods or wealth. When government takes this much of the people's money, it creates a drag on the economy, causing economic slump and unemployment. History reveals that no society has long survived a tax burden that reached one-third of the people's earnings. Looking back on the fallen empires of the past, one sees the first warning signs appear. As the burden grows heavier, there is growing a lack of respect for government and the law. Fraud becomes widespread and crime increases. Are we to say none of those things are taking place here?

Is it so radical to suggest that we have the knowledge and intelligence in this land of free enterprise to find that percentage of the people's earnings which must be left in their hands if free enterprise is to continue?

Most of the opposition to this idea has come from within government. One legislator has told us such a plan would make it impossible for government to "continue re-distributing the earnings of the people." I submit that that is not a proper function of government. You and I do not have the right to take the earnings of one to give to another, and therefore we cannot give such power to government.

A number of points, none of them valid, have been raised in an effort to cast doubt on this proposal.

The legislative analyst assails our figures—claiming we have exaggerated—that people are not paying 44.7

percent in taxes. We arrived at our figure by taking the total cost of all governmental institutions and simply determining what percentage that is compared to the total revenues of the people. There actually is no other true way than to relate the cost of government to the income of those who pay for government.

Nevertheless we rechecked with our original source, the Tax Foundation in New York, and submitted the legislative analyst figures to them.

Quoting from their reply: "an estimate of taxes as a proportion of personal income in California of 40 percent would not be far off. The figures for total revenues would of course be several percentage points higher."

In other words, "40 percent or 40-plus several percentage" points—the point is taxes are too high and every citizen knows it.

An equally spurious and somewhat demagogic objection is that our proposal benefits the rich at the expense of the poor. Our legislative leader cites the case of an individual who would only get a $2.50 rebate from the surplus while another would be $250. Well, possibly there would be such cases. But the man who would get $2.50 only had a $12.50 tax bill to begin with. The one getting $250 owed $1,250 and after his rebate he will still owe $1,000 while the other individual will owe only $10.

Again, let me point out this is not a case of government largesse—of handing out charity or gifts. We are talking about the return—as fairly as it can be worked out—of over-payments the people made.

As one of our cabinet members, Frank Walton, said the other day: "If you overpay your utility bill, the company returns the overpayment to you. It doesn't divide it up among your neighbors."

As I told you, families with earnings of $8,000 or less will get a 100 percent rebate.

Attempts have been made to confuse you by charging the plan we have proposed invades the prerogative of the legislature and will tie the legislature's hands in the future by fixing tax rates in the [California] Constitution. It will do no such thing. The Constitution will simply place a limit on the percentage of the combined income of all the people that the state can take in taxes. The people, by a simple majority vote, can raise that limit any time they choose and the legislature can do so in emergency situations. Beyond that, however, nothing in this proposal changes the legislature's right to alter the tax structure by raising or lowering specific taxes—adopting new ones or cancelling old ones. One assemblyman has protested because our program does not eliminate the oil depletion allowance. Of course it does not—the legislature has the power to do this and it always has had such power.

The truth about the nit-picking and carping criticism is that many of those who are talking the loudest in the legislative chambers do not even believe their own words. They have admitted to us that while they will continue to block the people's right to vote on this, they really cannot find anything wrong with our proposal, anything wrong, that is, except that philosophically they believe government should take even more of the people's earnings because only government has the wisdom to spend that money properly for the people's own good.

Because of this we have gone to you—the people, asking you to place this on the ballot by petition. Only a vote of the people can amend the Constitution, and two methods provide for such a vote. The legislature can, by a two-thirds majority, place it on the ballot as they did with eleven measures in the last election; or the people can do it by petition. We submitted this to the legislature and it has been blocked by the assembly leadership, just as that same leadership refused to implement the death penalty approved overwhelmingly by the people at the last election.

If you are wondering why we have decided on a special election, (which incidentally will cost about $3 million—not $10 million), it is to begin the income tax reduction by January 1. Waiting for the next general election would delay the cost one and possibly two years. Since the savings to you in that one part of the plan alone amounts to some $200 million a year, a $3 million investment in a special election seems like a good idea.

Those who say the Tax Control and Tax Limitation Plan will not work or that it will raise your local taxes are the same ones who said the welfare reforms would not work and that property taxes would have to be raised. Well, the reforms have worked better than we predicted they would. The President has taken our people to H.E.W. in Washington to try to put them into effect nationally and forty-two of our fifty-eight California counties were able to lower their taxes.

These are the same people who told us loudly and at great length two years ago that we faced a gigantic deficit unless we had a $750 million tax increase. We did not have the tax increase and we wound up the year with a $250 million surplus.

But you know, as I said earlier, that this household we call California must have the resources to meet its responsibilities; to see that education is provided for your children, care is given to those in need, and the battle to preserve the environment carried on.

You want an answer to the charge that a tax limit

would put the state in a fiscal straitjacket? Under the limit we have proposed, the state will be able to double its budget in the next ten years and triple it in fifteen. The revenues will be sufficient to meet all the increased costs due to inflation and population growth, and will provide an additional $41.5 billion for new programs and services in the next fifteen years. If that is a straitjacket, it's a pretty loose fit.

This is an idea whose time has come. Taxes are the biggest cost item your family has. It costs you more to pay for government than it does to feed, clothe, and provide housing for your entire family.

It is an arrogant denial of the democratic process for a few legislators to say the people must not even be allowed to vote on something as fundamental as their right to their own earnings.

The petitions now being circulated do not ask for approval of the plan; they simply ask that it be put on the ballot. The people then will have until next November to inform themselves and determine whether they do or do not want a return of their money and a reduction in the present tax burden.

1973

WHY THE CONSERVATIVE MOVEMENT IS GROWING

(We Are the Minority Party in Registration Only)

Speaking before convention of Southern GOP, Atlanta, Georgia, December 7th

9.

I can't tell you how delighted and pleased I am to be here. I realize in the climate of today, when anyone holding public office makes a statement of that kind, it's assumed that this is the political thing to say. But I suppose in some way we deserve that. There was a fellow running for Congress; and he went out soliciting votes and sat down by an old-timer on the courthouse bench in a little town and solicited his vote. He told him what he was there for and when he finished his pitch the old man said: "What do you intend to do about the geese?" The candidate looked, and the courthouse lawn was covered with geese. He said: "Well, now that's a lovely sight, isn't it?" He said: "I think they should be protected." And the old man said: "You just lost my vote. They mess up the lawn; they chase the kids; they peck at their legs. They ought to be destroyed." So the candidate moved over to another bench, sat down beside another old-timer, made the same pitch, and when he finished, he got the same question: "What are you going to do about the geese?" "Well," he said, "look at them out there messing up the lawn. I think they ought to be destroyed." The fellow said: "You just lost my vote. I raise geese. They're an important part of this community." He got to the third bench, made the same pitch and, believe it or not, he got the same question about the geese. This time, he put his arm around the fellow's shoulders and said: "Brother, on that question, I'm with you."

There was a time earlier this afternoon, though, when I thought in this age of cynicism that maybe we could look back to a President of ours, Cal Coolidge, on how to handle some situations. He was having a press conference once and a reporter asked him: "Do you have anything to say about prohibition?" And Cal said: "No." "What about the farm situation?" the reporter asked. Cal said "No." "Well," the reporter said, "you don't seem to have any comments about anything, do you?" And Cal said: "No comment and don't quote me."

Tonight, there are those in this land who have already hung the picture of our party's mascot, the elephant, alongside the dinosaur, in the gallery of extinct species. I think they're living in a dreamworld. Not too many years ago, you could have run a full-grown elephant right through this room and you never would have stepped on a Republican toe.

Indeed, there are very few of you who would have been here not too many years ago, and I include myself. It seems so long ago. But it was only about a decade past that Barry Goldwater made his long and lonely journey across this land, speaking a truth that needed telling. Men and women who recognize and respect the truth listened and were moved. And they realized that the leadership of the party of their fathers had taken the party of Jefferson and Jackson down a strange road, where they couldn't follow without betraying their most fundamental beliefs. Now, those who had counted on the Solid South, in election after election, and taken for granted that Southerners would vote for the party name, even though that party leadership now was taking the party against their conscience. Those people look upon a gathering such as this and speak sneeringly of something called the "Southern strategy." Well, there is a Southern strategy and this country is better for it.

Today, almost one-fourth of the Republicans in Congress represent southern and border states: John Tower, Jesse Helms of North Carolina, Howard Baker and Bill Brock of Tennessee, Bill Scott of Virginia. We've elected governors. Our toastmaster here tonight, Governor [James E.] Holshouser, Win Dunn of Tennessee and Mills Godwin of Virginia, who just recently followed the lead of men like Senator Strom Thurmond of South Carolina, and John Connally of Texas. And I will suggest there are other statesmen who still bear the other party's label, who one of these days will follow the course of men like Strom Thurmond and realize their destiny, too, lies with this party. They'll recognize the truth that was spoken by Winston Churchill when he changed parties in his own country. Winston, in that inimitable way of his, said: "Some men change principle for party and some change party for principle."

Sure you are still outnumbered. We're outnumbered in California, three to two. But you know sometimes that makes life a little more simple. When you're outnumbered and surrounded and someone yells "charge," you don't have to ask which direction. Any way you're facing, you'll find a target. And that kind of turnout would be true in the last election (1972). We just went out in any direction and found millions of patriotic Democrats and Independents who saw very clearly the difference in philosophy that was offered for their choosing. And they made their choice on their belief and not on their party label.

Now, a pall has been cast over the mandate that was so clearly given just a year ago. A cloud of doubt, mistrust, and cynicism has been generated by something called

Watergate. We're told that the illegal and immoral acts of a few individuals must be the burden, a political hair shirt worn by the entire Republican Party. Watergate and its aftermath have been before the courts and the Congress for almost a year now. Those allegations of illegal and immoral acts which have been proven are condemned by us. No one's indignation is greater than ours. Such campaign excesses are contrary to all our beliefs and principles. Over too many years, we've been on the receiving end of stuffed ballot boxes in cities like Chicago and St. Louis. Now the time has come to put Watergate in its proper perspective. It has been debated in the court of public opinion. And it is now before the bar of justice. *Let the facts be known. Let those who are guilty of wrongdoing accept the consequences of their actions.* Let justice take its course in the courts—the only place where a final judgment can be fairly rendered. But, for America's sake, let's get on with the business of government! There is the energy crisis, making America self-sufficient in fuel and power and no longer subject to blackmail from foreign lands, slowing down inflation, reducing the tax burden that is bleeding away the vitality of our free enterprise system, protecting the law abiding on our streets and in their homes. And above all, continuing the great start this administration has made toward achieving a lasting peace in the world. And, that includes maintaining a defense second to none.

These are the vital issues that will shape our lives and the lives of our people and our destiny as a nation for the next generation. Public cynicism about political affairs didn't start with Bobby Baker or Billy Sol Estes or Watergate. And it will not end there. The time has come to say to some politicians: "It is time to become statesmen, for the leaders of both houses to sit down with the Administration." Let them put Watergate on one side of the scale and weigh it against the free world leadership that is ours whether we like it or not.

It was the United States that brought a cease-fire in the Middle East a few days ago. It was an American President who stopped the Soviet Union from moving armed forces into that troubled area. And an American President has brought an easing of tensions worldwide such as we haven't known since before World War II. A few days ago, I was in Australia, Indonesia and Singapore, talking to the leaders of those countries on behalf of this Administration. They looked at me, and they asked if Americans were totally unaware of the part that we play in maintaining the stability in the whole of Southeast Asia. The Domino Theory. They believe it. They'll tell you what would happen if America's position is weakened in the world; if our forces were withdrawn from those areas of southeast Asia, how the dominos would begin to fall.

There are some who would destroy a man in order to destroy a mandate of all the people. In the Democratic Convention of 1972, we watched long-time party stalwarts of that party as they were denied participation in the deliberations of that convention; some were even denied admittance. But the first who were thrown out of that convention were Thomas Jefferson and Andrew Jackson.

The battle we won in 1972 must be won again. Millions of Democrats must be made to see that philosophically they have more in common with us than with those who would erode our defenses, pawning our weapons to pay for some new experiment in social reform. And make no mistake about it, there's been no change in the Democratic leadership since that convention of 1972. They are the same people who rediscover poverty every election and promise to cure it. They've cured it so often that they've now made a profession of it. They thrive on failures, on righting wrongs, aiding victims and so forth. It must be understood that success in those tasks would put them out of business. No matter how many programs are set up and operating, their proponents never claim success for them. To do so would be to say the problems have been solved, meaning the programs are no longer needed. And the programs, not the problems, are their very reason for being.

They're against violence and lawlessness, but they blame the victims of crime, not the criminals, because the victim is a member of society, and it's society that they blame for crime.

Less than a year ago, America was fighting a bloody war in southeast Asia that had dragged on for almost a decade. It had been spawned in indecision, and it had been directed for years by leaders who refused to win it and didn't know how in hell to end it. Well, it has been ended; our troops are home. And hundreds of the bravest men any nation has ever produced have been released from years of torture and captivity. But it wasn't ended by some street demonstration; it wasn't ended by a congressional resolution, nor was peace obtained because of a speech by the chairman of the Senate Foreign Relations Committee. It was brought to an honorable end by forceful policies and the effective negotiations of a Republican administration in Washington—in the same way that a Republican administration ended another war that wasn't of our doing twenty years ago in 1953.

We've heard so much demagoguery going on. I wonder how many of us remember some of the things in the last campaign. One candidate had some television spots filmed. He appeared in a market buying a basketful of groceries. Then he brought them up in front of the camera, and he compared the price that he had to pay for these groceries with the price before this Administration took office. The idea was to lay the blame for inflation on Republican policies. But the inflation we are struggling with today was a deliberate, planned policy under the New Deal, the Fair Deal, the New Frontier, and the Great Society.

We were told that planned deficits, federal spending, and a little annual inflation were good for us. Do you know that the only time we've ever had fiscal stability in these forty years was when we had a Republican Congress and a Republican President in Washington at the same time, a single two-year period under the Administration of Dwight Eisenhower?

We all know that inflation is the direct result of government spending; we all know it's a cruel tax falling on those least able to pay. But there's another facet that is not so well known. Except for those who are on fixed incomes, it is true that in all these years of inflation, wages have gone up faster than the rate of inflation. For example, a $10,000 a year income, the average individual's earning in 1966, has by today gone up to $13,500. Inflation has only gone up a little over $3,000 in that period. So the individual has not only kept pace with inflation; he's a little better off than he was except for the other part, the part that has made some of our so-called economic experts favor a planned inflation. That man, as he went up $3,500 in his earnings, keeping ahead of inflation, moved up through our progressive tax brackets $950 worth, so that today he has $466 *less* in purchasing power than he had in 1966. It was taxes, not inflation alone, that did this. And confiscatory taxes bear a Democratic trademark.

Since the inception of the federal income tax in 1914,

it has been increased thirteen times under Democratic administrations. It has been reduced eight times under Republican administrations.

In 1969, this administration reduced the taxes for the working men and women who our opponents claim are their special concern. Nine million of the lowest earners were relieved of paying any income tax at all.

The next brackets above them received a 70 percent reduction. It was only when you got to those above $50,000, who according to our opponents are all Republicans, that you found them paying a higher tax under a Republican administration. It would seem that our opponents are guilty of a little political demagoguery at times.

James Buchanan has written that even the keenest, most analytical surgeon, when operating on a Democratic politician, can't separate demagogic from solid tissue without causing the death of the patient.

Over four decades of almost uninterrupted Democratic philosophy, a gigantic bureaucracy has grown virtually beyond the consent of the governed. And now it is almost beyond the control of elected officials. When those four decades began, there were 203 Americans for every federal employee. When Richard Nixon took office, there was one for every 67. Add in state and local employees. and one out of six of the nation's workforce is a government employee. Not even the Office of Management and Budget in Washington knows how many boards, commissions, agencies, and bureaus there are in the federal government. The Federal Register, listing all their regulations, has almost as many pages as the Encyclopedia Britannica.

Forms and questionnaires pour out to businessmen from Washington by the billions. They number about ten every year for each man, woman, and baby in the United States. Small businessmen alone spend an estimated 130 million man-hours in this required government paperwork. It adds billions in cost to the things we buy.

And yet, a young Senator from Massachusetts journeyed to Alabama on the Fourth of July, and there, in the presence of Governor [George] Wallace, he made a speech complaining about big, centralized government. To hear him tell it, he was against it. George Wallace sat there listening; he must have thought they sent the wrong sound track.

Working men and women in America have been told over and over again by some of their own union leaders, by the Democratic leadership, that their leadership offers them the best chance for prosperity. Our sons and daughters, in too many social science courses, are taught the same fairy tale. Invoking memories of the Great Depression, history is being rewritten in classrooms all over America. The truth is the only full employment that we have ever known under our opponents' leadership has been the result of, and during, a war.

They would like to lay the food shortage at our door. But who was it who spawned programs and spent billions of dollars to reduce the number of farmers and to keep those who remained on the farm from producing food for a hungry world?

Forty years ago, the loyal opposition, our party, pointed out the threat to freedom inherent in the continued enlargement of centralization of power in Washington. We argued for limited government, and lower taxes, most of all, for the preservation of our federal system of sovereign states, operating under their own governments in the best interest of the people.

If you will permit me just a personal experience, I'd like to cite some of the adventures that we've had in California for the last several years which I think could demonstrate the difference in philosophy between the two parties. In 1967, our Administration took over a government that had been a "Little Sir Echo" to the great social experiments in Washington for the previous eight years. The state was spending one million dollars a day more than it was taking in. Gimmicks had been employed to put off the inevitable tax increase. The last of such devices was a change in bookkeeping which got them through the 1966 election without a tax increase by funding twelve months spending with fifteen months revenue. For eight years, price had been no object. They'd added an average of five thousand new employees a year to state government. Welfare costs alone were going up almost four times as fast as revenues. Now, I've always believed that government could and should be run with the same common sense rules that apply to business or even budgeting a household. But when you start talking about common sense in connection with government, you cause some traumatic shocks.

I found myself nose to nose in a confrontation with the Democratic majority in control of both houses of our Legislature, those who had helped bring about the fiscal insolvency of our state. We announced a program of cut, squeeze, and trim and this brought thunder down upon our heads, from the entrenched bureaucracy as well as the Legislature. It was charged that education would degenerate and progress in our state would come to a halt. When we proposed reforming welfare, the Legislature, with the help of the Welfare Rights Organization, said that our program would increase the caseload, not decrease it, that local county taxes would go up, that the state would run a $700 million deficit and that the poor would be starving in the streets. Other than that, they didn't find much wrong with the program.

It's seven years later, seven years of Republican philosophy, and an uphill fight with the Democratic Legislature. We haven't been adding five thousand employees a year; we have virtually the same number we started with seven years ago and they're handling a 30 to 40 percent workload increase. We increased state support for education 93 percent, while enrollment has gone up less than 6 percent. We've built a thousand highway projects with money that formerly was spent on administrative overhead. Our support for local mental health care clinics is eight times what it was seven years ago. Two and a half years ago, we finally achieved our welfare reform. The caseload isn't going up 40,000 a month; there are now 387,000 fewer people on welfare than when we started. The truly needy aren't starving in the streets; they've had a 30 percent increase in their grants. County property taxes have gone down in forty-five of our fifty-eight counties. In addition, the state is subsidizing local government to finance almost a billion dollar reduction in the homeowners' taxes. The $700 million deficit they predicted became an $800 million surplus which we're returning to the people in the form of a one-time tax rebate.

Giving back that $800 million wasn't as easy as I make it sound. When you suggest to a Democratic Legislature that they give that kind of money back to the people it's a little like getting between the hog and the bucket. One legislator indignantly proclaimed that this was an unnecessary expenditure of public funds. But another, a senator, really expressed their political philosophy. He said, "Reducing taxes and giving this money back will interfere with our ability to redistribute the earnings of the people." What would have happened if the Democratic philosophy had prevailed during those seven years?

As this country of ours prepares to celebrate its 200th anniversary, we suddenly realize how great a heritage was left us by our Founding Fathers. The old world still looks upon us as a young, upstart nation. But the Constitutional system created by that little band of men, whose like has seldom been seen in the world, has proven to have great durability. Today, our young, upstart country is the oldest continuing Republic in the world.

The next election campaign is important. But it is not nearly as important as the next generation or the next century. Will we pass on the heritage that was entrusted to us and that has been guarded so well for almost these two hundred years? I believe that the Republican party offers the best guarantee that we will. And you who have chosen this party in the South have an opportunity to ensure a dynamic resurgence of the philosophy of limited, responsible government. You don't have to sell your Democratic neighbors and friends on the Republican philosophy. Most of them already subscribe to it. What really is needed is to show them that what they believe is what we officially as a party stand for. Let us shine the light of truth on Democratic political demagoguery. It has been said, for example, that we're the party of the rich. Then why is it that five out of eight Wall Street bankers are Democrats?

In two, three, four, five, or ten dollar contributions, in election after election, including the last one, we outnumbered the Democrats in that kind of small contributor five to one.

We are the minority party in registration only. If your friends still retain membership in the Democratic party and need some convincing, may I suggest you ask a question of them. Ask them how they feel about this statement: "We advocate the immediate and drastic reduction of governmental expenditures by abolishing useless commissions and offices, consolidating departments and bureaus, eliminating extravagance, to accomplish savings not less than 25 percent in the cost of the federal government." Well, that statement was made in 1932 as a candidate by Franklin Delano Roosevelt. That was once the philosophy that characterized the Democratic party. Which party endorses that philosophy today? Certainly not those who highjacked the convention a year ago June in Miami. On the basis of our philosophy, we are in step with the yearnings and the dreams of the overwhelming majority of Americans. Let us shatter the present stereotype. Let us tell our friends that private enterprise, not government, is the great provider; that the way to get a bigger slice of the pie is not by reducing someone else's slice, but by producing a bigger pie; that we have compassion for those who need our help, but we will no longer sentence a segment of our society to a life of hopelessness on the dole; that we are mindful of the fact that for someone to get something he hasn't earned, someone else must earn something he doesn't get.

We've come to a moment in our history when party labels are unimportant. Philosophy is all important. Little men with loud voices cry doom, seeing little that is good in America. They create fear and uncertainty among us. Millions of Americans, especially our own sons and daughters, are seeking a cause they can believe in. There is a hunger in this country today—a hunger for spiritual guidance. People yearn once again to be proud of their country and proud of themselves, and to have confidence in themselves. And there's every reason why they should be proud. Some may have failed America, but America has never failed us, and there is so much to be proud of in this land.

In the days after World War II, when our economic strength and military power were all that stood between the world and a return to the Dark Ages, Pope Pius XII said: "The American people have a genius for splendid and unselfish action, and into their hands, the hands of America, God has placed the destinies of an afflicted mankind."

We do have a rendezvous with destiny. Either we will preside over the great nightfall for all mankind, or we will accept the leadership that has been thrust upon us. I believe that is the obligation and responsibility of the Republican Party today.

If I could just tell you something that I said to some people in Mississippi a few weeks ago. It's not been too many months, not quite a year, that we sat up until the late hours and watched on television when that first plane came into Clark Field. We saw those men when the plane door opened. We didn't know what we were going to see. Would they be zombies, would they be robots, as the result of seven, eight, nine years of torture and confinement? And then that first American came down the ramp, saluted the flag, and said: "God Bless America." Nancy and I have had an experience. About 150 of those returning prisoners of war were from California. We had them, and some who weren't from California, as guests in our home, just after their return. It was an unforgettable experience. We saw men come into our home, who for nine years had been the most intimate of buddies in prison camps. And suddenly they looked at each other, and we heard them acknowledge this was the first time they had ever seen each other face to face. Their intimate friendship had been built up through bamboo walls, tapping on the walls, with the code and the signals that they had invented. They told us of the things they did to harrass the enemy with their code.

There were other stories. They told us of men that had been tortured, lying on the other side of the wall in the next cell near death. And all they could do was lie on their side of the cell, hour after hour, taking turns all night long—tapping on the wall, just to tell them they were not alone, to keep in there, to hang on.

Some said: "You know, we thought you'd throw rocks at us when we came home." They didn't feel they could serve any longer; they were imprisoned. So they resisted torture as long as they could, but they said eventually the enemy got what he wanted. Someone, one night in our home said to them: "Well, if you knew you were going to have to talk and give in, why didn't you do that first; why did you take that torture?" And they looked with astonishment and said: "Holding out was the only thing left for us to do; the only thing we could still do for our country." Later, I asked Nancy, where do we find men like this? And almost as quickly as I asked the question, I knew the answer. We find them on the farms, in small towns, in the city streets of America—just ordinary guys named Joe, produced by this society of ours.

There is truly nothing for us to fear but fear itself.

1974

REBUILDING A PROSPEROUS AMERICA

(The Cause of America's Economic Woes)

Speaking to the American Trucking Association Board of Directors, San Francisco, California, October 16th

10.

In the past year or two, we have been going through a prolonged period of uncertainty in America and the world. If you glance at any newspaper, you quickly see an array of problems that would tax the wisdom of Solomon.

There is the energy problem—something you are rather familiar with—declining productivity, strikes, high taxes, crime. All these have an impact on business. The threat of war still hangs over the world scene.

But the fundamental challenge facing America today is simply the restoration of America's financial stability in a world economy dangerously out of kilter because of inflation.

Putting our economic house in order is America's greatest imperative, and it must take precedence over everything else.

Unless we bring inflation under control, we can never expect to deal with any of the other problems we face as a nation or as individuals.

The President [Ford] has declared this to be a national priority and I doubt that anyone would disagree. The program he outlined to Congress includes a number of constructive steps: financial incentives to encourage capital investment for economic expansion, jobs and prosperity, increased food production, and efforts to conserve energy and reduce America's reliance on foreign oil. All are necessary steps along the long road toward economic stability.

In all honesty, however, I must voice opposition to the proposed income tax surcharge, however temporary that tax may be.

To combat inflation, we should be reducing excessive government spending, especially at the federal level, and I submit it is counter-productive to increase government's revenues.

In his economic address to Congress, the President mentioned the fact that the federal government operated at a deficit in nineteen of the twenty-five years he served in Congress. By doing so, he touched on the primary cause of our current economic troubles. The truth is: there is one reason for inflation in America and that is simply that government for too long has been spending too much money.

Two generations ago, in the middle of the Great Depression, America first began moving away from this country's historic commitment to balanced budgets and a free economy. It was then that the Keynesian philosophy of planned inflation became official government policy.

Fostered first by the economic dislocation of the Depression, and later by the pressures of World War II, our country went into a decade-long period in which government vastly increased its spending, its size, and its power.

Our economic values were turned around. Instead of a model of thrift and solvency, government became a gross example of spend-thrift waste and excess.

The experts who claimed they knew best told us that a little inflation is good for us. So we had a little inflation and then a little bit more. It was like giving a drunk another drink to sober him up.

Some of our nation's most able leaders, Dwight Eisenhower, Everett Dirksen and others, spoke out time and again against chronic federal deficits and a government that keeps on taking a bigger and bigger share of the national income.

But Congress was listening to the kind of people who told us we did not need to worry about the national debt because "we owe it to ourselves."

For awhile inflation is like a warm bath—we sit back and relax. Everything seems easy and pleasant. In the euphoria of inflation's early days, we failed to notice that output per manhour had slipped. By the 1960s we were lowest among the fourteen major industrial nations in the free world. The country that introduced mass production, showed the world how to build things better and sell them cheaper, suddenly found everyone but us had what we used to call "American know-how."

Many products we used to sell so easily in foreign markets suddenly became noncompetitive. And the world's greatest trading nation found itself for the first time in this century with a balance of payments deficit.

It is necessary to recall these historic trends if we are to understand what has happened to our economy. If you want to know which way to go in the future, you have to know which path you took in the past and where you stepped in a gopher hole along the way.

The tragedy is that our inflation problems are not the fault of the free market system. We stumbled into inflation because we strayed too far away from the free market concept. Too many of us, and that includes business, turned to government for answers that seemed easier than the hard competition of the marketplace.

For too many years, government has been growing in

size and power, with no regard for the economic consequences. And government loved it.

But it is time for us to realize we have had too much government, too much red tape, too many taxes, and too many regulations. Private business and industry is the most over-regulated, over-taxed, and under-appreciated part of America's society. The simple truth is that free enterprise in America is no longer free.

If we are ever to bring inflation under control, we have got to start rooting the causes of inflation out of our system. And the greatest single cause of inflation is government itself. Unnecessary restrictions, red tape, and regulations are robbing our people of the prosperity that is rightfully theirs.

In trying to perfect one of his inventions, Thomas Edison once tried 28,000 experiments and all were failures.

When he was asked if he was not discouraged, he said, "No. Now I know 28,000 things that won't work."

Those who advocate more and more government regulation have been experimenting for forty years, trying to create an economic system in which everyone can somehow be made more prosperous by the toil of someone else. It is time they recognized how many things don't work.

Instead, they have cast industry and business in the role of archvillain, accusing you of monopoly powers, excess profits, and of defrauding the consumer.

But the real danger today is government's monopoly power over industry and business. No one is regulating the regulators.

In Washington, the United States Senate resorted to a filibuster to halt a so-called consumer protection bill that would have vastly increased government's power to control every facet of production and merchandizing in America. They will try again. That bill will come back and eventually be passed unless we make up our minds to turn government around and tell them "enough already."

Right now, there is a lot of talk about government action in the rapid transit field. Everyone is looking greedily at gasoline taxes to pay not only for streets and highways, but also for rapid transit, air pollution controls, and even for planning—which is a term they use to cover anything else they may think of.

Government's track record in solving problems does not exactly inspire confidence. Let us look at one of your competitor industries that was in business long before trucks were invented.

A hundred years ago the railroads were thriving. We have accepted a rewrite of history that would have us believe government had to regulate the railroads because of the excesses of early industrial barons who built and ran the railroads. The truth is government was involved in railroading from the start and the railroads are a classic example of what government can do to ruin business.

The President has called for a review of all our regulatory agencies. I support that.

It is time to start eliminating agencies which hurt more than help the consumer, the taxpayers, and the businesses they regulate.

The Interstate Commerce Commission is a good place to start. I challenge anyone to prove there is a need to continue the ICC or that it serves any useful purpose. If it had been in business during the pioneer days, the 49ers would still be trying to find out what the rules are for crossing the Mississippi River.

This combination of red tape and high taxes is strangling industry's ability to compete, to meet the demands of customers, to pay the wages of employees, and to fulfill a necessary public service at the least possible cost.

For half a century the railroads begged for relief from excessive government regulations and claimed they could resolve most, if not all their problems, if they were free to operate as a private enterprise. Their pleas fell on deaf ears, and now we no longer have any private passenger rail service in this country.

So government took over the passenger trains and the first thing it did was exempt itself from the rules and restrictions that made it impossible to run a profitable private railroad industry.

The consumer does not gain when government takes over. He loses.

Anyone who doubts that should take a look at the plight of the airlines. The Civil Aeronautics Board has decided it will no longer allow lower youth fares or discounts on international flights.

So what happened? Our international air carriers lost about $8 million in revenues. And the passengers found themselves paying higher fares.

Government regulations and red tape have perpetuated higher rates and higher costs, not just in transportation, but in almost every industry regulated by government. And these days, almost every industry is regulated by government, coming, going, and in-between.

Government regulations encrusted with bureaucratic barnacles are actually stifling the competition they were designed to encourage.

Small businessmen in America must spend 130 million man hours a year filling out government forms. This adds $30 to $50 billion to the cost of doing business. And that means higher prices for the consumer. But the citizen taxpayer gets hit with a double whammy. Government has to spend between $15 and $20 billion a year to find places to stack all the forms it requires business to fill out.

Government is the only business in the world which can continue to exist while ignoring every sensible rule of economics.

When a business or an individual spends more than it makes, it goes bankrupt. When government does it, it sends you the bill. And when government does it for forty years the bill comes in two ways—higher taxes and inflation. Make no mistake about it: inflation is a tax and not by accident. Lenin once said, "Through inflation government can quietly and unobservedly confiscate the prosperity of its citizens."

Someone once said our government taxes everything except its imagination. But the encrusted bureaucracy, the ones with a vested self-interest in bigger government, go that one step further. They have got an answer for everything except one that will work.

Remember the great fuel shortage? You had better because it has not gone away for long. Almost two decades ago, the oil and energy industries were warning us that America was heading toward an energy crunch. When it finally happened, government was the first to cry, "Why weren't we warned?" And the next line was, "We in government must do something." Something, of course, was massive governmental intervention, rationing, and even a demand that the government go into the oil business.

Fortunately, the worst of the fuel crisis has eased. But does anyone believe it would have if we had instituted gasoline rationing? They would still be trying to get the ration books distributed. May I warn you—don't relax. Right now there are proposals in Congress to have government name two members to the board of each oil company. If they do—whose business is next?

The time has come to resist the Utopian schemers who pay only lip service to free enterprise.

It is time to ask ourselves: do we really believe in the free market? Or have we grown so soft we no longer relish its rugged competitiveness? Do we believe in closed cartels, a controlled economy where government sets the price the producer will get for his product, and the price the consumer must pay? And if there is any slippage on either end of the transaction, government puts up the difference in the form of a subsidy paid for by the consumers and the taxpayers.

I know you have heard this kind of talk before. I know your own industry spokesmen have criticized overregulation and high taxes. And some of you have heard me sound off on this subject because it is something I have been preaching for years.

But the time for just sounding the alarm is over. We have to start doing something to bring government under control.

There is only a very little time to make the right decisions, to free the productive capacity of America, to loosen government's stranglehold on our economy and on our pocketbooks.

You do not have to have deficit government if you raise enough hell so that those who run government are more concerned about what the taxpayers think than the demands of special interest groups and their bureaucratic counterparts in government.

I know government can be controlled if the people

will work at making "government by the people" more than just a slogan.

Government can be brought under control if enough people are willing to stand the gaff and take the heat, and fight for common sense solutions.

The reason there is a cynical lack of confidence in government is because too many politicians are elected to office, but never try to carry out their campaign promises. Campaigning becomes their occupation instead of working for the changes our society must have if it is to survive.

There is only one way to make government bite the bullet on inflation, on high taxes, on all those things that should be a matter of concern. And that is to hold all elected officials accountable. Match their performance with their promises, and if you find some who don't measure up, vote them out of office.

Either you will control your government, or government will control you.

1976

GOVERNMENT AND THE FAMILY

(The Need to Restore Basic Values)

National Television Address, July 6th

11.

Just two days ago, on Sunday, you and I achieved a milestone in the history of mankind and in the history of freedom. We the people of the United States of America have been free for two hundred years plus two days and we've proven to the world that freedom works.

Now, this might not sound like much of an accomplishment to those of us who were born here and accept freedom as the natural state of mankind. But it should. The places and the periods in which man has known freedom are few and far between; just scattered moments on the span of time. And most of those moments have been ours, in this land, in these two hundred years.

The original colonists came here driven by a hunger for freedom. They've been followed down to the present by modern-day immigrants possessed of that same hunger and courage it takes to tear up roots and start anew in a strange land. Some of those immigrants are better described as refugees. They crawl over walls, make their way through mine fields and barbed wire, and risk their lives in leaky, makeshift boats to escape the new tyranny of the police state.

Those original colonists were unique. In all the world the march of empire, the opening of new lands was accomplished by military forces, followed by adventurers and soldiers of fortune. Only here did the people not precede by force of arms. Those who came to this untamed land brought the family. And families built a nation. I'm convinced that today the majority of Americans want really what those first Americans wanted—a better life for themselves and their children, a minimum of governmental authority. Very simply, they want to be left alone in peace and safety to take care of the family by earning an honest dollar and putting away some savings. This may not sound too exciting, but there is a magnificence about it. On the farm, and on the street corner, in the factory and in the kitchen, millions of us asking nothing more, but certainly nothing less, than to live our own lives, according to our own values, at peace with ourselves, our neighbors, and the world.

We have come from every corner of the world, from every racial and ethnic background and we've created a new breed. Yes, we have our faults—plenty of them—but selfishness isn't one of them. We are a generous people, with our friends, our neighbors and with strangers throughout the world, as victims of catastrophes in most every country can testify. There is a great deal to love and to be proud of in our land.

But there seems to be a discontent in the land today. Government, which once did those things which strengthened family and traditional values, now seems to have lost faith in us. And many of us seem to have lost confidence in ourselves.

There's a story told about the early days of the automobile—the horseless carriage. A motorist, complete with linen duster and goggles, pulled up in front of a farmhouse. He called out to the old fellow on the porch and asked, "Do you know where this road takes me?" The old boy said, "Nope." "Well," he asked, "do you know where that road back down there behind the cornfield goes?" Again, "Nope." Annoyed, he said, "You don't seem to know much of anything do you?" The old boy said, "I ain't lost." And he wasn't—not him or those other Americans of that day. They knew who they were and where they were going. Some would have us believe those Americans are no longer relevant—that there is no place for them or their rugged individualism in today's world. And some who think *that* are to be found in government.

The Americans who keep this country going—the ones who fight the wars; drive the trucks and raise the kids; the farmer and fireman, craftsman, and cop, they are wondering—for the first time—if the governmental institutions they have upheld and defended really care about them or their values.

Oh, they haven't fallen for the line of a few fashionable intellectuals and academics who in recent years would have us believe ours is a sick society—a bad country. They know better. Someone said to me the other day, "'tis a great country for the Irish." I'll personally testify to that. Indeed, it's a great country for Americans of Polish ancestry, German, Scandinavian, Greek, Chinese, Italian, and all the scores of ancestries that go to make this breed we call American. We aren't giving up on America. But we are beginning to wonder if the American government is giving up on us.

We've worked and made this the most prosperous, productive land in all the world. But now the dollars we earn don't increase in number as fast as they *decrease* in value. The savings we counted on to see us through our non-earning years melts away like ice in a summer sun. And we're told that's due to inflation, as if inflation were some kind of plague or natural disaster for which no one is to blame. Well, it is a killer, it kills jobs, it kills savings. It kills hopes and dreams, but someone *is* to blame.

Inflation is theft by legislation. It is government's way of getting more tax revenue without raising the rates. Don't raise the tax rate on your home—just appraise your home as worth more than it was the year before. Income tax rates can stay where they are, but a cost of living increase in pay moves you up to a surtax bracket where you pay a higher percentage of your earnings in tax, reducing your standard of living.

Every time a piece of inflationary legislation is passed by Congress, the American family's ability to plan for the future is hurt. Every time the buying power of a paycheck is reduced because the government is pursuing inflationary policies, government is acting against the values of thrift, of honesty, of savings—the values that our people brought with them to this country, the values they instilled in their children. Government programs that can't be paid for out of a balanced budget *must* be paid for *out of your pocket.*

Our society is now one in which, increasingly, older Americans live away from their families. And there is no group in this country which has been more viciously savaged by anti-family governmental action than America's elderly. Inflation can quite literally kill someone who is living on a fixed income. The big spenders in Washington have brought us to the place where older Americans are slowly but surely being pushed to the wall. And their suffering is shared by their children, who may be married with children of their own.

Inflation isn't a vague term from some economic textbook. It is a bitter, government-created fact of life the American family has to live with. Is it any wonder the American people are asking if anyone in Washington really cares?

Oddly enough, they probably do. Those we call bureaucrats are not evil people. They really are trying to be helpful to those they've decided need their help. But this means imposing on others, using the power of taxation to confiscate and redistribute earnings and restricting freedom. In short, this makes government the master, not the servant.

One of government's legitimate functions is to protect us from each other, to see that no one is discriminated against or denied one's God-given rights. To that end, we have adopted legislation to guarantee civil rights and eliminate discrimination of all kinds. Certainly no one of us would challenge government's right and responsibility to eliminate discrimination in hiring or education. But in its zeal to accomplish this worthy purpose, government orders what is in effect a quota system both in hiring and in education. They don't call it a quota system. It is an "affirmative action" program with "goals and timetables" for the hiring of particular groups.

If you happen to belong to an ethnic group not recognized by the federal government as entitled to special treatment, you are a victim of reverse discrimination. Goals and timetables are in reality a bureaucratic order for a quota system. For example, if your ancestry or national origin is Czechoslovakian, Polish, Italian, or if you are of a Jewish faith, you may find yourself the victim of discrimination contrary to the Civil Rights Law. No American should be discriminated against because of religion, sex, race, or ethnic background in hiring, in schooling, or in any other way; and I'd like to have the opportunity to put an end to this federal distortion of the principle of equal rights.

There have been other decisions of government—

some still pending—which strike at basic values and, indeed, at the very heart of the family. One of the pending measures is a legislative proposal which in the name of child care would insert the government into the family's decisions with regard to children, decisions which properly are the right of the parent.

I realize there is a great difference of opinion regarding the subject of abortion. I personally believe that interrupting a pregnancy is the taking of a human life and can only be justified in self-defense—that is, if the mother's own life is in danger. But even those who disagree must certainly be concerned about one facet of government's involvement in abortion. The pregnancy of an underage girl automatically makes her eligible for welfare on the Aid to Dependent Children program. This, in turn, makes her eligible for Medicaid and a free abortion regardless of her family's means. To add insult to injury, welfare rules forbid government from informing her parents. Thus, government is in the position of conspiring with an underage child to provide her with an abortion, while keeping knowledge of her situation from her parents.

Let me read you a letter I received from a mother while I was still Governor. She wrote: "Who do they think they are—not telling the parents? Who in God's name gave them the right to keep the health and welfare of your own child from you? I, as a mother, have the right to carry in my body an unborn child. I have a right to stay up night after night holding and pacing the floor with this child, feeling the pain of fear. I have a right to look into her tiny face and love her so much that I could squeeze her to death. I have a right to watch her grow day after day, year after year, and then one day to look up and see a 15-year-old young lady standing in front of me. A 15-year-old who might some day find herself in trouble, and some fool standing there saying I don't have a right to know. I repeat—who do they think they are?"

I wonder what the early immigrants who came to this country would say if they knew that their descendants live in a society where their children are forbidden by government to pray in schools.

I could offer more examples—unfortunately too many—of government action *against* rather than *for* the strengthening of family life, governmental actions which not only harm the family but also destroy the sense of neighborhood and community that means so much to all of us. Forced school busing comes to mind immediately. It is so obviously wrong that overwhelming majorities of Americans, black and white, are against it. Yet, courts continue to impose it.

Parents have a right—and a responsibility—to direct the education of their children. This should include the choice of school their children attend. I have said repeatedly that as President I would propose legislation—in keeping with the Fourteenth Amendment—to eliminate forced busing. Should that prove inadequate, then I would propose a Constitutional Amendment declaring that no state nor the federal government shall refuse admission to a public institution to any person, otherwise qualified, solely on account of race, color, ethnic origin, sex, or creed.

That does not mean I am opposed to all federal action in the field of education. But such action should be so indirect as to avoid any possibility of federal bureaucratic control.

For too many years a philosophy of government has dominated Washington and especially the Congress—a philosophy that works against the values of the family and the values that were so basic to the building of this country. I believe this is the central issue of this campaign and of our time.

After eight years as Governor of a state that is literally a cross section of America—great cities teeming with industry, small towns and sprawling suburbs, a rich agricultural economy and 22 million people of every race, religion, and ethnic background—after those eight years, I know that government can work *for* the family and not against it. I know that economic justice *can* once again become a reality instead of a dream for hard-working Americans.

I know that government can be energetic without being intrusive, helpful without being domineering, efficient without being dictatorial.

Some weeks ago on a TV broadcast similar to this, I told of how our Administration had found California on the verge of bankruptcy and how we had been forced to raise taxes in the face of that emergency. I also spoke of the measures we then employed to make government more responsive and efficient and how, as a result, we were able to return more than $5.5 billion to the people in tax cuts and rebates.

But there is more to government than just practicing economy, important as that is. Here are a few things we did as we straightened out the fiscal mess. The state income tax had begun at the first $2000 of earnings. But when we left office, a family had to be earning more than $8000 before it was subject to any income tax.

We subsidized local governments to provide a $1750 exemption in the homeowners tax. And we provided a rebate for renters.

We increased supplemental aid to the elderly, the

blind and disabled to make it the highest of any state in the Union. And, we gave additional property tax relief to senior citizens, based on their income, ranging up to 92 percent of the tax on their homes.

We increased state support for schools twenty-four times as much as the increase in enrollment. The state scholarship fund for deserving young people is nine times as big as it was, and we put more young people twenty-one and under on boards and commissions than any other administration in California history.

More members of minority communities were appointed to executive and policy-making positions than in all the previous administrations put together. We moved from eleventh to third among the states in the rehabilitation of the handicapped and their placement in private enterprise jobs. And we increased support for alcohol and drug abuse programs, rehabilitation of juveniles and adults, and treatment of the mentally ill.

More than 800,000 needy Californians on county health care were included in Medicaid, and forty-three of our fifty-eight counties were able to reduce property taxes two years in a row. The second year, there were forty-five.

We had a problem in California that is also a national problem—the constant increase in welfare. It continues to go up in good times and bad, in numbers of recipients and in cost. Voices in Washington—Democrat and Republican—refer to it as "the welfare mess". In California it *was* a mess, with the caseload increasing by some 40,000 people a month. Every attempt at controlling its growth was resisted and frustrated by bureaucrats who seemed to be actually recruiting to increase the rolls.

Finally, with the help of a citizen's task force, we designed a program to reform welfare; to eliminate cheaters; to encourage the able-bodied to work; to find runaway fathers and make them responsible for their family's support. In less than three years, we not only halted the runaway growth, we reduced the rolls by more than 300,000 people, saved the taxpayers $2 billion and were able to increase the grants to the truly deserving needy by an average of 43 percent.

We learned, of course, that there are people who'll cheat, and there are those who'll accept a lower standard of living in order to get by without working. But we also learned that the overwhelming majority of welfare recipients would like nothing better than to be self-supporting, with a job and a place in our productive society. They may be fed and sheltered by welfare, but as human beings, they are being destroyed by it.

There is a giant bureaucratic complex that thinks of them as "clients," to be permanently maintained as government dependents. This complex measures its own well being and success by how much the welfare rolls increase. To be truly successful, the goal should be to reduce the rolls by eliminating the need for welfare. This is the kind of common sense that's been lacking in Washington for much too long. I believe what we achieved in California can be done at the national level if government will once again have faith in the people and their ability to solve problems.

There are those who want to approach the nation's problems on a politics as usual basis: a little government help here, a shrewd political move there, a little special treatment to this group or that group, a political "strategy" of one kind or another. But we are not going to get out of the mess we are in simply by doing the same old things in a new way.

And then there are those whose approach to government combines soothing rhetoric, pleasant smiles, and reorganization gimmicks. Well, you can't get to the heart of an issue by being vague about it. And you don't discipline an irresponsible and wasteful Congress by putting an indulgent friend in the White House. You don't fix bad policies by rearranging or replacing one bureaucrat with another. You have to replace bad ideas with good ones.

I'm not a politician by profession. I am a citizen who decided I had to be personally involved in order to stand up for my own values and beliefs. My candidacy is based on my record, and for that matter, my entire life.

I'm not asking you to help me because I say, "Trust me, don't ask questions, and everything will be fine." I ask you to trust yourselves, trust your own heads, hearts. Trust your own knowledge of what's happening in America, and your hopes for the future.

Let me be completely candid: no presidential candidate has a patent on virtue. But I believe I offer something more than words, and that is my record as Governor of a state which, if it were a nation, would be the seventh ranking economic power in the world. I believe I can do the job that has to be done.

Many of you—perhaps most of you—who are watching this evening consider yourselves Democrats. I'd like to say a few words to you directly.

During the six months I've been campaigning, I have had some wonderful moments. But I must say that among the most satisfying were those in which I discovered I had received votes not only from members of my own party, but from a great many independents and Democrats as well. This happened in the industrial North, in the South, and in the West. It indicates the issues I was talking about—our basic values, Washington's excesses, our declining national defense—all go beyond party lines; that is there is a new coalition, a new majority across this land ready to answer the nation's needs.

I was once a Democrat myself and believed *that* party represented our values faithfully: I don't believe I changed. But the intellectual and political leadership of the Democratic party changed. The party was taken over by elitists who believed only they could plan properly the lives of the people. We were sheep and they were the shepherds. And, if we don't watch out, the shepherds are going to outnumber the sheep. I am a former Democrat and now a Republican. Millions of you have decided neither party faithfully represents what you believe. The answer is for all of us to vote for our values and not for labels next November.

There are those who say what we are attempting to do cannot be done. But when I hear that I remind myself of a famous moment in American history. The British had been defeated at Yorktown in the last great battle of the War for Independence. As General George Washington marched out to receive the surrender of the British commander, the British musicians solemnly played a tune entitled, "The World Turned Upside Down." And, against all odds and the predictions of all the experts, that's just what the colonists had done.

Well, we can turn the world right side up, the world of the family and the neighborhood and the America we love.

It may take a struggle and some sacrifice, but isn't it worth it? We can do it for ourselves, for our children and in repayment for all those who did the back-breaking jobs that built this nation. They worked their hearts out to give us a country where the right to be left alone, to pursue happiness as we defined it, would be respected by men and by the law.

We ask nothing of freedom but freedom itself, and that means the right to control our own destiny without undue interference by an arrogant officialdom.

There are those who no longer have faith in our ability to do this. They still believe in government *for* the people, but *of* and *by* themselves; that, given freedom of choice, we'll choose unwisely; that ours is a sick society, salvageable only by their omnipotence.

Well, let them explain how a sick society produced the men who journeyed out into space and set foot on the moon; or those other men, the ones we waited for a few years ago, who came back to us proud and unbroken after enduring torture at the hands of savage captors for a longer period than any men in our history.

Have we forgotten how we waited in front of our TV sets through the long night hours for that first plane to land at Clark Field in the Philippines? We were filled with hope and fear, fear of what we might see of what the years of torture might have done to those we called the POW's.

Finally, the moment arrived. The plane was on the ground and we waited—it seemed forever—for the door to open and the first man to appear. Then, with some difficulty—but on his own—Jeremiah Denton, now Rear Admiral Jeremiah Denton, made his way down the ramp. He saluted our country's flag, thanked us for bringing them all home and then asked God's blessing on America.

As the planes continued to bring our men home, Nancy and I were to share an experience that will live in our hearts forever. We were permitted to officially welcome the more than 250 who were Californians by having them as guests in our home. Not all together, but in groups, on four such occasions in all, until we had been privileged to meet and know all of them. It was an unforgettable and inspiring experience. On one of those evenings, we watched two of our guests come together in our living room, apparently strangers until they heard each other's names. Then they threw their arms around each other. They were the closest of friends, knew the most intimate details of each other's lives and families. Their friendship had been built over the years of imprisonment by tapping coded messages on the mud and bamboo wall that separated their cells. They had never seen each other until they came face-to-face there in our living room.

On those four occasions, we heard tales of indescribable torture told without any attempt at dramatics, with no rancor or bitterness and definitely no attempt to beg sympathy. One man, for trying to escape, had been buried up to his neck and left for weeks, his food thrown on the ground before his face.

We heard of men tortured beyond the breaking point until, lying on their cell floors, they wanted to die because they had eventually told their captors some of what they wanted to know. But in the adjoining cells, others who had the same experience at one time or another took turns hour after hour just tapping on the wall to let them know they understood and to hang in there and not give up.

When they were asked why, if they knew they'd eventually break, why they didn't give their captors the information they wanted without undergoing the torture, they seemed surprised. They said, "We were prisoners. The only way we had left to fight the enemy was to hold out as long as we could."

One young man (a fighter pilot who looked as if he should be a cheerleader, maybe on a college campus) had shattered his arm and shoulder when he bailed out after his plane was hit by anti-aircraft fire. They wanted him to talk to two of our anti-war protesters who were guests in Hanoi. He refused. They stood him on a stool, tied his shattered arm to a hook in the wall and then kicked the stool from beneath his feet—not once, but time after time until he gave in. In the meeting that followed, knowing his words were being carefully monitored, he said he tried in every way he could to indicate to these fellow Americans they weren't hearing the truth, but he said, "I spoke to ears that refused to hear."

One night after our guests had gone and Nancy and I were alone, I asked, "Where did we find them, where did we find such men?" The answer came to me almost as quickly as I'd asked the question. We found them where we've always found them when such men are needed—on Main Street, on our farms, in shops and stores, in offices, oil stations, and factories. They are simply the product of the freest society man has ever known.

In the dark days following World War II, when we alone, with our industrial power and military might, stood between the world and a return to the Dark Ages, Pope Pius XII said, "The American people have a genius for great and unselfish deeds. Into the hands of America God has placed the destiny of an afflicted mankind."

God Bless America.

1977

RESHAPING THE AMERICAN POLITICAL LANDSCAPE

(A Majority of Americans Agree With Conservative Principles)

Speaking at the American Conservative Union Banquet, Washington, D.C., February 6th

12.

Three weeks ago here in our nation's capitol I told a group of conservative scholars that we are currently in the midst of a reordering of the political realities that have shaped our time. We know today that the principles and values that lie at the heart of conservatism are shared by the majority.

Despite what some in the press may say, we who are proud to call ourselves "conservative" are not a minority of a minority party; we are part of the great majority of Americans of both major parties and of most of the independents as well.

A Harris poll released September 7, 1975 showed 18 percent identifying themselves as liberal and 31 percent as conservative, with 41 percent as middle of the road. A few months later, on January 5, 1976, by a 43-19 plurality those polled by Harris said they would "prefer to see the country move in a more conservative direction than liberal one."

Last October 24th, the Gallup organization released the result of a poll taken right in the midst of the presidential campaign. Respondents were asked to state where they would place themselves on a scale ranging from "right-of-center" (which was defined as "conservative") to left-of-center (which was defined as "liberal").

- 37 percent viewed themselves as left of center or liberal.
- 12 percent placed themselves in the middle.
- 51 percent said they were right of center, that is, conservative.

What I find interesting about this particular poll is that it offered those polled a range of choices on a left-right continuum. This seems to me to be a more realistic approach than dividing the world into strict left and rights. Most of us, I guess, like to think of ourselves as avoiding both extremes, and the fact that a majority of Americans chose one or the other position on the right end of the spectrum is really impressive.

These polls confirm that most Americans are basically conservative in their outlook. But once we have said this, we conservatives have not *solved* our problems; we have merely stated them clearly. Yes, conservatism is the majority view. But the fact is that conservatism can and does mean different things to those who call themselves conservatives.

You know, as I do, that most commentators make a distinction between what they call "social" conservatism and "economic" conservatism. The so-called social issues—law and order, abortion, busing, quota systems—are usually associated with the blue-collar, ethnic, and religious groups who are traditionally associated with the Democratic Party. The economic issues—inflation, deficit spending, and big government—are usually associated with Republican Party members and independents who concentrate their attention on economic matters.

Now I am willing to accept this view of two major kinds of conservatism or, better still, two different conservative constituencies. But at the same time let me say that the old lines that once clearly divided these two kinds of conservatism are disappearing.

In fact, the time has come to see if it is possible to present a program of action based on political principle that can attract those interested in the so-called "social" issues and those interested in "economic" issues. In short, isn't it possible to combine the two major segments of contemporary American conservatism into one politically effective whole?

I believe the answer is yes; it *is* possible to create a political entity that will reflect the views of the great, hitherto, conservative majority. We went a long way toward doing it in California. We can do it in America. This is not a dream—a wistful hope. It is and has been a reality. I have seen the conservative future and it works!

Let me say again what I said to our conservative friends from the academic world: what I envision is not simply a melding together of the two branches of American conservatism into a temporary uneasy alliance, but the creation of a new, lasting majority.

This will mean compromise. But not a compromise of basic principle. What will emerge will be something new, something open and vital and dynamic, something the great conservative majority will recognize as its own, because at the heart of this undertaking is principled politics.

I have always been puzzled by the inability of some political and media types to understand exactly what is meant by adherence to political principle. All too often in the press and the television evening news it is treated as a call for "ideological purity." Whatever ideology may mean—and it seems to mean a variety of things, depending upon who is using it—it always conjurs up in my mind a picture of a rigid, irrational clinging to abstract theory in the face of reality. We have to recognize that in this country "ideology" is a scare-word. And, for good reason. Marxist-Leninism is, to give but one example, an ideology. All the facts of the real world have to be fitted to the Procrustean bed of Marx and Lenin. If the facts don't happen to fit the ideology, the facts are chopped off and discarded.

I consider this to be the complete opposite to principled conservatism. If there is any political viewpoint in this world which is free of slavish adherence to abstraction, it is American conservatism.

When a conservative states that the free market is the best mechanism ever devised by the mind of man to meet material needs, he is merely stating what a careful examination of the real world has told him is the truth.

When a conservative says that totalitarian Communism is an absolute enemy of human freedom, he is not theorizing—he is reporting the ugly reality captured so unforgettably in the writings of Alexander Solzhenitsyn.

When a conservative says it is bad for the government to spend more than it takes in, he is simply showing the same common sense that tells him to come in out of the rain.

When a conservative says that busing does not work, he is not appealing to some theory of education—he is merely reporting what he has seen down at the local school.

When a conservative quotes Jefferson that government that is closest to the people is best, it is because he knows that Jefferson risked his life, his fortune, and his sacred honor to make certain that what he and his fellow patriots learned from experience was not crushed by an ideology of empire.

Conservatism is the antithesis of the kind of ideological fanatacism that has brought so much horror and destruction to the world. The common sense and common decency of ordinary men and women, working out their own lives in their own way—this is the heart of American conservatism today. Conservative wisdom and principles are derived from willingness to learn—not just from what is going on *now,* but from what has happened before.

The principles of conservatism are sound because they are based on what men and women have discovered through experience in not just one generation or a dozen, but in all the combined experience of mankind. When we conservatives say that we know something about political affairs, and that what we know can be stated as principles, we are saying that the principles we hold dear are those that have been found, through experience, to be ultimately beneficial for individuals, for families, for communities and for nations—found through the often bitter testing of pain, or sacrifice and sorrow.

One thing that must be made clear in post-Watergate is this: the American new conservative majority we represent is *not* based on abstract theorizing of the kind that turns off the American people, but on common sense, intelligence, reason, hard work, faith in God, and the guts to say, yes, there *are* things we do strongly believe in, that we are willing to live for, and, yes, if necessary, to die for. This is not "ideological purity." It is simply what built this country and kept it great.

Let us lay to rest, once and for all, the myth of a small group of ideological purists trying to capture a majority. Replace it with the reality of a majority trying to assert its rights against the tyranny of powerful academics, fashionable left-revolutionaries, some economic illiterates who happen to hold elective office, and the social engineers who dominate the dialogue and set the format in political and social affairs. If there is any ideological fanatacism in American political life, it is to be found among the enemies of freedom on the left and right—those who would sacrifice principle to theory, those who worship only the god of political, social, and economic abstractions, ignoring the realities of everyday life. They are *not* conservatives.

Our first job is to get this message across to those who share most of our principles. If we allow ourselves to be portrayed as ideological shock troops without correcting this error we are doing ourselves and our cause a disservice. Wherever and whenever we can, we should gently but firmly correct our political and media friends who have been perpetuating the myth of conservatism as a narrow ideology. Whatever the word may have meant in the past, today conservatism means principles evolving from experience and a belief in change when necessary, but not just for the sake of change.

Once we have established this, the next question is: What will be the political vehicle by which the majority can assert its rights?

I have to say I cannot agree with some of my friends—perhaps including some of you here tonight—who have answered that question by saying this nation needs a new political party.

I respect that view and I know that those who have reached it have done so after long hours of study. But I believe that political success of the principles we believe in can best be achieved in the Republican Party. I believe the Republican Party can and should provide the political mechanism through which the goals of the majority of Americans can be achieved. For one thing, the biggest single grouping of conservatives is to be found in that party. It makes more sense to build on that grouping than to break it up and start over. Rather than a third party, we can have a new first party made up of people who share our principles. I have said before that if a formal change in name proves desirable, then so be it. But tonight, for purpose of discussion, I'm going to refer to it simply as the New Republican Party.

And let me say this so there can be no mistake as to what I mean: the New Republican Party I envision will not, and cannot, be one limited to the country club big business image that, for reasons, both fair and unfair, it is burdened with today. The New Republican Party I am speaking about is going to have room for the man and woman in the factories, for the farmer, for the cop on the beat, and the millions of Americans who may never have thought of joining our party before, but whose interests coincide with those represented by principled Republicanism. If we are to attract more working men and women of this country, we will do so not simply by "making room" for them, but by making certain they have a say in what goes on in the party. The Democratic Party turned its back on the majority of social conservatives during the 1960s. The New Republican Party of the late '70s and '80s must welcome them, seek them out, enlist them, not only as rank-and-file members but as leaders and as candidates.

The time has come for Republicans to say to black voters: look, we offer principles that black Americans can, and do, support. We believe in jobs, real jobs; we believe in education that is really education; we believe in treating all Americans as individuals and not as stereotypes or voting blocks—and we believe that the long-range interest of black America lies in looking at what each major party has to offer, and *then* deciding on the merits. The Democratic Party takes the black vote for granted. Well, it's time black America and the New Republican Party move toward each other and create a situation in which no black vote can be taken for granted.

The New Republican Party I envision is one that will energetically seek out the best candidates for every elective office—candidates who not only agree with, but understand, and are willing to fight for a sound, honest economy, for the interests of American families and neighborhoods and communities and a strong national defense. And these candidates must be able to communicate those principles to the American people in language they understand. Inflation isn't a textbook problem. Unemployment isn't a textbook problem. They should be discussed in human terms.

Our candidates must be willing to communicate with every level of society, because the principles we espouse are universal and cut across traditional lines. In every congressional district there should be a search made for young men and women who share these principles, and they should be brought into positions of leadership in the local Republican Party groups. We can find attractive, articulate candidates if we look, and when we find them, we will begin to change the sorry state of affairs that has led to a Democratic-controlled Congress for more than forty years. I need not remind you that you can have the soundest principles in the world, but if you don't have candidates who can communicate those principles, candidates who are articulate as well as principled, you are going to lose election after election. I refuse to believe that the good Lord divided this world into Republicans who defend basic values and Democrats who win elections. We have to find the tough, bright young men and women who are sick and tired of the clichés and the pomposity and the mind-numbing economic idiocy of the liberals in Washington.

It is at this point, however, that we come across a question that is really the essential one: what will be the basis of this New Republican Party? To what set of values and principles can our candidates appeal? Where can Americans who want to know where we stand look for guidance?

Fortunately, we have an answer to that question. That answer was provided last summer by the men and women of the Republican Party—not just the leadership, but the ones who have built the party on local levels all across the country. The answer was provided in the 1976 Platform of the Republican Party.

This was not a document handed down from on high. It was hammered out in free and open debate among all those who care about our party and the principles it stands for.

The Republican Platform is unique. Unlike any other party platform I have ever seen, it answers not only programmatic questions for the immediate future of the party, but also provides a clear outline of the underlying principles upon which those programs are based.

The New Republican Party can and should use the Republican Platform of 1976 as the major source from which a declaration of principles can be created and offered to the American people.

Tonight I want to offer to you my own version of what such a declaration might look like. I make no claim to originality. This declaration I propose is relatively short, taken, for the most part, word for word from the Republican Platform. It concerns itself with basic principles, not with specific solutions.

"We, the members of the New Republican Party, believe that the preservation and enhancement of the values that strengthen and protect individual freedom, family life, communities and neighborhoods and the liberty of our beloved nation should be at the heart of any legislative or political program presented to the American people. Toward that end, we, therefore, commit ourselves to the following propositions and offer them to each American believing that the New Republican Party, based on such principles, will serve the interest of all the American people.

"We believe that liberty can be measured by how much freedom Americans have to make their own decisions—even their own mistakes. Government must step in when one's liberties impinge on one's neighbor's. Government must protect constitutional rights, deal with other governments, protect citizens from aggressors, assure equal opportunity, and be compassionate in caring for those citizens who are unable to care for themselves.

"Our federal system of local-state-national government is designed to sort out on what level these actions should be taken. Those concerns of a national character—such as air and water pollution that do not respect state boundaries, or the national transportation system, or efforts to safeguard your civil liberties—must, of course, be handled on the national level.

"As a general rule, however, we believe that government action should be taken first by the government that resides as close to you as possible.

"We also believe that Americans, often acting through voluntary organizations, should have the opportunity to solve many of the social problems of their communities. This spirit of freely helping others is uniquely American and should be encouraged in every way by government.

"Families must continue to be the foundation of our nation.

"Families—not government programs—are the best way to make sure our children are properly nurtured, our elderly are cared for, our cultural and spiritual heritages are perpetuated, our laws are observed and our values are preserved.

"Thus it is imperative that our government's programs, actions, officials and social welfare institutions never be allowed to jeopardize the family. *We fear the government may be powerful enough to destroy our families; we know that it is not powerful enough to replace them.*" The New Republican Party must be committed to working always in the interest of the American family.

"Every dollar spent by government is a dollar earned (by individuals). Government must always ask: Are your dollars being wisely spent? Can we afford it? Is it not better for the country to leave your dollars in your pocket?

"Elected officials, their appointees, and government workers are expected to perform their public acts with honesty, openness, diligence, and special integrity.

"Government must work for the goal of justice and the elimination of unfair practices, but no government has yet designed a more productive economic system or one which benefits as many people (than the American market system).

"The beauty of our land is our legacy to our children. It must be protected by us so that they can pass it on intact to their children.

"The United States must always stand for peace and

liberty in the world and the rights of the individual. We must form sturdy partnerships with our allies for the preservation of freedom. We must be ever-willing to negotiate differences, but equally mindful that there are American ideals that cannot be compromised. Given that there are other nations with potentially hostile design, we recognize that we can reach our goals only while maintaining a superior nation defense, second to none."

In his inaugural speech President Carter said that he saw the world "dominated by a new spirit. . . ." He then said, and I quote, "The passion for freedom is on the rise. . . ."

Well, I don't know how he knows this, but if it is true, then it is the most unrequited passion in human history. The world is being dominated by a new spirit, all right, but it isn't the spirit of freedom.

It isn't very often you see a familiar object that shocks and frightens you. But the other day I came across a map of the world created by Freedom House, an organization monitoring the state of freedom in the world for the past thirty-five years. It is an ordinary map, with one exception: it shows the world nations in white for free, shaded for partly free and black for not free.

Almost all of the great Eurasian land mass is completely colored black, from the western border of East Germany, through middle and eastern Europe, through the awesome spaces of the Soviet Union, on to the Bering Strait in the north, down past the immensity of China, still further, down to Vietnam and the South China Sea—in all that huge, sprawling, inconceivably-immense area not a single political or personal or religious freedom exists. The entire continent of Africa, from the Mediterranean to the Cape of Good Hope, from the Atlantic to the Indian

Ocean, all that vastness is almost totally unfree. In the tiny nation of Tanzania alone, according to a report in the *New York Times,* there are three thousand people in detention for political crimes—that is more than the total being held in South Africa. The Mid-East has only one free state: Israel. If a visitor from another planet were to approach earth, and if this planet showed free nations in light and unfree nations in darkness, the pitifully small beacons of light would make him wonder what was hidden in that terrifying, enormous blackness.

We know what is hidden: Gulag. Torture. Families—and human beings—broken apart. No free press, no freedom of religion. The ancient forms of tyranny revived and made even more hideous and strong through what Winston Churchill once called "a perverted science." Men rotting for years in solitary confinement because they have different political and economic beliefs, solitary confinement that drives the fortunate ones insane and makes the survivors wish for death.

Only now and then do we in the West hear a voice, from out of that darkness. Then there is silence—the silence of human slavery. There is no more terrifying sound in human experience, with one possible exception. Look at that map again. The very heart of the darkness is the Soviet Union and from that heart comes a different sound. It is the whirling sound of machinery and the whisper of the computer technology we ourselves have sold them. It is the sound of building, building of the strongest military machine ever devised by man. Our military strategy is designed to hopefully prevent a war. Theirs is designed to win one. A group of eminent scientists, scholars, and intelligence experts offer a survey showing that the Soviet Union is driving for military superiority and are derided as hysterically making a "worst case" concerning Soviet intentions and capabilities.

But is it not precisely the duty of the national government to be prepared for the worst case? Two Senators, after studying the North Atlantic Treaty Organization, have reported to the Armed Forces committee that Soviet forces in Eastern Europe have the capability to launch, with little warning, a "potentially devastating" attack in central Europe from what is termed a "standing start."

Reading their report one can almost see the enormous weight of the parts of the earth that are under tyranny shifting in an irresistable tilt toward that tiny portion of land in freedom's light. Even now in Western Europe we have Communists in the government of Italy. France appeases terrorists, and England—for centuries the model or the sword of freedom in Western Europe—weak, dispirited, turning inward.

A worst case? How could you make a *good* case out of the facts as they are known? The Soviet Union, poised on the edge of free Europe, capable of striking from a standing start, has modern tanks in far greater numbers than the outmoded vehicles of NATO. We have taken comfort from NATO's superiority in the air, but now the Soviet Union has made a dramatic swing away from its historic defensive air posture to one capable of supporting offensive action. NATO's southern flank is described in the Senate report with a single word: "shambles."

The report is simple reality, as it was, with different names and faces, in Europe in the late 1930s when so many refused to believe and thought if we did not look the threat would go away.

We don't want hysteria. We don't want distortion of Soviet power. We want truth. And above all we want peace. And to have that the United States has to immediately reexamine its entire view of the world and develop a strategy of freedom. We cannot be the second-best super-power for the simple reason that he who is second is last. In this deadly game, there are no silver medals for second.

President Carter, as a candidate, said he would cut five to seven billion dollars from the defense budget. We must let him know that while we agree there must be no fat in our armed forces, those armed forces must be capable of coping with the new reality presented to us by the Russians; and cutting seven billion dollars out of our defense budget is not the way to accomplish this. Some years ago, a young President said we will make any sacrifice, bear any burden, and we will to preserve our freedom.

Our relationship with mainland China is clouded. The so-called "gang of four" are up one day and down the next, and we are seeing the pitfalls of making deals with charismatic personalities and living legends. The charisma fades as the living legends die, and those who take their place are interested not in our best wishes but in power. The key word for China today is turmoil. We should watch and observe and analyze as closely and rationally as we can.

But in our relationships with the mainland of China we should always remember that the conditions and possibilities for and the realities of freedom exist to an infinitely greater degree with our Chinese friends in Taiwan. We can never go wrong if we do what is morally right, and the moral way—the honorable way—is to keep our commitment, our solemn promise to the people of Taiwan. Our liberal friends have made much of the lack of freedom in some Latin American countries. Senator Edward

Kennedy and his colleagues here in Washington let no opportunity pass to let us know about horrors in Chile.

Well, I think when the United States of America is considering a deal with a country that hasn't had an election in almost eight years, where the press is under the thumb of a dictatorship, where ordinary citizens are abducted in the night by secret police, where military domination of the country is known to be harsh on dissenters and when these things are documented, we should reject overtures from those who rule such a country.

But the country I'm describing is not Chile—it is *Panama.*

We are negotiating with a dictatorship that comes within the portion of that map colored black for no freedom. No civil rights. One man rule. No free press.

Candidate Carter said he would never relinquish "actual control" of the Panama Canal. President Carter is negotiating with a dictator whose record on civil and human rights is as I have just described, and the negotiations concern the rights guaranteed to us by treaty which we will give up under a threat of violence. In only a few weeks we will mark the second anniversary of the death of freedom for the Vietnamese. An estimated 300,000 of them are being "reeducated" in concentration camps to forget about freedom.

There is only one major question on the agenda of national priorities and that is the state of our national security. I refer, of course, to the state of our armed forces—but also to our state of mind, to the way we perceive the world. We cannot maintain the strength we need to survive, no matter how many missiles we have, no matter how many tanks we build, unless we are willing to reverse the trend of deteriorating faith in and continuing abuse of our national intelligence agencies. Let's stop the sniping and the propaganda and the historical revisionism and let the CIA and the other intelligence agencies do their job.

Let us reverse the trend of public indifference to problems of national security. In every Congressional district citizens should join together, enlist and educate neighbors and make certain that Congressmen know we care. The front pages of major newspapers on the East Coast recently headlined and told in great detail of a takeover, the takeover of a magazine published in New York—not a nation losing its freedom. You would think, from the attention it received in the media, that it was a matter of blazing national interest whether the magazine lived or died. The tendency of much of the media to ignore the state of our national security is too well documented for me to go on.

My friends, the time has come to start acting to bring about the great conservative majority party we know is waiting to be created.

And just to set the record straight, let me say this about our friends who are now Republicans but who do not identify themselves as conservatives.

I want the record to show that I do not view the new revitalized Republican Party as one based on a principle of exclusion. After all, you do not get to be a majority party by searching for groups you *won't* associate or work with. If we truly believe in our principles, we should sit down and talk. Talk with anyone, anywhere, at any time, if it means talking about the principles of the Republican Party. Conservatism is not a narrow ideology nor is it the exclusive property of conservative activists.

We've succeeded better than we know. Little more

than a decade ago, more than two-thirds of Americans believed the federal government could solve all our problems with its multitude of bureaus, agencies, and programs, and do so without restricting our freedom or bankrupting the nation.

We warned of things to come, of the danger inherent in unwarranted government involvement in things not its proper province. What we warned against has come to pass. And today more than two-thirds of our citizens are telling us, and each other, that social engineering by the federal government has failed. The Great Society is great only in power, in size, and in cost. And so are the problems it set out to solve. Freedom has been diminished and we stand on the brink of economic ruin.

Our task now is not to sell a philosophy, but to make the majority of Americans, who already share that philosophy, see that modern conservatism offers them a political home. We are not a cult; we are members of a majority. Let's act and talk like it.

The job is ours and the job must be done. If not by us, who? if not now, when?

Our party must be the party of the individual. It must not sell out the individual to cater to the group. No greater challenge faces our society today than insuring that each one of us can maintain his dignity and his identity in an increasingly complex, centralized society.

Extreme taxation, excessive controls, oppressive government competition with business, galloping inflation, frustrated minorities, and forgotten Americans are not the products of free enterprise. They are the residue of centralized bureaucracy, of government by a self-anointed elite.

Our party must be based on the kind of leadership that grows and takes its strength from the people. Any organization is in actuality only the lengthened shadowed of its members. A political party is a mechanical structure created to further a cause. The cause, not the mechanism, brings and holds the members together. And our cause must be to rediscover, reassert, and reapply America's spiritual heritage to our national affairs.

Then with God's help we shall indeed be as a city upon a hill with the eyes of all people upon us.

1977

UNITED STATES FOREIGN POLICY AND WORLD REALITIES

(Assessment of Major Problem Areas in Foreign Policy)

Speaking to the Foreign Policy Association,
New York City, New York, June 9th

13.

Your format for guest speakers is one of which I heartily approve: that we should have a dialogue rather than a monologue. I am aware, of course, that there must be some of the latter before we get to your questions. So I would like to share with you some observations on United States foreign policy and world realities as we face them today.

In his commencement address at Notre Dame University, President Carter said he believes that, since Vietnam, "we have found our way back to our own principles and values, and we have regained our lost confidence."

He also called for an American foreign policy that is based on "constant decency" in U.S. values and "on optimism in its historic vision."

I hope he is right on botn counts. Our historic desire for all men and women to share in our tradition of individual human rights and freedom, with government the servant and not the master, should continue to guide us.

Yet it must be tempered by the reality that other powers with which we must deal simply do not and probably never will agree with our concept of constitutional republicanism, let alone human rights.

President Carter's commendable concern for human rights has been well stated, but to make it the cornerstone of United States foreign policy offers problems that are both balky and contradictory.

If human rights around the world are going to be our principal concern, then we must adhere to a single, not a double standard in our policy. For example, if we deplore alleged violations of human rights in Chile, Argentina, and Brazil, can we ignore them in Panama?

Can we, on humanitarian grounds, carry on a constant drumbeat of criticism toward South Africa and Rhodesia at the same time we talk of recognizing a regime in Cambodia that has butchered as much as a third of its population? We negotiate with the conquerors of South Vietnam who routinely violate human rights, and who cynically signed and then scrapped the Paris Peace Accords. We nudge closer to recognizing Castro's Cuba, which, Amnesty International estimates, holds 4,000 to 5,000 of its citizens political prisoner.

The Christian Institute, by the way, counts only 317 political prisoners in South Africa. And yet, partly because of past mistakes here at home and partly because of our basic belief in majority rule, we insist on applying our own political standards to South Africa. We do not insist on these standards for the rest of that continent, where one-party, one-tribe, or military dictatorship are less the exception than the rule. In forty-odd of the newly emerged African states they believe in one man, one vote—once.

Human rights are basic, applicable to all, and we should apply them with consistency. But so far, with the exception of some earlier and highly publicized comments about the Soviet Union's treatment of dissenters, the new Administration's foreign policy has aimed most of its human rights criticisms at governments that are no threat to others and that, despite not always behaving as we might like, have nevertheless been our friends.

Perhaps the most important reality facing us today is

the shrinking global influence of the West. The signs of it are all about us, but as our Ambassador to the North Atlantic Treaty Organization, Robert Strausz-Hupé, said on his recent retirement from that post, ". . . throughout the West, it seems to have engendered in the Western public at large that sense of fatalistic indifference which, so I have read, living by the side of a volcano induces in the local population."

That indifference presents the Western world with its greatest challenge in ages. I am talking not only of Western loss of natural resources and materials, though that is occurring, but beyond it to the decline of the Western concepts of political responsibility and individual freedom. Perhaps President Carter in his quest for human rights has recognized this decline and wants to reverse it. I hope so, but I am disturbed by the unevenness with which the policy has been applied.

While Western influence has been declining, Western living standards continue to improve and, indeed, have begun to spread to less developed countries. That much is to the good. We should be able to make the productive genius of Western industry and technology work for the betterment of all mankind.

But, despite our miracles of agricultural production, sending men to the moon, and creating for hundreds of millions of people the highest standard of living the world has ever seen, complacency we cannot afford.

Halfway around the world our principal challenger, the Soviet Union, is ready to offer us continued and new challenges.

In the decades since World War II, there have been two main thrusts in the external affairs of the Soviet Union. In the early years following the war, conflicts (of varying degrees of intensity) involving the major powers occurred—for the most part—along the edges of that part of the world dominated by Soviet communism. For example:

- The USSR's attempt to expand its own empire by absorbing northern Iran. That did not work.
- Its efforts to overthrow the constitutional government of Greece through civil war. That did not work either.
- Its demand for two border provinces from Turkey. Another blank.
- Its attempts to replace Tito in Yugoslavia, which were all thwarted by U.S. counter measures.
- The Soviet blockade of Berlin, which was broken by the Allied airlift.

The Soviet Union did, of course, succeed in consolidating its hold on much of Central and Eastern Europe.

These events all happened a number of years ago, and they were reflective of Russia's historic concern for its own defense and security.

Since that time, the Soviet Union, whenever possible, has moved outward, turning non-Western peoples against the West and against the United States in particular, and taking advantage of those conflicts it did not have a hand in starting.

Western nations with colonial holdings have systematically relinquished them. This is consistent with our own views of self-determination, but it has created political voids the Soviets have not been bashful about filling.

This Soviet policy of seeking to alienate non-Western peoples from the West and to mobilize them against the West whenever and wherever possible, to many observers seems to have been a thoroughly consistent one since the end of World War II, and it is certainly consistent with Lenin's goal of ultimate worldwide Communist victory.

The Soviet Union has a global objective. That fact alone makes our idealism vulnerable. We Americans would dearly love to let everyone live in peace and harmony. We cling to the belief that if only a few essentials of democracy are adhered to in any land, reason will prevail. This may be described as a global objective, I suppose, but it is no substitute for a coherent global policy in the face of real challenges.

The United Kingdom's new Foreign Secretary, David Owen, put the West's problem succinctly when he said recently, "The basic premise from which we in the West must start is that the Soviet Union is a world power with national interests and ambitions to match, which inevitably bring it into competition and sometimes confrontation with the West. To this we must add that Communist ideology invests the natural rivalry between East and West with a dynamic of increasing struggle."

Despite its huge arms buildup in the past few years and a massive civil defense program designed to let it survive a nuclear war, the Soviet Union does not want to fight a war if it can be avoided. Instead, the Soviet buildup seems to be designated primarily for political leverage—to achieve their aims indirectly.

What they want to accomplish—namely, the gradual encirclement of the West and reduction of its strategic and economic influence—they believe can be accomplished by several means. "Proxy" wars are important. The wars in Korea and Indochina are examples. So was the Angolan civil war following Portugal's withdrawal from its former colony. So was the so-called Katangan incursion into Zaire recently, though that one failed. And so is the growing Soviet influence in Ethiopia in its battle with independence-minded Eritrea province.

Detente between the United States and the Soviet Union may actually have improved the climate for Soviet promotion of proxy wars and skirmishes. American public opinion had turned against the Vietnam War. Our people, weary, wanted peace and no more nuclear threats. We were content with maintaining the status quo between the major powers. After all, we do not want to conquer anyone. We just want to be at peace with the world. And we tend to believe the other fellow sees things through the same set of eyes we do. In the case of detente, we believed that if we exposed the Soviet Union's people to more of our own people—through various exchange programs—the magic of democracy would somehow rub off on them.

Our assumption was false. First, the Soviet Union does not see itself as a status quo power but a dynamic one, interested in the ultimate goal of its philosophical fathers, the global triumph of its political system. And, interestingly enough, the trappings of that system—a police state; a judicial system that functions for the state, not the individual; and monolithic control of public opinion—are not so very different from those of Czarist Russia.

Even a cursory reading of the Soviet press shows you that it rails constantly against what it calls the "imperialists" of the West, the United States, and its allies.

We saw detente as a relaxation of tensions and an opportunity, through trade and cultural exchanges, to gradually modify the Soviet system. They saw it otherwise. For them, it provided a measure of security. It signified to them the growing strength of the Soviet Union in world affairs and a corresponding weakening of the

West. Detente, to the Soviet Union, became not a sign of compromise, but a victory for the USSR and a growing sign of Western weakness caused by the internal contradictions of capitalism. And all of this is part of the steady propaganda drum roll heard by the Soviet citizen.

Whatever we call it, detente is not what we thought it was. But what should we do about it? Scrap the trade agreements? Stop the exchanges? No, these can have some positive benefits, provided of course the trade does not involve products and technology which could be turned against us militarily one day. As for arms agreements, we should continue to discuss them with the Soviets and continue to seek reductions in deadly arms. But we must do so with our eyes open, and any agreements that are reached must be reciprocal and unambiguous.

What should be the underlying principle of our policies? I believe we should pursue policies that lie in our best interests and those of the West. For, so long as we are also committed to help less developed countries reach their destiny too, these policies will be beneficial to all the world.

Where will the new challenges come, and how should we deal with them? President Carter, in his recent speech (to which I referred earlier) said, "It is a new world—but America should not fear it. It is a new world—and we should help to save it." Call it a new world, or a new awakening to reality; it will involve challenges from which we must not shrink. They may come at any time, in any one or a combination of places.

In the southern tier of Europe there could be dramatic shifts in power. Though Portugal's future is not completely certain, it is stabilized at this time. But in Spain, free elections are soon to be held, and the Communist party, which claims 200,000 members, is now operating legally and doing its best to gain strength among any in that land who are discontent.

Italy's political and economic instability is both chronic and acute. The Communists control the governments of many major cities. Very likely we will see Communist ministers in the governments of Italy, Spain, Greece, and Cyprus within the next few years. Portugal already has one. This has ominous mutual defense implications for NATO, and we daydream if we think that so-called Eurocommunism is somehow independent of the Soviet Union.

In Yugoslavia the question is, after Tito, what? The USSR covets that land and can be counted on to exploit—to the maximum—the ethnic divisions in it.

Though the Soviets have lost much of their influence in the Middle East and may be thwarted from attempting to exploit worries arising from the election victory of the Likkud coalition in Israel, they can be expected to exploit every opportunity for gain.

In the Far East, waterways hold the key to strength from Thailand to Indonesia, with Singapore being the so-called "choke point" between two oceans. To the north, the Japanese are increasingly apprehensive that not only will we withdraw our troops from South Korea, but we will pull our Pacific defense perimeter back to Hawaii, and not even defend Japan itself if called upon.

In fact, the small quadrangle where China, the USSR, Korea, and Japan meet could become an area of future conflict. The pending withdrawal of United States troops could act as a catalyst for adventuresome challengers. Have we forgotten that the Korean War was a proxy war?

It was only one year ago that the largest Soviet naval exercise ever took place—in the East China Sea, the Sea of Okhotsk, and in the Pacific, east of Japan and northwest of the Carolines. It was organized around a simulated disruption of commerce and the nuclear destruction of U.S. bases.

In Africa, the Soviets, partly because of U.S. Executive and Congressional indecisiveness over Angola, have hit upon a winning formula: use Cuban troops as proxy mercenaries to stir up things.

Today there are Cuban troops in Angola, Guinea, Guinea-Bissau, the Congo, and Ethiopia! They are being transferred, too, to Mozambique (along with Soviet arms which are being unloaded at the capital of Maputo) for what they presumably expect to be the final assault on Rhodesia. There is not much doubt that the next target will then be Southwest Africa and, finally, South Africa. Yet our interest in what, at heart, is part of the American civil rights issue, clouds our ability to see this international danger to the Western world.

Is there any doubt about the fate of human rights if Southern Africa falls into the orbit of the Soviet Union and becomes, in the next few years, a series of Russian client states?

And is there any doubt about the consequences to economies of the West if the Soviet Union controls all the sea lanes from the Persian Gulf around to the Atlantic?

Closer to home, in the Western Hemisphere, we have Fidel Castro encouraging Puerto Rican terrorists, the Prime Minister of Jamaica turning his country ever leftward, and the Soviet Union and Castro egging on the dictator of Panama to insist that we give him the canal.

Most of these potential areas of international challenge (and possibly conflict) have three things in common:

- They are farther removed from Soviet borders than those we experienced in the years immediately following World War II.
- They involve our access to strategic resources—oil and minerals.
- They are located on or near the open sea.

These are the realities we must deal with; areas of potential challenge where the West in general and the United States in particular have operated without too much difficulty in the past. This may change.

The USSR has acquired an ability to intervene far from its own borders. For years it did not have this ability. Leonid Brezhnev, in a secret meeting of Eastern European Communist Party leaders in 1973 (quoted in a British intelligence report) said, "Trust us, comrades, for by 1985 as a consequence of what we are now achieving with detente, we will have achieved most of our objectives in Western Europe. We will have consolidated our position. We will have improved our economy. And a decisive shift in the correlation of forces will be such that, come 1985, we will be able to exert our will wherever we need to."

The facts emanating from the years since Brezhnev made that statement make it plain his words were not sheer bravado. They must be taken seriously.

In doing so, our asserting a strong belief in human rights is an important part of our moral ethic. But we need our friends, and before rebuking them, I believe we should keep in mind an American Indian maxim, the origin of which is lost in time. It is this: "Before I criticize a man, may I walk a mile in his moccasins."

Earlier, I quoted from my friend Ambassador Strausz-Hupé. Let me quote him again. "Ideally," he said, "the desire to do great things in common—to build a perfect society and to cure the world's ills—should move the Western people towards union."

This becomes an imperative as we look at the challenges before us—not only for the survival of the West, but for the growth and development of less developed countries that need our help. If our concern for basic human rights is to be fulfilled, there must be a favorable world environment in which we can pursue it. Only if we are ready to meet challenges, peacefully and effectively, from those who have quite a different view of mankind, can we meet our destiny as a free people. And only by remaining second to none in our defense capability will we have that opportunity.

Western civilization is not perfect, but it is the only civilization the earth has yet seen which has struck some kind of balance between the material and moral aspirations of its people. It is worth working for. It is worth sharing with others. And if need be it is worth fighting for.

1980

WE NEED A REBIRTH IN LEADERSHIP

(Three Grave Threats to Our Way of Life)

From the Presidential Nomination Acceptance Address, Republican National Convention, Detroit, Michigan, July 17th

14.

With a deep awareness of the responsibility conferred by your trust, I accept your nomination for the Presidency of the United States. I do so with deep gratitude.

I'm very proud of our party tonight. This convention has shown to all America a party united, with positive programs for solving the nation's problems; a party ready to build a new consensus with all those across the land who share a community of values embodied in these words: family, work, neighborhood, peace, and freedom.

Now, I know we've had a quarrel or two, but only as to the method of attaining a goal. There was no argument here about the goal. As President, I will establish a liaison with the fifty governors to encourage them to eliminate, wherever it exists, discrimination against women. I will monitor federal laws to insure their implementation and to add statutes if they are needed.

More than anything else, I want my candidacy to unify our country, to renew the American spirit and sense of purpose. I want to carry our message to every American, regardless of party affiliation, who is a member of this community of shared values.

Never before in our history have Americans been called upon to face three grave threats to our very existence, any one of which could destroy us. We face a disintegrating economy, a weakened defense, and an energy policy based on the sharing of scarcity.

The majoı issue of this campaign is the direct political, personal, and moral responsibility of Democratic Party leadership—in the White House and in the Congress—for this unprecedented calamity which has befallen us. They tell us they've done the most that humanly could be done. They say that the United States has had its day in the sun, that our nation has passed its zenith. They expect you to tell your children that the American people no longer have the will to cope with their problems, that the future will be one of sacrifice and few opportunities.

My fellow citizens, I utterly reject that view. The American people, the most generous on earth, who created the highest standard of living, are not going to accept the notion that we can only make a better world for others by moving backward ourselves. And those who believe we can have no business leading this nation.

I will not stand by and watch this great country destroy itself under mediocre leadership that drifts from one crisis to the next, eroding our national will and purpose. We have come together here because the American people deserve better from those to whom they entrust our nation's highest offices, and we stand united in our resolve to do something about it.

We need a rebirth of the American tradition of leadership at *every* level of government and in private life as well. The United States of America is unique in world history because it has a genius for leaders—many leaders—on many levels.

But back in 1976, Mr. Carter said, "Trust *me*." And a lot of people did. And now many of those people are out of work. Many have seen their savings eaten away by inflation. Many other on fixed incomes, especially the elderly, have watched helplessly as the cruel tax of inflation wasted away their purchasing power. And, today, a great many who trusted Mr. Carter wonder if we can survive the Carter policies of national defense.

"Trust me" government asks that we concentrate our hopes and dreams on one man, that we trust him to do what's best for us. But my view of government places trust not in one person or one party, but in those values that transcend persons and parties. The trust is where it belongs—in the people. The responsibility to live up to that trust is where *it* belongs, in their elected leaders. That kind of relationship, between the people and their elected leaders, is a special kind of compact.

Three-hundred-and sixty years ago, in 1620, a group of families dared to cross a mighty ocean to build a future for themselves in a new world. When they arrived at Plymouth, Massachusetts, they formed what they call a "compact," an agreement among themselves to build a community and abide by its laws.

This single act—the voluntary binding together of free people to live under the law—set the pattern for what was to come.

A century and a half later, the descendants of those people pledged their lives, their fortunes and their sacred honor to found this nation. Some forfeited their fortunes and their lives; none sacrificed honor.

Four score and seven years later, Abraham Lincoln called upon the people of all America to renew their dedication and their commitment to a government of, for and by the people.

Isn't it once again time to renew our compact of freedom, to pledge to each other all that is best in our lives; all that gives meaning to them—for the sake of this, our beloved and blessed land?

Together, let us make this a new beginning. Let us make a commitment to care for the needy; to teach our children the virtues handed down to us by our families; to have the courage to defend those values and virtues and the willingness to sacrifice for them.

Let us pledge to restore to the federal government the capacity to do the people's work without dominating their lives. I pledge to you a government that will not only work well but wisely, its ability to act tempered by prudence, and its willingness to do good balanced by the knowledge that government is never more dangerous than when our desire to have it help us blinds us to its great power to harm us.

You know, the first Republican president once said, "While the people retain their virtue and their vigilance, no administration by any extreme of wickedness or folly can seriously injure the government in the short space of four years."

If Mr. Lincoln could see what's happened in these last three and a half years, he might hedge a little on that statement. But with the virtues that are our legacy as a free people, and with the vigilance that sustains liberty, we still have time to use our renewed compact to overcome the injuries that have been done to America these past three and a half years.

First, we must overcome something the present Administration has cooked up: a new and altogether indigestible economic stew, one part inflation, one part high unemployment, one part recession, one part runaway taxes, one part deficit spending, seasoned with an energy crisis. It's an economic stew that has turned the national stomach. It is as if Mr. Carter had set out to prove, once and for all, that economics is indeed a "dismal science."

Ours are not problems of abstract economic theory. These are problems of flesh and blood, problems that cause pain and destroy the moral fiber of real people who should not suffer the further indignity of being told by the government that it is all somehow their fault. We do not have inflation because—as Mr. Carter says—we've lived too well.

The head of a government which has utterly refused to live within its means and which has, in the last few days, told us that this coming year's deficit will be $60 billion, dares to point the finger of blame at business and labor, both of which have been engaged in a losing struggle just trying to stay even.

High taxes, we are told, are somehow good for us, as if, when government spends our money it isn't inflationary, but when we spend it, it is.

Those who preside over the worst energy shortage in our history tell us to use less, so that we will run out of oil, gasoline, and natural gas a little more slowly. Well, now, conservation is desirable, of course, because we must not waste energy. But conservation is not the sole answer to our energy needs.

America must get to work producing more energy. The Republican program for solving economic problems is based on growth and productivity.

Large amounts of oil and natural gas lay beneath our land and off our shores, untouched because the present Administration seems to believe the American people would rather see more regulation, more taxes, and more controls than more energy.

Coal offers a great potential. So does nuclear energy produced under rigorous safety standards. It could supply electricity for thousands of industries and millions of jobs and homes. It must not be thwarted by a tiny minority opposed to economic growth which often finds friendly ears in regulatory agencies for its obstructionist campaigns.

Now, make no mistake. We will not permit the safety of our people or our environmental heritage to be jeopardized. But we are going to reaffirm that the economic prosperity of our people is a fundamental part of our environment.

Our problems are both acute and chronic; yet all we hear from those in positions of leadership are the same tired proposals for more government tinkering, more meddling, and more control—all of which led us to this sorry state in the first place.

Can anyone look at the record of this Administration and say, "Well done"? Can anyone compare the state of our economy when the Carter Administration took office with where we are today and say, "Keep up the good work"? Can anyone look at our reduced standing in the world today and say, "Let's have four more years of this"?

I believe the American people are going to answer these questions, as you've answered them, in the first week of November, and their answer will be, "No—we've had enough." And then it will be up to us—beginning next January 20—to offer an administration and congressional leadership of competence and more than a little courage.

We must have the clarity of vision to see the difference between what is essential and what is merely desirable; and then the courage to bring our government back under control.

It is essential that we maintain both the forward momentum of economic growth and the strength of the safety net between those in our society who need help. We also believe it is essential that the integrity of all aspects of Social Security be preserved.

Beyond these essentials, I believe it is clear our federal government is overgrown and overweight. Indeed, it is time our government should go on a diet. Therefore, my first act as Chief Executive will be to impose an immediate and thorough freeze on federal hiring. Then we are going to enlist the very best minds from business, labor, and whatever quarter to conduct a detailed review of every department, bureau, and agency that lives by federal appropriation.

And we are also going to enlist the help and ideas of many dedicated and hard-working government employees at all levels who want a more efficient government just as much as the rest of us do. I know that many of them are demoralized by the confusion and waste they confront in their work as a result of failed and failing policies.

Our instructions to the groups we enlist will be simple and direct. We will remind them that government programs exist at the sufferance of the American taxpayer and are paid for with money earned by working men and women, and programs that represent a waste of their money—a theft from their pocketbooks—must have that waste eliminated or that program must go. It must go by Executive Order where possible, by congressional action where necessary.

Everything that can be run more effectively by state and local government we shall turn over to state and local government, along with the funding sources to pay for it. We are going to put an end to the money merry-go-round where our money becomes Washington's money, to be spent by state and cities exactly the way the federal bureaucrats tell us it has to be spent.

I will not accept the excuse that the federal government has grown so big and powerful that it is beyond the control of any President, any Administration or Congress. We are going to put an end to the notion that the American taxpayer exists to fund the federal government. The federal government exists to *serve* the American people and to be accountable to the American people. On January 20, we are going to reestablish that truth.

Also on that date we are going to initiate action to get substantial relief for our taxpaying citizens and action to put people back to work. None of this will be based on any new form of monetary tinkering or fiscal sleight of hand. We will simply apply to government the common sense that we all use in our daily lives.

Work and family are at the center of our lives, the foundation of our dignity as a free people. When we deprive people of what they have earned, or take away their jobs, we destroy their dignity and undermine their families. We can't support families unless there are jobs, and we can't have jobs unless the people have both money to invest and the faith to invest it.

These are concepts that stem from an economic system that for more than two hundred years has helped us master a continent, create a previously undreamed of prosperity for our people, and has fed millions of others around the globe and that system will continue to serve us in the future, if our government will stop ignoring the basic values on which it was built and stop betraying the trust and good will of the American workers who keep it going.

The American people are carrying the heaviest peacetime tax burden in our nation's history—and it will grow even heavier, under present law, next January. We are taxing ourselves into economic exhaustion and stagnation, crushing our ability and incentive to save, invest, and produce.

This must stop. We *must* halt this fiscal self-destruction and restore sanity to our economic system.

I've long advocated a 30 percent reduction in income tax rates over a period of three years. This phased tax reduction would begin with a 10 percent "down payment" tax cut in 1981, which the Republicans in Congress and I have already proposed.

A phased reduction of tax rates would go a long way toward easing the heavy burden on the American people. But we shouldn't stop here.

Within the context of economic conditions and appropriate budget priorities during each fiscal year of my Presidency, I would strive to go further. This would include improvement in business depreciation taxes so we can stimulate investment in order to get plants and equipment replaced, put more Americans back to work, and put our nation back on the road to being competitive in world commerce. We will also work to reduce the cost of government as a percentage of our Gross National Product.

The first task of national leadership is to set realistic and honest priorities in our policies and our budget, and I pledge that my Administration will do that.

When I talk of tax cuts, I am reminded that every major tax cut in this century has strengthened the economy, generated renewed productivity, and ended up yielding new revenues for the government by creating new investment, new jobs, and more commerce among our people.

The present Administration has been forced by us

Republicans to play follow the leader with regard to a tax cut. But in this election year we must take with the proverbial "grain of salt" any tax cut proposed by those who have already given us the greatest tax increase in our nation's history.

When those in leadership give us tax increases and tell us we must also do with less, have they thought about those who've always had less—especially the minorities? This is like telling them that just as they step on the first rung of the ladder of opportunity, the ladder is being pulled out from under them. That may be the Democratic leadership's message to the minorities, but it won't be our message. Ours will be: we have to move ahead, but we're not going to leave *anyone* behind.

Thanks to the economic policies of the Democratic Party, millions of Americans find themselves out of work. Millions more have never even had a fair chance to learn new skills, hold a decent job, or secure for themselves and their families a share in the prosperity of this nation.

It's time to put America back to work, to make our cities and towns resound with the confident voices of men and women of all races, nationalities, and faiths bringing home to their families a paycheck they can cash for honest money.

For those without skills, we'll find a way to help them get new skills.

For those without job opportunities, we'll stimulate new opportunities, particularly in the inner cities where they live.

For those who've abandoned hope, we'll restore hope, and we'll welcome them into a great national crusade to make America great again.

When we move from domestic affairs, and cast our eyes abroad, we see an equally sorry chapter in the record of the present Administration:

- A Soviet combat brigade trains in Cuba, just 90 miles from our shores;
- A Soviet army of invasion occupies Afghanistan, further threatening our vital interests in the Middle East;
- America's defense strength is at its lowest ebb in a generation, while the Soviet Union is vastly outspending us in both strategic and conventional arms;
- Our European allies, looking nervously at the growing menace from the East, turn to us for leadership and fail to find it;
- And, incredibly, more than fifty of our fellow Americans have been held captive for over eight months by a dictatorial foreign power that holds us up to ridicule before the world.

Adversaries large and small test our will and seek to confound our resolve, but we are given weakness when we need strength, vacillation when the times demand firmness.

The Carter Administration lives in the world of make-believe. Every day, drawing up a response to that day's problems, troubles, regardless of what happened yesterday and what'll happen tomorrow.

But you and I live in a real world, where disasters are overtaking our nation without any real response from Washington.

This is make-believe, self-deceit and, above all, transparent hypocrisy.

For example, Mr. Carter says he supports the volunteer Army, but he lets military pay and benefits slip so low that many of our enlisted personnel are actually eligible for food stamps. Reenlistment rates drop and, just recently, after he fought all week *against* a proposed pay increase for our men and women in the military, he then helicoptered out to our carrier the U.S.S. Nimitz, which was returning from long months of duty in the Indian Ocean, and told the crew of that ship that he advocated better pay for them and their comrades. Where does he really stand, now that he's back on shore?

Well, I'll tell you where I stand. I do not favor a peacetime draft or registration, but I do favor pay and benefit levels that will attract and keep highly motivated men and women in our volunteer forces and back them up with an active reserve trained and ready for instant call in case of emergency.

You know, there may be a sailor at the helm of the ship of state, but the ship has no rudder. Critical decisions are made at times almost in comic fashion, but who can laugh?

Who was not embarrassed when the Administration handed a major propaganda victory in the United Nations to the enemies of Israel, our staunch Middle East ally for three decades, and then claimed that the American vote was a "mistake," the result of a "failure of communication" between the President, his Secretary of State, and his U.N. Ambassador?

Who does not feel a growing sense of unease as our allies, facing repeated instances of an amateurish and confused Administration, reluctantly conclude that America is unwilling or unable to fulfill its obligation as leader of the free world?

Who does not feel rising alarm when the question in any discussion of foreign policy is no longer, "Should we do something?" but "Do we have the capacity to do anything?"

The Administration which has brought us to this state is seeking your endorsement for four more years of weakness, indecision, mediocrity, and incompetence. No American should vote until he or she has asked: Is the United States stronger and more respected now than it was three and a half years ago? Is the world a safer place in which to live?

It is the responsibility of the President of the United States, in working for peace, to insure that the safety of our people cannot successfully be threatened by a hostile foreign power. As President, fulfilling that responsibility will be my number one priority.

We're not a warlike people. Quite the opposite. We always seek to live in peace. We resort to force infrequently and with great reluctance—and only after we've determined that it is absolutely necessary. We are awed—and rightly so—by the forces of destruction at loose in the world in this nuclear era.

But neither can we be naive or foolish. Four times in my lifetime America has gone to war, bleeding the lives of its young men into the sands of island beachheads, the fields of Europe and the jungles and rice paddies of Asia. We know only too well that war comes not when the forces of freedom are strong, it is when they are weak that tyrants are tempted.

We simply cannot learn these lessons the hard way again without risking our destruction.

Of all the objectives we seek, first and foremost is the establishment of lasting world peace. We must always stand ready to negotiate in good faith, ready to pursue any reasonable avenue that holds forth the promise of lessening tensions and furthering the prospects of peace. But let our friends and those who may wish us ill take note: the United States has an obligation to its citizens and to the people of the world never to let those who would destroy freedom dictate the future course of life on this planet. I would regard my election as proof that we have renewed our resolve to preserve world peace and freedom. That this nation will once again be strong enough to do that.

This evening marks the last step, save one, of a campaign that has taken Nancy and me from one end of this great nation to the other, over many months and thousands and thousands of miles. There are those who question the way we choose a President, who say that our process imposes difficult and exhausting burdens on those who seek the office. I have not found it so.

It is impossible to capture in words the splendor of this vast continent which God has granted as our portion of His creation. There are no words to express the extraordinary strength and character of this breed of people we call Americans.

Everywhere, we've met thousands of Democrats, Independents, and Republicans from all economic conditions, walks of life, bound together in that community of shared values of family, work, neighborhood, peace, and freedom. They are concerned, yes; they're not frightened. They're disturbed, but not dismayed. They are the kind of men and women Tom Paine had in mind when he wrote, during the darkest days of the American Revolution, "We have it in our power to begin the world over again."

Nearly 150 years after Tom Paine wrote those words,

an American President told the generation of the Great Depression that it had a "rendezvous with destiny." I believe this generation of Americans today also has a rendezvous with destiny.

Tonight, let us dedicate ourselves to renewing the American compact. I ask you not simply to "trust me," but to trust your values—our values—and to hold me responsible for living up to them. I ask you to trust that American spirit which knows no ethnic, religious, social, political, regional, or economic boundaries; the spirit that burned with zeal in the hearts of millions of immigrants from every corner of the earth who came here in search of freedom.

Some say that spirit no longer exists. But I've seen it—I've felt it—all across the land, in the big cities, in small towns, and in rural America. It's still there, ready to blaze into life if you and I are willing to do what has to be done; we have to do the practical things, the down to earth things, such as creating policies that will stimulate our economy, increase productivity, and put America back to work.

The time is now to limit federal spending, to insist on a stable monetary reform, and to free ourselves from imported oil.

The time is now to resolve that the basis of a firm and principled foreign policy is one that takes the world as it is and seeks to change it by leadership and example, not by harangue, harassment, or wishful thinking.

The time is now to say that we shall seek new friendships and expand and improve others; but we shall not do so by breaking our word or casting aside old friends and allies.

And the time is now to redeem promises once made to the American people by another candidate, in another time and another place. He said:

"For three long years I have been going up and down this country preaching that government—federal, state, and local—costs too much. I shall not stop that preaching. As an immediate program of action, we must abolish useless offices. We must eliminate unnecessary functions of government.

"We must consolidate subdivisions of government and, like the private citizen, give up luxuries which we can no longer afford." And then he said:

"I propose to you my friends, and through you, that government of all kinds, big and little, be made solvent and that the example be set by the President of the United States and his Cabinet."

Those were Franklin Delano Roosevelt's words as he accepted the Democratic nomination for President in 1932.

The time is now, my fellow Americans, to recapture our destiny, to take it into our own hands. And to do this it will take many of us, working together. I ask you tonight, all over this land, to volunteer your help in this cause so that we can carry our message throughout the land.

Isn't it time that we, the people, carry out these unkept promises? Let us pledge to each other and to all America on this July day forty-eight years later that now we intend to do just that.

I have thought of something that's not a part of my speech and worried over whether I should do it. Can we doubt that only a Divine Providence placed this land, this island of freedom, here as a refuge for all those people in the world who yearn to breathe free? Jews and Christians enduring persecution behind the Iron Curtain, the boat people of Southeast Asia, Cuba, and of Haiti, the victims of drought and famine in Africa, the freedom fighters in Afghanistan, and our own countrymen held in savage captivity.

I'll confess that I've been a little afraid to suggest what I'm going to suggest. I'm more afraid not to. Can we begin our crusade joined together in a moment of silent prayer?

God bless America.

1981

ECONOMIC RECOVERY WILL TAKE TIME

(The Government and Economic Policy Decisions)

From the Inaugural Address, as President, January 20th

15.

To a few of us here today this is a solemn and most momentous occasion. And, yet, in the history of our nation it is a commonplace occurrence.

The orderly transfer of authority as called for in the Constitution routinely takes place as it has for almost two centuries, and few of us stop to think how unique we really are.

In the eyes of many in the world, this every-four-year ceremony we accept as normal is nothing less than a miracle.

Mr. President, I want our fellow citizens to know how much you did to carry on this tradition.

By your gracious cooperation in the transition process, you have shown a watching world that we are a united people pledged to maintaining a political system which guarantees individual liberty to a greater degree than any other. And I thank you and your people for all your help in maintaining the continuity which is the bulwark of our republic.

The business of our nation goes forward.

These United States are confronted with an economic affliction of great proportions.

We suffer from the longest and one of the worst sustained inflations in our national history. It distorts our economic decisions, penalizes thrift, and crushes the struggling young and the fixed-income elderly alike. It threatens to shatter the lives of millions of our people.

Idle industries have cast workers into unemployment, human misery, and personal indignity.

Those who do work are denied a fair return for their labor by a tax system which penalizes successful achievement and keeps us from maintaining full productivity.

But great as our tax burden is, it has not kept pace with public spending. For decades we have piled deficit upon deficit, mortgaging our future and our children's future for the temporary convenience of the present.

To continue this long trend is to guarantee tremendous social, cultural, political, and economic upheavals.

You and I, as individuals, can, by borrowing, live beyond our means, but for only a limited period of time. Why then should we think that collectively, as a nation, we are not bound by that same limitation?

We must act today in order to preserve tomorrow. And let there be no misunderstanding—we're going to begin to act beginning today.

The economic ills we suffer have come upon us over several decades.

They will not go away in days, weeks, or months, but they will go away. They will go away because we as Americans have the capacity now, as we have had in the past, to do whatever needs to be done to preserve this last and greatest bastion of freedom.

In this present crisis, government is not the solution to our problems; government *is* the problem.

From time to time we've been tempted to believe that society has become too complex to be managed by self-rule, that government by an elite group is superior to government for, by, and of the people.

But if no one among us is capable of governing himself, then who among us has the capacity to govern someone else?

All of us together—in and out of government—must bear the burden. The solutions we seek must be equitable with no one group singled out to pay a higher price.

We hear much of special interest groups. Well, our concern must be for a special interest group that has been too long neglected.

It knows no sectional boundaries, or ethnic and racial divisions, and it crosses political party lines. It is made up of men and women who raise our food, patrol our streets, man our mines and factories, teach our children, keep our homes, and heal us when we're sick.

Professionals, industralists, shopkeepers, clerks, cabbies, and truck drivers. They are, in short, "We the people"—this breed called Americans.

Well, this Administration's objective will be a healthy, vigorous, growing economy that provides equal opportunities for all Americans with no barriers born of bigotry or discrimination.

Putting America back to work means putting all Americans back to work. Ending inflation means freeing all Americans from the terror of runaway living costs.

All must share in the productive work of this "new beginning," and all must share in the bounty of a revived economy.

With the idealism and fair play which are the core of our system and our strength, we can have a strong, prosperous America at peace with itself and the world.

So as we begin, let us take inventory.

We are a nation that has a government—not the other way around. And this makes us special among the nations of the earth.

Our government has no power except that granted it

by the people. It is time to check and reverse the growth of government which shows signs of having grown beyond the consent of the governed.

It is my intention to curb the size and influence of the federal establishment and to demand recognition of the distinction between the powers granted to the federal government and those reserved to the states or to the people.

All of us—all of us need to be reminded that the federal government did not create the states; the states created the federal government.

Now, so there will be no misunderstanding, it's not my intention to do away with government.

It is rather to make it work—work with us, not over us; to stand by our side, not ride on our back. Government can and must provide opportunity, not smother it; foster productivity, not stifle it.

If we look to the answer as to why for so many years we achieved so much, prospered as no other people on earth, it was because here in this land we unleashed the energy and individual genius of man to a greater extent than has ever been done before.

Freedom and the dignity of the individual have been more available and assured here than in any other place on earth. The price for this freedom at times has been high, but we have never been unwilling to pay that price.

It is no coincidence that our present troubles parallel and are proportionate to the intervention and intrusion in our lives that result from unnecessary and excessive growth of government.

It is time for us to realize that we are too great a nation to limit ourselves to small dreams. We're not, as some would have us believe, doomed to an inevitable decline. I do not believe in a fate that will fall on us no matter what we do. I do believe in a fate that will fall on us if we do nothing.

So, with all the creative energy at our command, let us begin an era of national renewal. Let us renew our determination, our courage, and our strength. And let us renew our faith and our hope. We have every right to dream heroic dreams.

Those who say that we're in a time when there are no heroes—they just don't know where to look. You can see heroes every day going in and out of factory gates. Others, a handful in number, produce enough food to feed all of us and then the world beyond.

You meet heroes across a counter—and they're on both sides of that counter. There are entrepreneurs with faith in themselves, and faith in an idea, who create new jobs, new wealth, and opportunity.

There are individuals and families whose taxes support the government and whose voluntary gifts support church, charity, culture, art, and education. Their patriotism is quiet but deep. Their values sustain our national life.

Now, I have used the words "they" and "their" in speaking of these heroes. I could say "you" and "your" because I'm addressing the heroes of whom I speak—you, the citizens of this blessed land.

Your dreams, your hopes, your goals are going to be the dreams, hopes, and the goals of this Administration, so help me God.

We shall reflect the compassion that is so much a part of your makeup.

How can we love our country and not love our countrymen? And loving them, reach out a hand when they fall, heal them when they're sick, and provide opportunity to make them self-sufficient so they will be equal in fact and not just in theory?

Can we solve the problems confronting us? Well, the answer is an unequivocal and emphatic "yes".

To paraphrase Winston Churchill, I did not take the oath I've just taken with the intention of presiding over the dissolution of the world's strongest economy.

In the days ahead I will propose removing the roadblocks that have slowed our economy and reduced productivity.

Steps will be taken aimed at restoring the balance between the various levels of government. Progress may be slow—measured in inches and feet, not miles—but we will progress.

It is time to reawaken this industrial giant, to get government back within its means and to lighten our punitive tax burden.

And these will be our first priorities, and on these principles there will be no compromise.

On the eve of our struggle for independence, a man who might've been one of the greatest among the Founding Fathers, Dr. Joseph Warren, president of the Massachusetts Congress, said to his fellow Americans, "Our country is in danger, but not to be despaired of. On you depend the fortunes of America. You are to decide the important question upon which rest the happiness and the liberty of millions yet unborn. Act worthy of yourselves."

Well I believe we the Americans of today are ready to act worthy of ourselves, ready to do what must be done to insure happiness and liberty for ourselves, our children and our children's children.

And as we renew ourselves here in our own land we

will be seen as having greater strength throughout the world. We will again be the exemplar of freedom and a beacon of hope for those who do not now have freedom.

To those neighbors and allies who share our freedom, we will strengthen our historic ties and assure them of our support and firm commitment.

We will match loyalty with loyalty. We will strive for mutually beneficial relations. We will not use our friendship to impose on their sovereignty, for our own sovereignty is not for sale.

As for the enemies of freedom, those who are potential adversaries, they will be reminded that peace is the highest aspiration of the American people. We will negotiate for it, sacrifice for it; we will not surrender for it—now or ever.

Our forbearance should never be misunderstood. Our reluctance for conflict should not be misjudged as a failure of will.

When action is required to preserve our national security, we will act. We will maintain sufficient strength to prevail if need be, knowing that if we do, we have the best chance of never having to use that strength.

Above all, we must realize that no arsenal or weapon in the arsenals of the world is so formidable as the will and moral courage of free men and women.

It is a weapon our adversaries in today's world do not have.

It is a weapon that we as Americans do have.

Let that be understood by those who practice terrorism and prey upon their neighbors.

I am told that tens of thousands of prayer meetings are being held on this day; for that I am deeply grateful. We are a nation under God, and I believe God intended for us to be free. It would be fitting and good, I think, if on each Inaugural Day in future years, there should be declared a day of prayer.

This is the first time in our history that this ceremony has been held, as you've been told, on this West Front of the Capitol.

Standing here, one faces a magnificent vista, opening up on this city's special beauty and history.

At the end of this open mall are those shrines to the giants on whose shoulders we stand.

Directly in front of me, the monument to a monumental man, George Washington, father of our country. A man of humility who came to greatness reluctantly. He led America out of revolutionary victory into infant nationhood.

Off to one side, the stately memorial to Thomas Jefferson. The Declaration of Independence flames with his eloquence.

And then beyond the Reflecting Pool, the dignified columns of the Lincoln Memorial. Whoever would understand in his heart the meaning of America will find it in the life of Abraham Lincoln.

Beyond those monuments, monuments to heroism, is the Potomac River, and on the far shore the sloping hills of Arlington National Cemetery with its row upon row of simple white markers bearing crosses or Stars of David. They add up to only a tiny fraction of the price that has been paid for our freedom.

Each one of those markers is a monument to the kind of hero I spoke of earlier.

Their lives ended in places called Belleau Wood, the Argonne, Omaha Beach, Salerno, and halfway around the world, on Guadalcanal, Tarawa, Pork Chop Hill, the Chosin Reservoir, and in a hundred rice paddies and jungles of a place called Vietnam.

Under such a marker lies a young man, Martin Treptow, who left his job in a small town barber shop in 1917 to go to France with the famed Rainbow Division.

There, on the Western front, he was killed trying to carry a message between battalions under heavy artillery fire.

We are told that on his body was found a diary.

On the flyleaf under the heading, "My Pledge," he had written these words:

"America must win this war. Therefore I will work, I will save, I will sacrifice, I will endure, I will fight cheerfully and do my utmost, as if the issue of the whole struggle depended on me alone."

The crisis we are facing today does not require of us the kind of sacrifice that Martin Treptow and so many thousands of others were called upon to make.

It does require, however, our best effort, and our willingness to believe in ourselves and to believe in our capacity to perform great deeds; to believe that together with God's help we can and will resolve the problems which now confront us.

And, after all, why wouldn't we believe that? We are Americans.

God bless you and thank you.

1981

AMERICA'S NEW BEGINNING

(A Program for Economic Recovery)

State of the Union Message, delivered before a Joint Session of Congress, Washington, D.C., February 18th

16.

Only a month ago, I was your guest in this historic building, and I pledged to you my cooperation in doing what is right for this nation we all love so much. I am here tonight to reaffirm that pledge and to ask that we share in restoring the promise that is offered to every citizen by this, the last, best hope of man on earth.

All of us are aware of the punishing inflation which has, for the first time in some sixty years, held to double-digit figures for two years in a row. Interest rates have reached absurd levels of more than 20 percent and over 15 percent for those who would borrow to buy a home. All across this land one can see newly built homes standing vacant, unsold because of mortgage interest rates.

Almost eight million Americans are out of work. These are people who want to be productive. But as the months go by, despair dominates their lives. The threats of layoff and unemployment hang over other millions, and all who work are frustrated by their inability to keep up with inflation.

One worker in a Midwest city put it to me this way. He said: "I'm bringing home more dollars than I thought I could ever earn but I seem to be getting worse off." Well, he is. Hourly earnings of the American worker, after adjusting for inflation, have declined 5 percent over the past five years. And, furthermore, in the last five years, federal personal taxes for the average family increased 67 percent.

We can no longer procrastinate and hope things will get better. They will not. If we do not act forcefully, and now, the economy will get worse.

Can we who man the ship of state deny it is out of control? Our national debt is approaching $1 trillion. A few weeks ago I called such a figure—a trillion dollars—incomprehensible. I've been trying to think of a way to illustrate how big it really is. The best I could come up with is to say that a stack of $1,000 bills in your hand only four inches high would make you a millionaire. A trillion dollars would be a stack of $1,000 bills 67 miles high.

The interest on the public debt this year will be over $90 billion. And unless we change the proposed spending for the fiscal year beginning October 1, we'll add another almost $80 billion to the debt.

Adding to our troubles is a mass of regulations imposed on the shopkeeper, the farmer, the craftsman, professionals, and major industry that is estimated to add $100 billion to the price of things we buy and reduces our ability to produce. The rate of increase in American productivity, once one of the highest in the world, is among the lowest of all major industrial nations. Indeed, it has actually declined the last three years.

I have painted a grim picture, but I believe I have painted it accurately. It is within our power to change this picture, and we can act in hope. There is nothing wrong with our internal strengths. There has been no breakdown in the human, technological, and natural resources upon which the economy is built.

Based on this confidence in a system which has never failed us—but which we have failed through a lack of confidence, and sometimes through a belief that we could fine tune the economy and get a tune more to our liking—I am proposing a comprehensive four-part program. I will now outline and give in some detail the principal parts of this program, but you will each be provided with a completely detailed copy of the program in its entirety.

This plan is aimed at reducing the growth in government spending and taxing, reforming and eliminating regulations which are unnecessary and counterproductive, and encouraging a consistent monetary policy aimed at maintaining the value of the currency.

If enacted in full, our program can help America create thirteen million new jobs, nearly three million more than we would have without these measures. It will also help us gain control of inflation.

It is important to note that we are only reducing the rate of increase in taxing and spending. We are not attempting to cut either spending or taxing to a level below that which we presently have. This plan will get our economy moving again, increase productivity, growth, and thus create the jobs our people must have.

I am asking that you join me in reducing direct federal spending by $41.4 billion in fiscal year 1982, along with $7.7 billion in user fees and off-budget savings for total savings of $49.1 billion. This will still allow an increase of $40.8 billion over 1981 spending.

I know that exaggerated and inaccurate stories about these cuts have disturbed many people, particularly those dependent on grant and benefit programs for their basic needs. Some of you have heard from constituents afraid that Social Security checks, for example, might be taken from them. I regret the fear that these unfounded stories have caused and welcome this opportunity to set things straight.

We will continue to fulfill the obligations that spring from our national conscience. Those who through no fault of their own must depend on the rest of us, the poverty-stricken, the disabled, the elderly, all those with true need, can rest assured that the social safety net of programs they depend on are exempt from any cuts.

The full retirement benefits of the more than thirty-one million Social Security recipients will be continued along with an annual cost of living increase. Medicare will not be cut, nor will supplemental income for the blind, aged, and disabled. Funding will continue for veterans' pensions.

School breakfasts and lunches for the children of low-income families will continue as will nutrition and other special services for the aging. There will be no cut in Project Head Start or summer youth jobs.

All in all, nearly $216 billion providing help for tens of millions of Americans will be fully funded. But government will not continue to subsidize individuals or particular business interests where real need cannot be demonstrated. And while we will reduce some subsidies to regional and local governments, we will at the same time convert a number of categorical grant programs into block grants to reduce wasteful administrative overhead and to give local government entities and states more flexibility and control. We call for an end to duplication in federal programs and reform of those which are not cost effective.

Already, some have protested there must be no reduction of aid to schools. Let me point out that federal aid to education amounts to only 8 percent of total educational funding. For this the federal government has insisted on a tremendously disproportionate share of control over our schools. Whatever reductions we've proposed in that 8 percent will amount to very little of the total cost of education. It will, however, restore more authority to states and local school districts.

Historically, the American people have supported by voluntary contributions more artistic and cultural activities than all the other countries in the world put together. I wholeheartedly support this approach and believe Americans will continue their generosity. Therefore, I am proposing a savings of $85 million in the federal subsidies now going to the arts and humanities.

There are a number of subsidies to business and industry I believe are unnecessary. Not because the activities being subsidized aren't of value, but because the marketplace contains incentives enough to warrant continuing these activities without a government subsidy. One such subsidy is the Department of Energy's synthetic fuels program. We will continue support of research leading to development of new technologies and more independence from foreign oil, but we can save at least $3.2 billion by leaving to private industry the building of plants to make liquid or gas fuels from coal.

We are asking that another major business subsidy, the Export-Import Bank loan authority, be reduced by one-third in 1982. We are doing this because the primary beneficiaries of taxpayer funds in this case are the exporting companies themselves—most of them profitable corporations.

And this brings me to a number of other lending programs in which government makes low-interest loans, some of them for an interest rate as low as 2 percent. What has not been very well understood is that the Treasury Department has no money of its own. It has to go into the private capital market and borrow the money to provide those loans. In this time of excessive interest rates the government finds itself paying interest several times as high as it receives from the borrowing agency. The taxpayers—your constituents—of course, are paying that high interest rate and it just makes all other interest rates higher.

By terminating the Economic Development Administration, we can save hundreds of millions of dollars in 1982 and billions more over the next few years. There is a lack of consistent and convincing evidence that E.D.A. and its regional commissions have been effective in creating new jobs. They have been effective in creating an array of planners, grantsmen, and professional middlemen. We believe we can do better just by the expansion of the economy and the job creation which will come from our economic program.

The Food Stamp Program will be restored to its original purpose, to assist those without resources to purchase sufficient nutritional food.

We will, however, save $1.8 billion in fiscal year 1982 by removing from eligibility those who are not in real need or who are abusing the program. Despite this reduction, the program will be budgeted for more than $10 billion.

We will tighten welfare and give more attention to outside sources of income when determining the amount of welfare an individual is allowed. This plus strong and effective work requirements will save $520 million next year.

I stated a moment ago our intention to keep the school breakfast and lunch programs for those in true need. But by cutting back on meals for children of families who can afford to pay, the savings will be $1.6 billion in fiscal year 1982.

Let me just touch on a few other areas which are typical of the kind of reductions we have included in this economic package. The Trade Adjustment Assistance program provides benefits for workers who are unemployed when foreign imports reduce the market for various American products causing shutdown of plants and layoff of workers. The purpose is to help these workers find jobs in growing sectors of our economy. And yet, because these benefits are paid out on top of normal unemployment benefits, we wind up paying greater benefits to those who lose their jobs because of foreign competition than we do to their friends and neighbors who are laid off due to domestic competition. Anyone must agree that this is unfair. Putting these two programs on the same footing will save $1.15 billion in just one year.

Earlier I made mention of changing categorical grants to states and local governments into block grants. We know of course that categorical grant programs burden local and state governments with a mass of federal regulations and federal paper work.

Ineffective targeting, wasteful administrative overhead—all can be eliminated by shifting the resources and decision-making authority to local and state government. This will also consolidate programs which are scattered throughout the federal bureaucracy. It will bring government closer to the people and will save $23.9 billion over the next five years.

Our program for economic renewal deals with a number of programs which at present are not cost effective. An example is Medicaid. Right now Washington provides the states with unlimited matching payments for their expenditures. At the same time we here in Washington pretty much dictate how the states will manage the program. We want to put a cap on how much the federal government will contribute but at the same time allow the states much more flexibility in managing and structuring their programs. I know from our experience in California that such flexibility could have led to far more cost effective reforms. This will bring a savings of $1 billion next year.

The space program has been and is important to America and we plan to continue it. We believe, however, that a reordering of priorities to focus on the most important and cost-effective NASA programs can result in a savings of a quarter of a billion dollars.

Coming down from space to the mailbox—the Postal Service has been consistently unable to live within its operating budget. It is still dependent on large federal subsidies. We propose reducing those subsidies by $632 million in 1982 to press the Postal Service into becoming more effective. In subsequent years, the savings will continue to add up.

The Economic Regulatory Administration in the Department of Energy has programs to force companies to convert to specific fuels. It has the authority to administer a gas rationing plan, and, prior to decontrol, it ran the oil price control program. With these and other regulations gone we can save several hundreds of millions of dollars over the next few years.

Now, I'm sure there is one department you've been waiting for me to mention. That is the Department of Defense. It is the only department in our entire program that will actually be increased over the present budgeted figure. But even here there was no exemption. The Department of Defense came up with a number of cuts which reduced the budget increase needed to restore our military balance. These measures will save $2.9 billion in 1982 outlays and by 1986 a total of $28.2 billion will have been saved. The aim will be to provide the most effective defense for the lowest possible cost.

I believe my duty as President requires that I recommend increases in defense spending over the coming years. Since 1970 the Soviet Union has invested $300 billion more in its military forces than we have. As a result of its massive military buildup, the Soviets now have a significant numerical advantage in strategic nuclear delivery systems, tactical aircraft, submarines, artillery, and anti-air craft defense. To allow this imbalance to continue is a threat to our national security.

Notwithstanding our economic straits, making the financial changes beginning now is far less costly than waiting and attempting a crash program several years from now.

We remain committed to the goal of arms limitation through negotiation and hope we can persuade our adversaries to come to realistic balanced and verifiable agreements. But, as we negotiate, our security must be fully protected by a balanced and realistic defense program.

Let me say a word here about the general problem of waste and fraud in the federal government. One government estimate indicated that fraud alone may account for anywhere from 1 to 10 percent—as much as $25 billion—of federal expenditures for social programs. If the tax dollars that are wasted or mismanaged are added to this fraud total, the staggering dimensions of this problem begin to emerge.

The Office of Management and Budget is now putting together an interagency task force to attack waste and fraud. We are also planning to appoint as Inspectors General highly trained professionals who will spare no effort to do this job.

No administration can promise to immediately stop a trend that has grown in recent years as quickly as government expenditures themselves. But let me say this: waste and fraud in the federal budget is exactly what I have called it before—an unrelenting national scandal—a scandal we are bound and determined to do something about.

Marching in lockstep with the whole program of reductions in spending is the equally important program of reduced tax rates. Both are essential if we are to have economic recovery. It is time to create new jobs, build and rebuild industry, and give the American people room to do what they do best. And that can only be done with a tax program which provides incentive to increase productivity for both workers and industry.

Our proposal is for a 10 percent across-the-board cut every year for three years in the tax rates for all individual income taxpayers making a total tax cut of 30 percent. This three-year reduction will also apply to the tax on unearned income leading toward an eventual elimination of the present differential between the tax on earned and unearned income.

The effective starting date for these 10 percent personal income tax rate reductions will be July 1st of this year.

Again, let me remind you that this 30 percent reduction in marginal rates, while it will leave the taxpayers with $500 billion more in their pockets over the next five years, is actually only a reduction in the tax increase already built into the system.

Unlike some past tax "reforms," this is not merely a

shift of wealth between different sets of taxpayers. This proposal for an equal reduction in everyone's tax rates will expand our national prosperity, enlarge national incomes, and increase opportunities for all Americans.

Some will argue, I know, that reducing tax rates now will be inflationary. A solid body of economic experts does not agree. And certainly tax cuts adopted over the past three-fourths of a century indicate these economic experts are right. The advice I have had is that by 1985 our real production of goods and services will grow by 20 percent and will be $300 billion higher than it is today. The average worker's wage will rise (in real purchasing power) by 8 percent and those are after-tax dollars. This, of course, is predicated on our complete program of tax cuts and spending reductions being implemented.

The third part of the tax package is aimed directly at providing business and industry with the capital needed to modernize and engage in more research and development. This will involve an increase in depreciation allowances and this part of our tax proposal will be retroactive to January 1.

The present depreciation system is obsolete, needlessly complex, and economically counterproductive. Very simply, it bases the depreciation of plant, machinery, vehicles, and tools on their original cost with no recognition of how inflation has increased their replacement cost. We are proposing a much shorter write-off time than is presently allowed. We propose a five year write-off for machinery; three years for vehicles and trucks; and a ten year write-off for plants.

In fiscal year 1982, under this plan business would acquire nearly $10 billion for investment and by 1985 the figure would be nearly $45 billion. These changes are essential to provide the new investment which is needed to create millions of new jobs between now and 1986 and to make America competitive once again in world markets. These are not make-work jobs; they are productive jobs with a future.

I'm well aware that there are many other desirable tax changes such as indexing the income tax brackets to protect taxpayers against inflation. There is the unjust discrimination against married couples if both are working and earning; tuition tax credits; the unfairness of the inheritance tax especially to the family-owned farm and the family-owned business; and a number of others. But our program for economic recovery is so urgently needed to begin to bring down inflation that I would ask you to act on this plan first and with great urgency. Then I pledge to you I will join with you in seeking these additional tax changes at an early date.

American society experienced a virtual explosion in government regulation during the past decades. Between 1970 and 1979, expenditures for the major regulatory agencies quadrupled. The number of pages published annually in the Federal Register nearly tripled and the number of pages in the Code of Federal Regulations increased by nearly two-thirds.

The result has been higher prices, higher unemployment, and lower productivity growth. Over-regulation causes small and independent businessmen and women, as well as large businesses, to defer or terminate plans for expansion; and, since they are responsible for most of our new jobs, those new jobs aren't created.

We have no intention of dismantling the regulatory agencies—especially those necessary to protect the environment and to assure the public health and safety. However, we must come to grips with inefficient and burdensome regulations—eliminate those we can and reform those we must keep.

I have asked Vice President Bush to head a Cabinet-level Task Force on Regulatory Relief. Second, I asked each member of my Cabinet to postpone the effective dates of the hundreds of regulations which have not yet been implemented. Third, in coordination with the Task Force, many of the agency heads have taken prompt action to review and rescind existing burdensome regulations. Finally, just yesterday, I signed an Executive Order that for the first time provides for effective and coordinated management of the regulatory process.

Although much has been accomplished, this is only a beginning. We will eliminate those regulations that are unproductive and unnecessary by Executive Order where possible and cooperate fully with you on those that require legislation.

The final aspect of our plan requires a national monetary policy which does not allow money growth to increase consistently faster than the growth of goods and services. In order to curb inflation, we need to slow the growth in our money supply.

We fully recognize the independence of the Federal Reserve System and will do nothing to undermine that independence. We will consult regularly with the Federal Reserve Board on all aspects of our economic program and will vigorously pursue budget policies that will make their job easier in reducing monetary growth.

A successful program to achieve stable and moderate growth patterns in the money supply will keep both inflation and interest rates down and restore vigor to our financial institutions and markets.

This, then, is our proposal. "America's New Beginning: A Program for Economic Recovery." I do not want it to be simply the plan of my Administration—I am here tonight to ask you to join me in making it our plan. Together, we can embark on this road not to make things easy, but to make things better.

Can we do the job? The answer is yes. But we must begin now. Our social, political, and cultural, as well as our economic institutions, can no longer absorb the repeated shocks that have been dealt them over the past decades.

We are in control here. There is nothing wrong with America that we can't fix. So, I'm full of hope and optimism that we will see this difficult new challenge to its end—that we will find those reservoirs of national will to once again do the right thing.

I'm sure there will be some who will raise the familiar old cry, "Don't touch my program—cut somewhere else."

I hope I've made it plain that our approach has been even handed, that only the programs for the truly deserving remain untouched.

The question is, are we simply going to go down the same path we've gone down before—carving out one special program here and another special program there. I don't think that is what the American people expect of us. More important, I don't think it is what they want. They are ready to return to the source of our strength.

The substance and prosperity of our nation is built by wages brought home from the factories and the mills, the farms and the ships.

They are the services provided in 10,000 corners of America; the interest on the thrift of our people and the returns from their risk-taking. The production of America is the possession of those who build, serve, create, and produce.

For too long now, we've removed from our people the decisions on how to dispose of what they created. We have strayed from first principles. We must alter our course.

The taxing power of government must be used to provide revenues for legitimate government purposes. It must not be used to regulate the economy or bring about social change. We've tried that and surely must be able to see it doesn't work.

Spending by government must be limited to those functions which are the proper province of government. We can no longer afford things simply because we think of them.

Next year we can reduce the budget by $41.1 billion, without harm to government's legitimate purposes and to our responsibility to all who need our benevolence. This, plus the reduction in tax rates, will help bring an end to inflation.

In the health and social services area alone, the plan we are proposing will substantially reduce the need for 465 pages of law, 1,400 pages of regulations and 5,000 federal employees who presently administer 7,600 separate grants at about 25,000 locations. Over seven million man and woman hours of work by state and local officials are required to fill our federal forms.

May I direct a question to those who have indicated unwillingness to accept this plan for a new beginning, for an economy recovery? Have they an alternative which offers a greater chance of balancing the budget, reducing and eliminating inflation, stimulating the creation of jobs, and reducing the tax burden? And, if they haven't, are they suggesting we can continue on the present course without coming to a day of reckoning in the very near future?

If we don't do this, inflation and a growing tax burden will put an end to everything we believe in and to our dreams for the future. We do not have an option of living with inflation and its attendant tragedy, of millions of productive people willing and able to work but unable to find buyers in the job market.

We have an alternative to that, a program for economic recovery, a program that will balance the budget, put us well on the road to our ultimate objective of eliminating inflation entirely, increasing productivity, and creating millions of new jobs.

True, it will take time for the favorable effects of our proposal to be felt. So we must begin now.

The people are watching and waiting. They don't demand miracles, but they do expect us to act. Let us act together.

1982

THE TIME FOR ACTION IS NOW

(The Federal Budget: A Strong and Positive Change)

State of the Union Message, delivered before a Joint Session of Congress, Washington, D.C., January 26th

17.

President Washington began this tradition in 1790 after reminding the nation that the destiny of self-government and the "preservation of the sacred fire of liberty" is "finally staked on the experiment entrusted to the hands of the American people." For our friends in the press, who place a high premium on accuracy, let me say: I did not actually hear George Washington say that, but it is a matter of historic record.

But from this podium, Winston Churchill asked the free world to stand together against the onslaught of aggression. Franklin Delano Roosevelt spoke of a day of infamy and summoned a nation to arms. And Douglas MacArthur made an unforgettable farewell to a country he had loved and served so well. Dwight Eisenhower reminded us that peace was purchased only at the price of strength, and John F. Kennedy spoke of the burden and glory that is freedom.

When I visited this chamber last year as a newcomer to Washington, critical of past policies which I believed had failed, I proposed a new spirit of partnership between this Congress and this Administration and between Washington and our state and local governments.

In forging this new partnership for America we could achieve the oldest hopes of our republic—prosperity for our nation, peace for the world, and the blessings of individual liberty for our children and, someday, for all of humanity.

It's my duty to report to you tonight on the progress that we have made in our relations with other nations, on the foundation we have carefully laid for our economic recovery, and, finally, on a bold and spirited initiative that I believe can change the face of American government and make it again the servant of the people.

Seldom have the stakes been higher for America. What we do and say here will make all the difference to auto workers in Detroit, lumberjacks in the Northwest, steelworkers in Steubenville who are in the unemployment lines, to black teenagers in Newark and Chicago, to hard pressed farmers and small businessmen, and to millions of everyday Americans who harbor the simple wish of a safe and financially secure future for their children.

To understand the State of the Union, we must look not only at where we are and where we're going but also where we've been. The situation at this time last year was truly ominous.

The last decade has seen a series of recessions. There was a recession in 1970, in 1974, and again in the spring of 1980. Each time, unemployment increased and inflation soon turned up again. We coined the word "stagflation" to describe this.

Government's response to these recessions was to pump up the money supply and increase spending.

In the last six months of 1980, as an example, the money supply increased at the fastest rate in postwar history—13 percent. Inflation remained in double digits and government spending increased at an annual rate of 17 percent. Interest rates reached a staggering 21.5 percent. There were eight million unemployed.

Late in 1981, we sank into the present recession—largely because continued high interest rates hurt the auto industry and construction. And there was a drop in productivity and the already high unemployment increased.

This time, however, things are different. We have an economic program in place completely different from the artificial quick-fixes of the past. It calls for a reduction of the rate of increase in government spending, and already that rate has been cut nearly in half. But reduced spending alone isn't enough. We've just implemented the first and smallest phase of a three-year tax-rate reduction designed to stimulate the economy and create jobs.

Already interest rates are down to 15.75 percent, but they must still go lower. Inflation is down from 12.4 percent to 8.9 and for the month of December it was running at an annualized rate of 5.2 percent.

If we had not acted as we did, things would be far worse for all Americans than they are today. Inflation, taxes and interest rates would all be higher.

A year ago, Americans' faith in their governmental process was steadily declining. Six out of ten Americans were saying they were pessimistic about their future.

A new kind of defeatism was heard. Some said our domestic problems were uncontrollable—that we had to learn to live with the seemingly endless cycle of high inflation and high unemployment.

There were also pessimistic predictions about the relationship between our Administration and this Congress. It was said we could never work together. Well, those predictions were wrong.

The record is clear, and I believe that history will remember this as an era of American renewal, remember this Administration as an Administration of change and remember this Congress as a Congress of destiny.

Together, we not only cut the increase in government

spending nearly in half, we also brought about the largest tax reductions and the most sweeping changes in our tax structure since the beginning of this century. And because we indexed future taxes to the rate of inflation, we took away government's built-in profit on inflation and its hidden incentive to grow larger at the expense of American workers.

Together, after fifty years of taking power away from the hands of the people in their states and local communities we have started returning power and resources to them.

Together, we have cut the growth of new federal regulations nearly in half. In 1981, there were 23,000 fewer pages in the Federal Register, which lists new regulations than there were in 1980. By deregulating oil, we've come closer to achieving energy independence and help bring down the costs of gasoline and heating fuel.

Together, we have created an effective federal strike force to combat waste and fraud in government. In just six months it has saved the taxpayers more than $2 billion, and it's only getting started.

Together, we've begun to mobilize the private sector—not to duplicate wasteful and discredited government programs but to bring thousands of Americans into a volunteer effort to help solve many of America's social problems.

Together, we've begun to restore that margin of military safety that insures peace. Our country's uniform is being worn once again with pride.

Together we have made a new beginning, but we have only begun.

No one pretends that the way ahead will be easy. In my inaugural address last year, I warned that the "ills we suffer have come upon us over several decades. They will not go away in days, weeks, or months, but they will go away . . . because we as Americans have the capacity now, as we've had it in the past, to do whatever needs to be done to preserve this last and greatest bastion of freedom."

The economy will face difficult moments in the months ahead. But, the program for economic recovery that is in place will pull the economy out of its slump and put us on the road to prosperity and stable growth by the latter half of this year.

That is why I can report to you tonight that in the near future the State of the Union and the economy will be better—much better—if we summon the strength to continue on the course that we've charted.

And so the question: If the fundamentals are in place, what now?

Two things. First, we must understand what's happening at the moment to the economy. Our current problems are not the product of the recovery program that's only just now getting under way, as some would have you believe; they are the inheritance of decades of tax and tax, and spend and spend.

Second, because our economic problems are deeply rooted and will not respond to quick political fixes, we must stick to our carefully integrated plan for recovery. And that plan is based on four common sense fundamentals: Continued reduction of the growth of federal spending; preserving the individual and business tax reductions that will stimulate saving and investment; removing unnecessary federal regulations to spark productivity; and maintaining a healthy dollar and a stable monetary policy—the latter a responsibility of the Federal Reserve System.

The only alternative being offered to this economic program is a return to the policies that gave us a trillion-dollar debt, runaway inflation, runaway interest rates, and unemployment.

The doubters would have us turn back the clock with tax increases that would offset the personal tax-rate reductions already passed by this Congress.

Raise present taxes to cut future deficits, they tell us. Well, I don't believe we should buy that argument. There are too many imponderables for anyone to predict deficits or surpluses several years ahead with any degree of accuracy. The budget in place when I took office had been projected as balanced. It turned out to have one of the biggest deficits in history. Another example of the imponderables that can make deficit projections highly questionable: A change of only one percentage point in unemployment can alter a deficit up or down by some $25 billion.

As it now stands, our forecasts, which we're required by law to make, will show major deficits, starting at less than $100 billion and declining, but still too high.

More important, we are making progress with the three keys to reducing deficits: economic growth, lower interest rates, and spending control. The policies we have in place will reduce the deficit steadily, surely, and, in time, completely.

Higher taxes would not mean lower deficits. If they did, how would we explain tax revenues more than doubled just since 1976, yet in that same six-year period we ran the largest series of deficits in our history. In 1980 tax revenues increased by $54 billion, and in 1980 we had one of our all-time biggest deficits.

Raising taxes won't balance the budget. It will encourage more government spending and less private investment. Raising taxes will slow economic growth, reduce production, and destroy future jobs, making it more difficult for those without jobs to find them and more likely that those who now have jobs could lose them.

So I will not ask you to try to balance the budget on the backs of the American taxpayers. I will seek no tax increases this year and I have no intention of retreating from our basic program of tax relief. I promised the American people to bring their tax rates down and keep them down—to provide them incentives to rebuild our economy, to save, to invest in America's future. I will stand by my word. Tonight I'm urging the American people: Seize these new opportunities to produce, to save, to invest, and together we'll make this economy a mighty engine of freedom, hope and prosperity again.

Now, the budget deficit this year will exceed our earlier expectations. The recession did that. It lowered revenues and increased costs. To some extent, we're also victims of our own success. We've brought inflation down faster than we thought we could, and, in doing this, we've deprived government of those hidden revenues that occur when inflation pushes people into higher income tax brackets. And the continued high interest rates last year cost the government about $5 billion more than anticipated.

We must cut out more nonessential government spending and root out more waste, and we will continue our efforts to reduce the number of employees in the federal work force by 75,000.

Starting in fiscal 1984, the federal government will assume full responsibility for the cost of the rapidly growing Medicaid program to go along with its existing responsibility for Medicare. As part of a financially equal swap, the states will simultaneously take full responsibility for aid to families with dependent children and food stamps. This will make welfare less costly and more responsive to genuine need because it will be designed and administered closer to the grass roots and the people it serves.

In 1984, the federal government will apply the full proceeds from certain excise taxes to a grass roots trust fund that will belong, in fair shares, to the fifty states. The total amount flowing into this fund will be $28 billion a year.

Over the next four years, the states can use this money in either of two ways. If they want to continue receiving federal grants in such areas as transportation, education, and social services, they can use their trust fund money to pay for the grants; or, to the extent they choose to forgo federal grant programs, they can use their trust fund money on their own, for those or other purposes. There will be a mandatory pass-through of part of these funds to local governments.

By 1988, the states will be in complete control of over forty federal grant programs. The trust fund will start to phase out, eventually to disappear, and the excise taxes will be turned over to the states. They can then preserve, lower, or raise taxes on their own and fund and manage these programs as they see fit.

In a single stroke, we will be accomplishing a realignment that will end cumbersome administration and spiraling costs at the federal level while we insure these programs will be more responsive to both the people they're meant to help and the people who pay for them.

Hand in hand with this program to strengthen the

discretion and flexibility of state and local governments, we're proposing legislation for an experimental effort to improve and develop our depressed urban areas in the 1980s and 1990s. This legislation will permit states and localities to apply to the federal government for designation as urban enterprise zones. A broad range of special economic incentives in the zones will help attract new business, new jobs, new opportunity to America's inner cities and rural towns. Some will say our mission is to save free enterprise. Well, I say we must free enterprise so that, together, we can save America.

Some will also say our states and local communities are not up to the challenge of a new and creative partnership. Well, that might have been true twenty years ago before reforms like reapportionment and the Voting Rights Act, the ten-year extension of which I strongly support. It's no longer true today. This Administration has faith in state and local governments and the constitutional balance envisioned by the Founding Fathers. We also believe in the integrity, decency, and sound good sense of grass roots Americans.

Our faith in the American people is reflected in another major endeavor. Our private sector initiatives task force is seeking out successful community models of school, church, business, union, foundation, and civic programs that help community needs. Such groups are almost invariably far more efficient than government in running social programs.

We're not asking them to replace discarded and often discredited government programs dollar for dollar, service for service. We just want to help them perform the good works they choose, and help others to profit by their example. Three hundred eighty-five thousand corporations and private organizations are already working on social programs ranging from drug rehabilitation to job training, and thousands more Americans have written us asking how they can help. The volunteer spirit is still alive and well in America.

Our nation's long journey towards civil rights for all our citizens—once a source of discord, now a source of pride—must continue with no backsliding or slowing down. We must and shall see that those basic laws that guarantee equal rights are preserved and, when necessary, strengthened. Our concern for equal rights for women is firm and unshakable.

We launched a new Task Force on Legal Equity for Women, and a fifty-state project that will examine state laws for discriminatory language. And for the first time in our history a woman sits on the highest court in the land.

So, too, the problem of crime—one as real and deadly serious as any in America today—demands that we seek transformation of our legal system, which overly protects the rights of criminals while it leaves society and the innocent victims of crime without justice.

We look forward to the enactment of a responsible Clean Air Act to increase jobs while continuing to improve the quality of our air. We are encouraged by the bipartisan initiative of the House and are hopeful of further progress as the Senate continues its deliberations.

So far I have concentrated largely on domestic matters. To view the State of the Union in perspective, we must not ignore the rest of the world. There isn't time tonight for a lengthy treatment of social or of foreign policy, subjects I intend to address in detail in the near future. A few words, however, are in order on the progress we've made over the past year re-establishing respect for our nation around the globe and some of the challenges and goals that we will approach in the year ahead.

At Ottawa and Cancún, I met with leaders of the major industrial powers and developing nations. Now some of those I met with were a little surprised that I didn't apologize for America's wealth. Instead I spoke of the strength of the free marketplace system and how that system could help them realize their aspirations for economic development and political freedom. I believe lasting friendships were made and the foundation was laid for future cooperation.

In the vital region of the Caribbean Basin, we're developing a program of aid, trade and investment incentives to promote self-sustaining growth and a better, more secure life for our neighbors to the south. Toward those who would export terrorism and subversion in the Caribbean and elsewhere, especially Cuba and Libya, we will act with firmness.

Our foreign policy is a policy of strength, fairness, and balance. By restoring America's military credibility, by pursuing peace at the negotiating table wherever both sides are willing to sit down in good faith, and by regaining the respect of America's allies and adversaries alike, we have strengthened our country's position as a force for peace and progress in the world.

When action is called for, we're taking it. Our sanctions against the military dictatorship that has attempted to crush human rights in Poland—and against the Soviet regime behind that military dictatorship—clearly demonstrated to the world that America will not conduct "business as usual" with the forces of oppression.

If the events in Poland continue to deteriorate, further measures will follow.

The budget plan I submit to you on February 8 will

realize major savings by dismantling the Departments of Energy and Education, and by eliminating ineffective subsidies for business. We will continue to redirect our resources to our two highest budget priorities: a strong national defense to keep America free and at peace and a reliable safety net of social programs for those who have contributed and those who are in need.

Contrary to some of the wild charges you may have heard, this Administration has not and will not turn its back on America's elderly or America's poor. Under the new budget, funding for social insurance programs will be more than double the amount spent only six years ago.

But it would be foolish to pretend that these or any programs cannot be made more efficient and economical.

The entitlement programs that make up our safety net for the truly needy have worthy goals and many deserving recipients. We will protect them. But there's only one way to see to it that these programs really help those whom they were designed to help, and that is to bring their spiraling costs under control.

Today we face the absurd situation of a federal budget with three-quarters of its expenditures routinely referred to as "uncontrollable," and a large part of this goes to entitlement programs.

Committee after committee of this Congress has heard witness after witness describe many of these programs as poorly administered and rife with waste and fraud. Virtually every American who shops in a local supermarket is aware of the daily abuses that take place in the food stamp program, which has grown by 16,000 percent in the last fifteen years. Another example is Medicare and Medicaid, programs with worthy goals but whose costs have increased from 11.2 billion to almost 60 billion, more than five times as much, in just ten years.

Waste and fraud are serious problems. Back in 1980, federal investigators testified before one of your committees that "corruption has permeated virtually every area of the Medicare and Medicaid health care industry." One official said many of the people who are cheating the system were "very confident that nothing was going to happen to them."

Well, something is going to happen. Not only the taxpayers are defrauded—the people with real dependency on these programs are deprived of what they need because available resources are going not to the needy but to the greedy.

The time has come to control the uncontrollable.

In August we made a start. I signed a bill to reduce the growth of these programs by $44 billion over the next three years, while at the same time preserving essential services for the truly needy. Shortly you will receive from me a message on further reforms we intend to install—some new, but others long recommended by our own Congressional committees. I ask you to help make these savings for the American taxpayer.

The savings we propose in entitlement programs will total some $63 billion over four years and will, without affecting Social Security, go a long way toward bringing federal spending under control.

But don't be fooled by those who proclaim that spending cuts will deprive the elderly, the needy, and the helpless. The federal government will still subsidize 95 million meals every day. That's one out of seven of all the meals served in America. Head Start, senior nutrition programs, and child welfare programs will not be cut from the levels we proposed last year. More than one-half billion dollars has been proposed for minority business assistance. And research at the National Institutes of Health will be increased by over $100 million. While meeting all these needs, we intend to plug unwarranted tax loopholes and strengthen the law which requires all large corporations to pay a minimum tax.

I am confident the economic program we've put into operation will protect the needy while it triggers a recovery that will benefit all Americans. It will stimulate the economy, result in increased savings, and provide capital for expansion, mortgages for home building, and jobs for the unemployed.

Now that the essentials of that program are in place, our next major undertaking must be a program—just as bold, just as innovative—to make government again accountable to the people, to make our system of federalism work again.

Our citizens feel they've lost control of even the most basic decisions made about the essential services of government, such as schools, welfare, roads, and even garbage collection. And they're right.

A maze of interlocking jurisdictions and levels of government confronts average citizens in trying to solve even the simplest of problems. They don't know where to turn for answers, who to hold accountable, who to praise, who to blame, who to vote for or against.

The main reason for this is the overpowering growth of federal grants-in-aid programs during the past few decades.

In 1960, the federal government had 132 categorical grant programs, costing $7 billion. When I took office, there were approximately 500, costing nearly $100 billion—13 programs for energy, 36 for pollution control, 66 for social services, 90 for education. And here in the Congress, it takes at least 166 committees just to try to keep track of them.

You know and I know that neither the President nor the Congress can properly oversee this jungle of grants-in-aid; indeed, the growth of these grants had led to the distortion in the vital functions of government. As one Democratic governor put it recently: "The national government should be worrying about arms control not potholes."

The growth in these federal programs has, in the words of one intergovernmental commission, made the federal government "more pervasive, more intrusive, more unmanageable, more ineffective and costly, and above all more unaccountable."

Well, let's solve this problem with a single bold stroke—the return of some $47 billion in federal programs to state and local government, together with the means to finance them and a transition period of nearly ten years to avoid unnecessary disruption.

I will shortly send this Congress a message describing this program. I want to emphasize, however, that its full details will have been worked out only after close consultation with Congressional, state, and local officials.

Now let me also note that private American groups have taken the lead in making January 30 a day of solidarity with the people of Poland—so, too, the European Parliament has called for March 21 to be an international day of support for Afghanistan. Well, I urge all peace-loving peoples to join together on those days, to raise their voices, to speak and pray for freedom.

Meanwhile, we're working for reduction of arms and military activities. As I announced in my address to the nation last November 18, we have proposed to the Soviet Union a far-reaching agenda for mutual reduction of military forces and have already initiated negotiations with them in Geneva on intermediate-range nuclear forces.

In those talks it is essential that we negotiate from a position of strength. There must be a real incentive for the Soviets to take these talks seriously. This requires that we rebuild our defenses.

In the last decade, while we sought the moderation of Soviet power through a process of restraint and accommodation, the Soviets engaged in an unrelenting buildup of their military forces.

The protection of our national security has required that we undertake a substantial program to enhance our military forces.

We have not neglected to strengthen our traditional alliances in Europe and Asia, or to develop key relationships with our partners in the Middle East and other countries.

Building a more peaceful world requires a sound strategy and the national resolve to back it up. When radical forces threaten our friends, when economic misfortune creates conditions of instability, when strategically vital parts of the world fall under the shadow of Soviet power, our response can make the difference between peaceful change or disorder and violence. That's why we've laid such stress not only on our own defense, but on our vital foreign assistance program. Your recent passage of the foreign assistance act sent a signal to the world that America will not shrink from making the investments necessary for both peace and security. Our foreign policy must be rooted in realism, not naïveté or self-delusion.

A recognition of what the Soviet empire is about is the starting point. Winston Churchill, in negotiating with the Soviets, observed that they respect only strength and resolve in their dealings with other nations.

That's why we've moved to reconstruct our national defenses. We intend to keep the peace—we will also keep our freedom.

We have made pledges of a new frankness in our public statements and worldwide broadcasts. In the face of a climate of falsehood and misinformation, we've promised the world a season of truth—the truth of our great civilized ideas: individual liberty, representative government, the rule of law under God.

We've never needed walls, or mine fields or barbwire to keep our people in. Nor do we declare martial law to keep our people from voting for the kind of government they want.

Yes, we have our problems; yes, we're in a time of recession. And it's true, there's no quick fix, as I said, to instantly end the tragic pain of unemployment. But we will end it—the process has already begun and we'll see its effect as the year goes on.

We speak with pride and admiration of that little band of Americans who overcame insuperable odds to set this nation on course two hundred years ago. But our glory didn't end with them—Americans ever since have emulated their deeds.

We don't have to turn to our history books for heroes. They're all around us. One who sits among you here tonight epitomized that heroism at the end of the longest imprisonment ever inflicted on men of our armed forces. Who will ever forget that night when we waited for television to bring us the scene of that first plane landing at Clark Field in the Philippines—bringing our POW's home. The plane door opened and Jeremiah Denton came slowly down the ramp. He caught sight of our flag, saluted it, said, "God bless America," and then thanked us for bringing him home.

Just two weeks ago, in the midst of a terrible tragedy on the Potomac, we saw again the spirit of American heroism at its finest—the heroism of dedicated rescue workers saving crash victims from icy waters. And we saw the heroism of one of our young government employees, Lenny Skutnik, who, when he saw a woman lose her grip on the helicopter line, dived into the water and dragged her to safety.

And then there are countless quiet, everyday heroes of American life—parents who sacrifice long and hard so their children will know a better life than they've known: church and civic volunteers who help to feed, clothe, nurse, and teach the needy; millions who've made our nation, and our nation's destiny, so very special—unsung heroes who may not have realized their own dreams themselves but then who reinvest those dreams in their children.

Don't let anyone tell that America's best days are behind her—that the American spirit has been vanquished. We've seen it triumph too often in our lives to stop believing in it now.

One hundred and twenty years ago the greatest of all our Presidents delivered his second State of the Union Message in this chamber. "We cannot escape history," Abraham Lincoln warned. "We of this Congress and this Administration will be remembered in spite of ourselves." The "trial through which we pass will light us down in honor or dishonor to the latest generation."

Well, that President and that Congress did not fail the American people. Together, they weathered the storm and preserved the Union. Let it be said of us that we, too did not fail; that we, too, worked together to bring America through difficult times. Let us so conduct ourselves that two centuries from now, another Congress and another President, meeting in this chamber as we're meeting, will speak of us with pride, saying that we met the test and preserved for them in their day the sacred flame of liberty—this last, best hope of man on Earth.

1982

FREEDOM IS OUR COMMON DESTINY

(Aid to the Caribbean Basin)

Speaking to the Organization of American States, Washington, D.C., February 24th

18.

It's a great honor for me to stand before you today. The principles which the Organization of American States embodies—democracy, self-determination, economic development, and collective security—are at the heart of U.S. foreign policy. The United States of America is a proud member of this organization. What happens anywhere in the Americas affects us in this country.

In that very real sense, we share a common destiny. We, the peoples of the Americas, have much more in common than geographical proximity. For over four hundred years, our peoples have shared the dangers and dreams of building a new world. From colonialism to nationhood, our common quest has been for freedom. Most of our forebears came to this hemisphere seeking a better life for themselves; they came in search of opportunity and, yes, in search of God.

Virtually all descendants of the land and immigrants alike have had to fight for independence. Having gained it, they've had to fight to retain it. There were times when we even fought each other. Gradually, however, the nations of this hemisphere developed a set of common principles and institutions that provided the basis for mutual protection.

Some twenty years ago, John F. Kennedy caught the essence of our unique mission when he said it was up to the New World to demonstrate that man's unsatisfied aspiration for economic progress and social justice can best be achieved by free men working within a framework of democratic institutions.

In the commitment to freedom and independence, the peoples of this hemisphere are one. In this profound sense, we are all Americans. Our principles are rooted in self-government and nonintervention. We believe in the rule of law. We know that a nation cannot be liberated by depriving its people of liberty. We know that a state cannot be free when its independence is subordinated to a foreign power. And we know that a government cannot be democratic if it refuses to take the test of a free election.

We have not always lived up to these ideals; all of us at one time or another in our history have been politically weak, economically backward, socially unjust or unable to solve our problems through peaceful means. My own country, too, has suffered internal strife including a tragic Civil War. We have known economic misery and once tolerated racial and social injustice—and, yes, at times we have behaved arrogantly and impatiently toward our neighbors.

These experiences have left their scars, but they also help us today to identify with the struggle for political and economic development in the other countries of this hemisphere. Out of the crucible of our common past, the Americas have emerged as more equal and more understanding partners. Our hemisphere has an unlimited potential for economic development and human fulfillment. We have a combined population of more than six hundred million people. Our continents and our islands boast vast reservoirs of food and raw materials, and the markets of the Americas have already produced the highest standard of living among the advanced as well as the developing countries of the world.

The example that we could offer the world would not only discourage foes, but also would project like a beacon of hope to all of the oppressed and impoverished nations of the world. We are the New World, a world of sovereign and independent states that today stand shoulder to shoulder with a common respect for one another and a greater tolerance of one another's shortcomings.

Some two years ago, when I was announced as a candidate for the Presidency, I spoke of an ambition I had to bring about an accord with our neighbors here on the North American continent. Now, I was not suggesting a common market or any kind of formal arrangement—accord was the only word that seemed to fit what I had in mind. I was aware that the United States has long enjoyed friendly relations with Mexico and Canada, that our borders have no fortifications. Yet it seemed to me that there was a potential for a closer relationship than had yet been achieved.

Three great nations share the North American continent with all its human and natural resources. Have we done all we can to create a relationship in which each country can realize its potential to the fullest?

Now I know in the past the United States has proposed policies that we declared would be mutually beneficial not only for North America but also for the nations of the Caribbean and Central and South America. But there was often a problem—no matter how good our intentions were, our very size may have made it seem that we were exercising a kind of paternalism.

At the time I suggested a new North American accord I said I wanted to approach our neighbors not as someone with yet another plan but as a friend seeking their ideas, their suggestions as to how we could become better neighbors. I met with President López Portillo in Mexico before my inauguration and with Prime Minister Trudeau in Canada shortly after I had taken office; we have all met several times since in the United States, in Mexico, in Canada. And I believe that we have established a relationship better than any our three countries have ever known before.

Today, I would like to talk about our other neighbors, neighbors by the sea, some two dozen countries of the Caribbean and Central America. These countries are not unfamiliar names from some isolated corner of the world far from home—they're very close to home. The country of El Salvador, for example, is nearer to Texas than Texas is to Massachusetts.

The Caribbean region is a vital strategic and commercial artery for the United States. Nearly half of our trade, two-thirds of our imported oil and over half of our imported strategic minerals pass through the Panama Canal or the Gulf of Mexico. Make no mistake, the well-being and security of our neighbors in this region are in our own vital interest.

Economic health is one of the keys to a secure future for our Caribbean Basin, and to the neighbors there. I'm happy to say that Mexico, Canada, and Venezuela have joined in this search for ways to help these countries realize their economic potential. Each of our four nations has its own unique position and approach: Mexico and Venezuela are helping to offset energy costs to Carribean Basin countries by means of an oil facility that is already in operation; Canada is doubling its already significant economic assistance. We all seek to insure that the peoples of this area have the right to preserve their own national identities, to improve their economic lot and to develop their political institutions to suit their own unique social and historical needs.

The Central American and Caribbean countries differ widely in culture, personality and needs. Like America itself, the Caribbean Basin is an extraordinary mosaic of Hispanics, Africans, Asians, and Europeans as well as native Americans. At the moment, however, these countries are under economic siege. In 1977, one barrel of oil was worth five pounds of coffee or 155 pounds of sugar. Well, to buy that same barrel of oil today, these small countries must provide five times as much coffee—nearly 26 pounds—or almost twice as much sugar—283 pounds.

This economic disaster is consuming our neighbors' money, reserves, and credit, forcing thousands of people to leave for other countries, for the United States—often illegally—and shaking even the most established democracies. And economic disaster has provided a fresh opening to the enemies of freedom, national independence, and peaceful development.

We've taken the time to consult closely with other governments in the region, both sponsors and beneficiaries, to ask them what they think will work. And we've labored long to develop an economic program that integrates trade, aid and investment, a program that represents a long-term commitment to the countries of the Caribbean and Central America, to make use of the magic of the marketplace, the market of the Americas, to earn their own way toward self-sustaining growth.

At the Cancún summit last October, I presented a fresh view of a development which stressed more than aid and government intervention. As I pointed out then, nearly all of the countries that have succeeded in their development over the past thirty years have done so on the strength of market-oriented policies and vigorous participation in the international economy. Aid must be complemented by trade and investment.

The program I'm proposing today puts these principles into practice. It is an integrated program that helps our neighbors help themselves, a program that will create conditions under which creativity and private entrepreneurship and self-help can flourish. Aid is an important part of this program because many of our neighbors needed to put themselves in a starting position from which they can begin to earn their own way. But this aid will encourage private-sector activities, not displace them.

The centerpiece of the program that I am sending to the Congress is free trade for Caribbean Basin products exported to the United States. Currently some 87 percent of Caribbean exports already enter U.S. markets duty-free under the generalized system of preferences. These exports, however, cover only the limited range of existing products, not the wide variety of potential products these talented and industrious peoples are capable of producing under the free-trade arrangement that I am proposing.

Exports from the area will receive duty-free treatment for twelve years. Thus, new investors will be able to enter the market knowing that their products will receive duty-free treatment for at least the payoff lifetime of their investments. Before granting duty-free treatment, we will discuss with each country its own self-help measures. The only exception to the free-trade concept will be textile and apparel products, because these products are covered now by other international agreements. However, we will make sure that our immediate neighbors have more liberal quota arrangements.

This economic proposal is as unprecedented as today's crisis in the Caribbean. Never before has the United States offered a preferential trading arrangement to any region. This commitment makes unmistakably clear our determination to help our neighbors grow strong.

The impact of this free-trade approach will develop slowly. The economies that we seek to help are small. Even as they grow, all the protections now available to U.S. industry, agriculture, and labor against disruptive imports will remain. And growth in the Caribbean will benefit everyone, with American exports finding new markets.

Second, to further attract investment, I will ask the Congress to provide significant tax incentives for investment in the Caribbean Basin. We also stand ready to negotiate bilateral investment treaties with interested Basin countries.

Third, I'm asking for a supplemental fiscal year 1982 appropriation of $350 million to assist those countries which are particularly hard hit economically. Much of this aid will be concentrated on the private sector. These steps will help foster the spirit of enterprise necessary to take advantage of the trade and investment portions of the program.

Fourth, we will offer technical assistance and training to assist the private sector in the Basin countries to benefit from the opportunities of this program. This will include investment promotion, export marketing and technology transfer efforts, as well as programs to facilitate adjustments to greater competition and production in agriculture and industry.

I intend to seek the active participation of the business community in this joint undertaking. The Peace Corps already has 861 volunteers in Caribbean Basin countries, and we will give special emphasis to recruiting volunteers with skills in developing local enterprise.

Fifth, we will work closely with Mexico, Canada, and Venezuela, all of whom have already begun substantial and innovative programs of their own, to encourage stronger international efforts to coordinate our own development measures with their vital contributions and with those of other potential donors like Colombia. We will also encourage our European, Japanese, and other Asian allies, as well as multilateral development institutions, to increase their assistance in the region.

Sixth, given our special valued relationship with Puerto Rico and the United States Virgin Islands, we will propose special measures to insure that they also will benefit and prosper from this program. With their strong traditions of democracy and free enterprise, they can play leading roles in the development of the area.

This program has been carefully prepared; it represents a farsighted act by our own people at a time of considerable economic difficulty at home. I wouldn't propose it if I were not convinced that it is vital to the security interests of this nation and of this hemisphere. The energy, the time, and the treasure we dedicate to assisting the development of our neighbors now can help to prevent the much larger expenditures of treasure, as well as human lives, which would flow from their collapse.

One early sign is positive: after a decade of falling income and exceptionally high unemployment, Jamaica's new leadership is reducing bureaucracy, dismantling unworkable controls, and attracting new investment. Continued outside assistance will be needed to tide Jamaica over until market forces generate large increases in output and employment; but Jamaica is making freedom work.

I've spoken up to now mainly of the economic and social challenges to development. But there are also other dangers. A new kind of colonialism stalks the world today and threatens our independence. It is brutal and totalitarian; it is not of our hemisphere, and it has established footholds on American soil for the expansion of its colonialist ambitions.

The events of the last several years dramatize two different futures which are possible for the Caribbean area: either the establishment or restoration of moderate constitutional governments with economic growth and improved living standards, or further expansion of political violence from the extreme left and the extreme right resulting in the imposition of dictatorships and inevitably more economic decline and human suffering.

A positive opportunity is illustrated by the two-thirds of the nations in the area which have democratic governments. A dark future is foreshadowed by the poverty and repression of Castro's Cuba, the tightening grip of the totalitarian left in Grenada and Nicaragua, and the expansion of Soviet-backed Cuban-managed support for violent revolution in Central America. The record is clear: nowhere in its whole sordid history have the promises of Communism been redeemed. Everywhere it has exploited and aggravated temporary economic suffering to seize power, and then to institutionalize economic deprivation and suppress human rights. Right now, six million people world-wide are refugees from Communist systems. Already more than a million Cubans alone have fled Communist tyranny.

Our economic and social program cannot work if our

neighbors cannot pursue their own economic and political future in peace, but must divert their resources instead to fight imported terrorism and armed attack. Economic progress cannot be made while guerrillas systematically burn, bomb, and destroy bridges, farms and power and transportation systems—all with the deliberate intention of worsening economic and social problems in hopes of radicalizing already suffering people.

Our Caribbean neighbors' peaceful attempts to develop are feared by the foes of freedom because their success will make the radical message a hollow one. Cuba and its Soviet backers know this. Since 1978, Havana has trained, armed, and directed extremists in guerrilla warfare and economic sabotage as part of a campaign to exploit troubles in Central America and the Caribbean. Their goal is to establish Cuban-style Marxist-Leninist dictatorships.

Last year, Cuba received 66,000 tons of war supplies from the Soviet Union, more than in any year since the 1962 missile crisis. Last month, the arrival of additional high-performance MIG-23 Floggers gave Cuba an arsenal of more than 200 Soviet warplanes, far more than the military aircraft inventories of all other Caribbean Basin countries combined.

For almost two years, Nicaragua has served as a platform for covert military actions. Through Nicaragua, arms are being smuggled into El Salvador and Guatemala. The Nicaraguan Government even admits the forced relocation of about 8,500 Mosquite Indians, and we have clear evidence that since late 1981 many Indian communities have been burned to the ground and men, women, and children killed.

The Nicaraguan junta cabled written reassurances to the O.A.S. in 1979 that it intended to respect human rights and hold free elections. Two years later, these commitments can be measured by the postponement of elections until 1985, by repression against free trade unions, against the media, minorities, and the defiance of all international civility by the continued export of arms and subversion to neighboring countries.

Two years ago, in contrast, the government of El Salvador began an unprecedented land reform. It has repeatedly urged the guerrillas to renounce violence, to join in the democratic process—an election in which the people of El Salvador could determine the government they prefer. Our own country and other American nations, through the O.A.S., have urged such a course. The guerrillas have refused. More than that, they now threaten violence and death to those who participate in such an election.

Can anything make more clear the nature of those who pretend to be supporters of so-called wars of liberation? A determined propaganda campaign has sought to mislead many in Europe, and certainly many in the United States, as to the true nature of the conflict in El Salvador. Very simply, guerrillas, armed and supported by and through Cuba, are attempting to impose a Marxist-Leninist dictatorship on the people of El Salvador as part of a larger imperialistic plan.

If we do not act promptly and decisively in defense of freedom, new Cubas will arise from the ruins of today's conflicts. We will face more totalitarian regimes, tied militarily to the Soviet Union, more regimes exporting subversion, more regimes so incompetent yet so totalitarian that their citizens' only hope becomes that of one day migrating to other American nations, as in recent years they have come to the United States.

I believe free and peaceful development of our

hemisphere requires us to help governments confronted with aggression from outside their borders to defend themselves. For this reason, I will ask the Congress to provide increased security assistance to help friendly countries hold off those who would destroy their chances for economic and social progress and political democracy.

Since 1947, the Rio Treaty has established reciprocal defense responsibilities linked to our common democratic ideals. Meeting these responsibilities is all the more important when an outside power supports terrorism and insurgency to destroy any possibility of freedom and democracy.

Let our friends and our adversaries understand that we will do whatever is prudent and necessary to insure the peace and security of the Caribbean area. In the face of outside threats, security for the countries of the Caribbean and Central American area is not an end in itself, but a means to an end. It is a means toward building representative and responsive institutions, toward strengthening pluralism and free private institutions—churches, free trade unions, and an independent press. It is a means to nurturing the basic human rights freedom's foes would stamp out.

In the Caribbean, we above all seek to protect those values and principles that shape the proud heritage of this hemisphere. I have already expressed our support for the coming election in El Salvador. We also strongly support the Central American Democratic Community formed this January by Costa Rica, Honduras, and El Salvador.

The United States will work closely with other concerned democracies, inside and outside the area, to preserve and enhance our common democratic values. We will not, however, follow Cuba's lead in attempting to resolve human problems by brute force. Our economic assistance, including the additions that are part of the program I've just outlined, is at more than five times the amount of our security assistance. The thrust of our aid is to help our neighbors realize freedom, justice, and economic progress.

We seek to exclude no one. Some, however, have turned from their American neighbors and their heritage. Let them return to the traditions and common values of this hemisphere and we all will welcome them. The choice is theirs.

As I have talked these problems over with friends and fellow citizens here in the United States, I'm often asked: "Well, why bother? Why should the problems of Central America or the Caribbean concern us? Why should we try to help?" Well, I tell them we must help because the people of the Caribbean and Central America are in a fundamental sense fellow Americans. Freedom is our common destiny and freedom cannot survive if our neighbors live in misery and oppression. In short, we must do it because we're doing it for each other.

Our neighbors' call for help is addressed to us all here in this country—to the Administration, to the Congress, to millions of Americans from Miami to Chicago, from New York to Los Angeles. This is not Washington's problem, it is the problem of all the people of this great land, and of all the other Americas, the great and sovereign republics of North America, the Caribbean Basin, and South America.

The Western Hemisphere does not belong to any one of us—we belong to the Western Hemisphere. We are brothers historically as well as geographically. Now, I'm aware that the United States has pursued good-neighbor policies in the past. These policies did some good, but they're inadequate for today. I believe that my country is now ready to go beyond being a good neighbor to being a true friend and brother in a community that belongs as much to others as to us. That, not guns, is the ultimate key to peace and security for us all.

We have to ask ourselves why has it taken so long for us to realize the God-given opportunity that is ours. These two great land masses—North and South, so rich in virtually everything we need—together our more than 600 million people can develop what is undeveloped, can eliminate want and poverty, can show the world that our many nations can live in peace, each with its own customs and language and culture, but sharing a love for freedom and a determination to resist outside ideologies that would take us back to colonialism.

We return to a common vision. Nearly a century ago, a great citizen of the Caribbean and the Americas, José Marti, warned that mankind is composed of two sorts of men: those who love and create, and those who hate and destroy. Today, more than ever, the compassionate, creative peoples of the Americas have an opportunity to stand together, to overcome injustice, hatred and oppression, and to build a better life for all the Americas.

I have always believed that this hemisphere was a special place with a special destiny. I believe we are destined to be the beacon of hope for all mankind. With God's help, we can make it so. We can create a peaceful, free, and prospering hemisphere based on our shared ideals and reaching from pole to pole of what we proudly call the New World.

1982

THE WILLINGNESS TO DEFEND OUR VALUES

(East-West Relations)

Speaking at Eureka College Commencement,
Eureka, Illinois, May 9th

19.

It goes without saying that this is a very special day for you who are graduating. Would you forgive me if I say it is a special day for me also? Over the years since I sat where you of the graduating class of 1982 are now sitting, I've returned to the campus many times, always with great pleasure and warm nostalgia. It isn't true that I just came back to clean out my locker in the gym.

On one of those occasions, I addressed a graduating class here, "'neath the elms," and was awarded an honorary degree. I informed those assembled that while I was grateful for the honor, it added to a feeling of guilt I'd been nursing for twenty-five years. I always figured the first degree I was given was honorary.

If it is true that tradition is the glue holding civilization together, then Eureka has made its contribution to that effort. Yes, it is a small college in a small community; it is no impersonal assembly-line diploma mill. As the years pass, if you let yourselves absorb the spirit and tradition of this place, you'll find the four years you have spent here living in your memory as a rich and important part of your life.

Oh, you'll have some regrets along with the happy memories. I let football and other extracurricular activities eat into my study time with the result that my grade average was closer to the "C" level required to maintain eligibility than it was to straight A's. Even now I wonder what I might have accomplished if I'd studied harder.

I know there are differences between the Eureka College of 1932 and the Eureka of 1982, but I'm also sure that in many ways—important ways—Eureka remains the same. For one thing, it is impossible for you now to believe what I've said about things being the same. We who preceded you understand that very well. We thought "old grads" who came back only five years after they got out—not fifty—couldn't understand what our life was like. Just take my word for it—as the years go by you'll be amazed at how fresh the memory of these years will remain in your mind, how easily you can relive the very emotions you experienced.

The class of '32 has no yearbook to record our final days on the campus. The class of '33 didn't put out a *Prism* because of the hardships of that Great Depression era. The faculty went without pay sometimes months on end. And yet this school made it possible for young men and women, myself included, to get an education even though we were totally without funds, our families destitute victims of the Depression.

Yes, this place is deep in my heart. Everything that has been good in my life began here.

Graduation day is called "commencement" and properly so, because it is both recognition of completion and of beginning. I would like to talk with you about this new phase—the society in which you are now going to take your place as full-time participants. You are no longer observers; you will be called upon to make decisions and express your views on global events because those events will affect your life.

I've spoken of similarities, and the 1980s, like the 1930s, may be one of those crucial junctures in history that will determine the direction of the future.

In about a month I will meet in Europe with the leaders of nations who are our closest friends and allies. At Versailles, leaders of the industrial powers of the world will seek better ways to meet today's economic challenges. In Bonn I will join my colleagues from the Atlantic Alliance nations to renew those ties which have been the foundation of Western, free-world defense for thirty-seven years. There will also be meetings in Rome and London.

These meetings are significant for a simple, yet important reason. Our own nation's fate is directly linked to that of our sister democracies in Western Europe. The values for which American and all democratic nations stand represent the culmination of Western culture.

Andrei Sakharov, the distinguished Nobel Laureate and courageous Soviet human rights advocate, has written in a message smuggled to freedom: "I believe in Western man, I have faith in his mind, which is practical and efficient and at the same time aspires to great goals. I have faith in his good intentions and his decisiveness."

The glorious tradition requires a partnership to preserve and protect it. Only as partners can we hope to achieve the goal of a peaceful community of nations. Only as partners can we defend the values of democracy and human dignity we hold so dear.

There is a single, major issue in our partnership which will underlie the discussions that I will have with European leaders: the future of Western relations with the Soviet Union. How should we deal with the Soviet Union in the years ahead? What framework should guide our conduct and policies toward it? What can we realistically expect from a world power of such deep fears, hostilities and external ambitions?

I believe the unity of the West is the foundation for any successful relationship with the East. Without Western unity, we'll squander our energies in bickering while the Soviets continue as they please. With unity, we have the strength to moderate Soviet behavior. We have done so in the past and we can do so again.

Our challenge is to establish a framework in which sound East-West relations will endure. I am optimistic we can build a more constructive relationship with the Soviet Union. To do so, however, we must understand the nature of the Soviet system and the lessons of the past.

The Soviet Union is a huge empire ruled by an elite that holds all power and all privilege. They hold it tightly because—as we have seen in Poland—they fear what might happen if even the smallest amount of control slips from their grasp. They fear the infectiousness of even a little freedom and because of this, in many ways, their system has failed. The Soviet empire is faltering because rigid, centralized control has destroyed incentives for innovation, efficiency, and individual achievement. Spiritually, there is a sense of malaise and resentment.

But in the midst of social and economic problems, the Soviet dictatorship has forged the largest armed force in the world. It has done so by preempting the human needs of its people, and, in the end, this course will undermine the foundations of the Soviet system. Harry Truman was right when he said of the Soviets that "when you try to conquer other people or extend yourself over vast areas, you cannot win in the long run."

Yet Soviet aggressiveness has grown as Soviet military

power has increased. To compensate, we must learn from the lessons of the past. When the West has stood firm and unified, the Soviet Union has taken heed. For thirty-five years Western Europe has lived free despite the shadow of Soviet military might. Through unity, you will remember from your modern history courses, the West secured the withdrawal of occupation forces from Austria and the recognition of its rights in Berlin.

Other Western policies have not been successful. East-West trade was expanded in the hope of providing incentives for Soviet restraint, but the Soviets exploited the benefits of trade without moderating their behavior. Despite a decade of ambitious arms-control efforts, the Soviet buildup continues. And despite its signature of the Helsinki agreements on human rights, the Soviet Union has not relaxed its hold on its own people or those of Eastern Europe.

During the 1970s, some of us forgot the warning of President Kennedy who said that the Soviets "have offered to trade us an apple for an orchard. We don't do that in this country." Well, we came perilously close to doing just that.

If East-West relations in the detente era in Europe have yielded disappointment, detente outside of Europe has yielded a severe disillusionment for those who expected a moderation of Soviet behavior. The Soviet Union continues to support Vietnam in its occupation of Kampuchea and its massive military presence in Laos. It is engaged in a war of aggression against Afghanistan. Soviet proxy forces have brought instability and conflict to Africa and Central America.

We are now approaching an extremely important phase in East-West relations as the current Soviet leadership is succeeded by a new generation. Both the current and the new Soviet leadership should realize aggressive policies will meet a firm Western response.

On the other hand, a Soviet leadership devoted to improving its people's lives, rather than expanding its armed conquests, will find a sympathetic partner in the West. The West will respond with expanded trade and other forms of cooperation.

But all this depends on Soviet actions. Standing in the Athenian marketplace 2,000 years ago, Demosthenes said, "What sane man would let another man's words rather than his deeds proclaim who is at peace and who is at war with him?"

Peace is not the absence of conflict, but the ability to cope with conflict by peaceful means. I believe we can cope. I believe that the West can fashion a realistic, durable policy that will protect our interests and keep the peace, not just for this generation, but for your children and grandchildren.

I believe such a policy consists of five points: military balance, economic security, regional stability, arms reduction, and dialogue. These are the means by which we can seek peace with the Soviet Union in the years ahead. Today, I want to set out this five-point program to guide the future of East-West relations.

First, a sound East-West military balance is absolutely essential. Last week NATO published a comprehensive comparison of its forces with those of the Warsaw Pact. Its message is clear: During the past decade, the Soviet Union has built up its forces across the board.

During the same period the defense expenditures of the United States declined in real terms. The U.S. has already undertaken steps to recover from that decade of neglect. And I should add that the expenditures of our European allies have increased slowly but steadily, something we often fail to recognize here at home.

The second point on which we must reach consensus with our allies deals with economic security. Consultations are under way among Western nations on the transfer of militarily significant technology and the extension of financial credits to the East, as well as on the question of energy dependence on the East.

We recognize that some of our allies' economic requirements are distinct from our own. But the Soviets must not have access to Western technology with military applications, and we must not subsidize the Soviet economy. The Soviet Union must make the difficult choices brought on by its military budgets and economic shortcomings.

The third element is regional stability with peaceful change. Last year in a speech in Philadelphia and in the summit meeting in Cancún, I outlined the basic American plan to assist the developing world. These principles for economic development remain the foundation of our approach. They represent no threat to the Soviet Union. Yet in many areas of the developing world we find that Soviet arms and Soviet-supported troops are attempting to destabilize societies and extend Moscow's influence.

High on our agenda must be progress toward peace in Afghanistan. The United States is prepared to engage in a serious effort to negotiate an end to the conflict caused by the Soviet invasion of that country. We are ready to cooperate in an international effort to resolve this problem, to secure a full Soviet withdrawal from Afghanistan, and to ensure self-determination for the Afghan people.

In southern Africa, working closely with our Western allies and the African states, we have made real progress toward independence for Namibia. These negotiations, if successful, will result in peaceful and secure conditions throughout southern Africa. The simultaneous withdrawal of Cuban forces from Angola is essential to achieving Namibian independence, as well as creating long-range prospects for peace in the region.

Central America also has become a dangerous point of tension in East-West relations. The Soviet Union cannot escape responsibility for the violence and suffering in the region caused by its support for Cuban activities in Central America, and its accelerated transfer of advanced military equipment to Cuba.

However, it was in Eastern Europe that the hopes of the 1970s were greatest, and it is there that they have been most bitterly disappointed. There was hope that the people of Poland could develop a freer society. But the Soviet Union has refused to allow the people of Poland to decide their own fate, just as it refused to allow the people of Hungary to decide theirs in 1956, or the people of Czechoslovakia in 1968.

If martial law in Poland is lifted, if all the political prisoners are released, and if a dialogue is restored with the Solidarity Union, the United States is prepared to join in a program of economic support. Water cannons and clubs against the Polish people are hardly the kind of dialogue that gives us hopes. It is up to the Soviets and their client regimes to show good faith by concrete actions.

The fourth point is arms reductions. I know that this weighs heavily on many of your minds. In our 1931 *Prism,* we quoted Carl Sandburg, who in his own beautiful way quoted the Mother Prairie, saying, "Have you seen a red sunset dip over one of my cornfields, the shore of night stars, the wave lines of dawn up a wheat valley?" What an idyllic scene that paints in our minds—and what a nightmarish prospect that a huge mushroom cloud might someday destroy such beauty. My duty as President is to ensure that the ultimate nightmare never occurs, that the prairies and the cities and the people who inhabit them remain free and untouched by nuclear conflict.

I wish more than anything there were a simple policy that would eliminate the nuclear danger. But there are only difficult policy choices through which we can achieve a stable nuclear balance at the lowest possible level.

I do not doubt that the Soviet people, and, yes, the Soviet leaders have an overriding interest in preventing the use of nuclear weapons. The Soviet Union within the memory of its leaders has known the devastation of total conventional war, and knows that nuclear war would be even more calamitous. Yet, so far, the Soviet Union has used arms control negotiations primarily as an instrument to restrict U.S. defense programs and, in conjunction with their own arms buildup, a means to enhance Soviet power and prestige.

Unfortunately, for some time suspicions have grown that the Soviet Union has not been living up to its obligations under existing arms control treaties. There is conclusive evidence the Soviet Union has provided toxins to the Laotians and Vietnamese for use against defenseless villagers in Southeast Asia. And the Soviets themselves are employing chemical weapons on the freedom fighters in Afghanistan.

We must establish firm criteria for arms control in the 1980s. If we are to secure genuine and lasting restraint on Soviet military programs through arms control, we must seek agreements which are verifiable, equitable, and militarily significant. Agreements that provide only the appearance of arms control breed dangerous illusions.

Last November, I committed the United States to seek significant reductions on nuclear and conventional forces.

In Geneva, we have since proposed limits on U.S. and Soviet intermediate-range missiles, including the complete elimination of the most threatening systems on both sides.

In Vienna, we are negotiating, together with our allies, for reductions of conventional forces in Europe.

In the forty-nation Committee on Disarmament, the United States seeks a total ban on all chemical weapons.

Since the first days of my Administration, we have been working on our approach to the crucial issue of strategic arms control negotiations with the Soviet Union. The study and analysis required have been complex and difficult. They had to be undertaken deliberately, thoroughly, and correctly. We have laid a solid basis for these negotiations; we are consulting with Congressional leaders and with our allies, and we are now ready to proceed.

The main threat to peace posed by nuclear weapons today is instability of the nuclear balance. This is due to the increasingly destructive potential of the massive Soviet buildup in its ballistic missile force.

Therefore, our goal is to enhance deterrence and achieve stability through significant reductions in the most destabilizing nuclear systems—ballistic missiles, and especially intercontinental ballistic missiles—while maintaining a nuclear capability sufficient to deter conflict, underwrite our national security, and meet our commitment to allies and friends.

For the immediate future, I am asking my START [Strategic Arms Reduction Talks] negotiating team to propose to their Soviet counterparts a practical, phased reduction plan. The focus of our efforts will be to reduce significantly the most destabilizing systems—ballistic missiles—the number of warheads they carry, and their overall destructive potential.

At the end of the first phase of the START reductions, I expect ballistic missile warheads—the most serious threat we face—to be reduced to equal ceilings at least a third below current levels. To enhance stability, I would ask that no more than half of those warheads be land-based. I hope that these warhead reductions, as well as significant reductions in missiles themselves, could be achieved as rapidly as possible.

In a second phase, we will seek to achieve an equal ceiling on other elements of our strategic nuclear forces, including limits on ballistic missile throwweight at less than current American levels. In both phases, we shall insist on verification procedures to ensure compliance with the agreement.

The monumental task of reducing and reshaping our strategic forces to enhance stability will take many years of concentrated effort. But I believe that it will be possible to reduce the risks of war by removing the instabilities that now exist and by dismantling the nuclear menace.

I have written to President Brezhnev and directed Secretary [of State] Haig to approach the Soviet Government concerning the initiation of formal negotiations on the reduction of strategic nuclear arms—START—at the earliest possible opportunity. We hope negotiations will begin by the end of June.

We will negotiate seriously, in good faith, and carefully consider all proposals made by the Soviet Union. If they approach these negotiations in the same spirit, I am confident that together we can achieve an agreement of enduring value that reduces the number of nuclear weapons, halts the growth in strategic forces, and opens the way to even more far-reaching steps in the future.

I hope the commencement today will also mark the commencement of a new era—in both senses of the word, a new start—toward a more peaceful, more secure world.

The fifth and final point I propose for East-West relations is dialogue. I have always believed that problems can be solved when people talk to each other instead of about each other. I have already expressed my own desire to meet with President Brezhnev in New York next month. If this cannot be done, I would hope we could arrange a future meeting where positive results can be anticipated.

And when we sit down, I will tell President Brezhnev that the United States is ready to build a new understanding based upon the principles I have outlined here today. I will tell him that his government and his people have nothing to fear from the United States. The free nations living at peace in the world community can vouch for the fact that we seek only harmony. And I will ask President Brezhnev why our two nations cannot practice mutual restraint. Why can't our peoples enjoy the benefits that would flow from real cooperation? Why can't we reduce the number of horrendous weapons?

Perhaps I should also speak to him of this school and the young graduates who are leaving it today—of your hopes for the future, of your deep desire for peace, and yet of your strong commitment to defend your values if threatened. Perhaps if he could someday attend such a ceremony as this, he would better understand America. In the only system he knows, you would be here by the decision of government, and on this day the government would be represented here telling many of you where you were going to work after your graduation.

But as we go to Europe for the talks and as we proceed on the important challenges facing this country, I want you to know I will be thinking of you and Eureka and what you represent. In one of my yearbooks I remember reading that, "The work of the prairie is to be the soil for the growth of a strong Western culture." I believe Eureka is fulfilling that work. You, the members of the 1982 graduating class, are this year's harvest.

Eureka is an institution, and you as individuals are sustaining the best of Western man's ideals. As a fellow graduate and in the office I hold, I will do my best to uphold these same ideals.

1982

A CRUSADE FOR FREEDOM

(Military Strength Is A Prerequisite For Peace)

Speaking to the British Parliament, London, England, June 8th

20.

The journey of which this visit forms a part is a long one. Already it has taken me to two great cities of the West—Rome and Paris—and to the Economic Summit at Versailles. There, once again, our sister democracies have proved that, even in a time of severe economic strain, free people can work together freely and voluntarily to address problems as serious as inflation, unemployment, trade and economic development in a spirit of cooperation and solidarity.

Other milestones lie ahead later this week. In Germany, we and our NATO allies will discuss measures for our joint defense and America's latest initiatives for a more peaceful, secure world through arms reductions.

Each stop of this trip is important but, among them all, this moment occupies a special place in my heart and the hearts of my countrymen—a moment of kinship and homecoming in these hallowed halls.

Speaking for all Americans, I want to say how very much at home we feel in your house. Every American would, because this is one of democracy's shrines. Here the rights of free people and the processes of representation have been debated and refined.

It has been said that an institution is the lengthening shadow of a man. This institution is the lengthening shadow of all the men and women who have sat here and all those who have voted to send representatives here.

This is my second visit to Great Britain as President of

the United States. My first opportunity to stand on British soil occurred almost a year and a half ago when your Prime Minister graciously hosted a diplomatic dinner at the British Embassy in Washington. Mrs. Thatcher said then that she hoped that I was not distressed to find staring down at me from the grand staircase a portrait of His Royal Majesty, King George III.

She suggested it was best to let bygones be bygones and—in view of our two countries' remarkable friendship in succeeding years—she added that most Englishmen today would agree with Thomas Jefferson that "a little rebellion now and then is a very good thing."

From here I will go to Bonn, and then Berlin, where there stands a grim symbol of power untamed. The Berlin Wall, that dreadful gash across the city, is in its third decade. It is the fitting signature of the regime that built it.

And a few hundred kilometers behind the Berlin Wall there is another symbol. In the center of Warsaw there is a sign that notes the distances to two capitals. In one direction it points toward Moscow. In the other it points toward Brussels, headquarters of Western Europe's tangible unity. The marker says that the distances from Warsaw to Moscow and Warsaw to Brussels are equal. The sign makes this point: Poland is not East or West. Poland is at the center of European civilization. It has contributed mightily to that civilization. It is doing so today by being magnificently unreconciled to oppression.

Poland's struggle to be Poland and to secure the basic rights we often take for granted demonstrates why we dare not take those rights for granted. Gladstone, defending the Reform Bill of 1866, declared: "You cannot fight against the future. Time is on our side." It was easier to believe in the inevitable march of democracy in

Gladstone's day—in that high noon of Victorian optimism.

We are approaching the end of a bloody century plagued by a terrible political invention—totalitarianism. Optimism comes less easily today, not because democracy is less vigorous but because democracy's enemies have refined their instruments of repression. Yet optimism is in order because, day by day, democracy is proving itself to be a not-at-all fragile flower.

From Stettin on the Baltic to Barna on the Black Sea, the regimes planted by totalitarianism have had more than thirty years to establish their legitimacy. But none—not one regime—has yet been able to risk free elections. Regimes planted by bayonets do not take root.

The strength of the Solidarity movement in Poland demonstrates the truth told in an underground joke in the Soviet Union. It is that the Soviet Union would remain a one-party nation even if an opposition party were permitted—because everyone would join that party.

America's time as a player on the stage of world history has been brief. I think understanding this fact has always made you patient with your younger cousins. Well, not always patient. I do recall that on one occasion Sir Winston Churchill said in exasperation about one of our most distinguished diplomats, "He is the only case I know of a bull who carries his china shop with him."

Witty as Sir Winston was, he also had that special attribute of great statesmen: the gift of vision, the willingness to see the future based on the experience of the past.

It is this sense of history, this understanding of the past, that I want to talk with you about today, for it is in remembering what we share of the past that our two nations can make common cause for the future.

We have not inherited an easy world. If developments like the Industrial Revolution, which began here in England, and the gifts of science and technology have made life much easier for us, they have also made it more dangerous. There are threats now to our freedom, indeed, to our very existence, that other generations could never even have imagined.

There is, first, the threat of global war. No President, no Congress, no Prime Minister, no Parliament, can spend a day entirely free of this threat. And I don't have to tell you that in today's world, the existence of nuclear weapons could mean, if not the extinction of mankind, then surely the end of civilization as we know it.

That is why negotiations on intermediate range nuclear forces now under way in Europe and the START talks—Strategic Arms Reduction Talks—which will begin later this month, are not just critical to American or Western policy; they are critical to mankind. Our commitment to early success in these negotiations is firm and unshakable and our purpose is clear: reducing the risk of war by reducing the means of waging war on both sides.

At the same time, there is a threat posed to human freedom by the enormous power of the modern state. History teaches the danger of government that overreaches: political control takes precedence over free economic growth; secret police, mindless bureaucracy—all combining to stifle individual excellence and personal freedom.

Now I am aware that among us here and throughout Europe there is legitimate disagreement over the extent to which the public sector should play a role in a nation's economy and life. But on one point all of us are united: our abhorrence of dictatorship in all its forms but most particularly totalitarianism and the terrible inhumanities it has caused in our time: the Great Purge, Auschwitz and Dachau, the Gulag and Cambodia.

Historians looking back at our time will note the consistent restraint and peaceful intentions of the West. They will note that it was the democracies who refused to use the threat of their nuclear monopoly in the '40s and early '50s for territorial or imperial gain. Had that nuclear monopoly been in the hands of the Communist world, the map of Europe, indeed, the world, would look very different today. And certainly they will note it was not the democracies that invaded Afghanistan or suppressed Polish Solidarity or used chemical and toxin warfare in Afghanistan or Southeast Asia.

If history teaches anything, it teaches that self-delusion in the face of unpleasant facts is folly. We see around us today the marks of our terrible dilemma—predictions of doomsday, anti-nuclear demonstrations, an arms race in which the West must, for its own protection, be an unwilling participant. At the same time, we see totalitarian forces in the world who seek subversion and conflict around the globe to further their barbarous assault on the human spirit.

What, then, is our course? Must civilization perish in a hail of fiery atoms? Must freedom wither in a quiet, deadening accommodation with totalitarian evil? Sir Winston Churchill refused to accept the inevitability of war or even that it was imminent. He said, "I do not believe that Soviet Russia desires war. What they desire is the fruits of war and the indefinite expansion of their power and doctrines. But what we have to consider here today while time remains, is the permanent prevention of war and the establishment of conditions of freedom and democracy as rapidly as possible in all countries."

This is precisely our mission today: to preserve freedom as well as peace. It may not be easy to see, but I believe we live now at a turning point.

In an ironic sense, Karl Marx was right. We are witnessing today a great revolutionary crisis—a crisis where the demands of the economic order are colliding directly with those of the political order. But the crisis is happening not in the free, non-Marxist West, but in the home of Marxism-Leninism, the Soviet Union.

It is the Soviet Union that runs against the tide of history by denying freedom and human dignity to its citizens. It also is in deep economic difficulty. The rate of growth in the Soviet gross national product has been steadily declining since the '50s and is less than half of what it was then. The dimensions of this failure are astounding: a country which employs one-fifth of its population in agriculture is unable to feed its own people.

Were it not for the tiny private sector tolerated in Soviet agriculture, the country might be on the brink of famine. These private plots occupy a bare 3 percent of the arable land but account for nearly one-quarter of Soviet farm output and nearly one-third of meat products and vegetables.

Overcentralized, with little or no incentives, year after year, the Soviet system pours its best resource into the making of instruments of destruction. The constant shrinkage of economic growth combined with the growth of military production is putting a heavy strain on the Soviet people.

What we see here is a political structure that no longer corresponds to its economic base, a society where productive forces are hampered by political ones.

The decay of the Soviet experiment should come as no surprise to us. Wherever the comparisons have been made between free and closed societies—West Germany and East Germany, Austria and Czechoslovakia, Malaysia and Vietnam—it is the democratic countries that are prosperous and responsive to the needs of their people.

And one of the simple but overwhelming facts of our time is this: of all the millions of refugees we have seen in the modern world, their flight is always away from, not toward, the Communist world. Today on the NATO line, our military forces face east to prevent a possible invasion. On the other side of the line, the Soviet forces also face east—to prevent their people from leaving.

The hard evidence of totalitarian rule has caused in mankind an uprising of the intellect and will. Whether it is the growth of the new schools of economics in America or England or the appearance of the so-called new philosophers in France, there is one unifying thread running through the intellectual work of these groups: rejection of the arbitrary power of the state, the refusal to subordinate the rights of the individual to the superstate, the realization that collectivism stifles all the best human impulses.

Since the Exodus from Egypt, historians have written of those who sacrificed and struggled for freedom: the stand at Thermopylae, the revolt of Spartacus, the storming of the Bastille, the Warsaw uprising in World War II.

More recently we have seen evidence of this same human impulse in one of the developing nations in Central America. For months and months the world news media covered the fighting in El Salvador. Day after day, we were treated to stories and film slanted toward the brave freedom fighters battling oppressive government forces in behalf of the silent, suffering people of that tortured country.

Then, one day those silent suffering people were offered a chance to vote to choose the kind of government they wanted. Suddenly the freedom fighters in the hills were exposed for what they really are: Cuban-backed guerrillas who want power for themselves and their backers, not democracy for the people.

They threatened death to anyone who voted, and destroyed hundreds of buses and trucks to keep people from getting to the polling places. But on election day, the people of El Salvador, an unprecedented 1.4 million of them, braved ambush and gunfire, trudging miles to vote for freedom.

They stood for hours in the hot sun waiting for their turn to vote. Members of our Congress who went there as observers told me of a woman wounded by rifle fire who refused to leave the line to have her wound treated until after she had voted.

A grandmother, who had been told by the guerrillas she would be killed when she returned from the polls, told the guerrillas, "You can kill me, kill my family, kill my neighbors, but you can't kill us all." The real freedom fighters of El Salvador turned out to be the people of that country, the young, the old, and the in-between. Strange, but there has been little if any news coverage of that war since the election.

Perhaps they'll say it's because there are newer struggles now. On distant islands in the South Atlantic, young men are fighting for Britain. And, yes, voices have been raised protesting their sacrifice for lumps of rock and earth so far away. But those young men aren't fighting for mere real estate.

They fight for a cause, for the belief that armed aggression must not be allowed to succeed, and that people must participate in the decisions of government under the rule of law. If there had been firmer support for that principle some forty-five years ago, perhaps our generation wouldn't have suffered the bloodletting of World War II.

In the Middle East, the guns sound once more, this time in Lebanon, a country that for too long has had to endure the tragedy of civil war, terrorism, and foreign intervention and occupation. The fighting in Lebanon on the part of all parties must stop, and Israel must bring its forces home. But this is not enough. We must all work to stamp out the scourge of terrorism that in the Middle East makes war an ever present threat.

But beyond the trouble spots lies a deeper, more positive pattern. Around the world today, the democratic revolution is gathering new strength. In India, a critical test has been passed with the peaceful change of governing political parties. In Africa, Nigeria is moving in remarkable and unmistakable ways to build and strengthen its democratic institutions. In the Caribbean and Central America, sixteen of twenty-four countries have freely elected governments. And in the United Nations, eight of ten developing nations which have joined the body in the past five years are democracies.

In the Communist world as well, man's instinctive desire for freedom and self-determination surfaces again and again. To be sure, there are grim reminders of how brutally the police state attempts to snuff out this quest for self-rule. 1953 in East Germany, 1956 in Hungary, 1968 in Czechoslovakia, 1981 in Poland.

But the struggle continues in Poland, and we know there are even those who strive and suffer for freedom within the confines of the Soviet Union itself. How we conduct ourselves here in the Western democracies will determine whether this trend continues.

No, democracy is not a fragile flower; still it needs

cultivating. If the rest of this century is to witness the gradual growth of freedom and democratic ideals, we must take actions to assist the campaign for democracy.

Some argue that we should encourage democratic change in right-wing dictatorships, but not in Communist regimes. To accept this preposterous notion—some well-meaning people have—is to invite the argument that, once countries achieve a nuclear capability, they should be allowed an undisturbed reign of terror over their own citizens. We reject this course.

As for the Soviet view, Chairman Brezhnev repeatedly has stressed that the competition of ideas and systems must continue, and that this is entirely consistent with relaxation of tension and peace. We ask only that these systems begin by living up to their own constitutions, abiding by their own laws, and complying with the international obligations they have undertaken. We ask only for a process, a direction, a basic code of decency—not for instant transformation.

We cannot ignore the fact that even without our encouragement, there have been and will continue to be repeated explosions against repression in dictatorships. The Soviet Union itself is not immune to this reality. Any system is inherently unstable that has no peaceful means to legitimize its leaders. In such cases, the very repressiveness of the state ultimately drives people to resist it—if necessary, by force.

While we must be cautious about forcing the pace of change, we must not hesitate to declare our ultimate objectives and to take concrete actions to move toward them. We must be staunch in our conviction that freedom is not the sole prerogative of a lucky few but the inalienable and universal right of all human beings. So states the United

Nations' Universal Declaration of Human Rights—which, among other things, guarantees free elections.

The objective I propose is quite simple to state: To foster the infrastructure of democracy—the system of a free press, unions, political parties, universities—which allows a people to choose their own way, to develop their own culture, to reconcile their own differences through peaceful means.

This is not cultural imperialism; it is providing the means for genuine self-determination and protection for diversity. Democracy already flourishes in countries with very different cultures and historical experiences. It would be cultural condescension, or worse, to say that any people prefer dictatorship to democracy.

Who would voluntarily choose not to have the right to vote; decide to purchase government propaganda handouts instead of independent newspapers; prefer government to worker-controlled unions; opt for land to be owned by the state instead of those who till it; want government repression of religious liberty; a single political party instead of a free choice; a rigid cultural orthodoxy instead of democratic tolerance and diversity?

Since 1917, the Soviet Union has given covert political training and assistance to Marxist-Leninists in many countries. Of course, it also has promoted the use of violence and subversion by these same forces.

Over the past several decades, West European and other Social Democrats, Christian Democrats and Liberals have offered open assistance to fraternal political and social institutions to bring about peaceful and democratic progress. Appropriately for a vigorous new democracy, the Federal Republic of Germany's political foundations have become a major force in this effort.

We in America now intend to take additional steps, as many of our allies have already done, toward realizing this same goal. The chairmen and other leaders of the National Republican and Democratic Party organizations are initiating a study with the bipartisan American Political Foundation to determine how the United States can best contribute—as a nation—to the global campaign for democracy now gathering force.

They will have the cooperation of Congressional leaders of both parties, along with representatives of business, labor, and other major institutions in our society. I look forward to receiving their recommendations and to working with these institutions and the Congress in the common task of strengthening democracy throughout the world.

It is time that we committed ourselves as a nation—in both the public and private sectors—to assisting democratic development.

We plan to consult with leaders of other nations as well. There is a proposal before the Council of Europe to invite parliamentarians from democratic countries to a meeting next year in Strasbourg. That prestigious gathering could consider ways to help democratic political movements.

This November in Washington there will take place an international meeting on free elections, and next spring there will be a conference of world authorities on constitutionalism and self-government hosted by the Chief Justice of the United States.

Authorities from a number of developing and developed countries—judges, philosophers, and politicians with practical experience—have agreed to explore how to turn principle into practice and further the rule of law.

At the same time, we invite the Soviet Union to consider with us how the competition of ideas and values—which it is committed to support—can be conducted on a peaceful and reciprocal basis. For example, I am prepared to offer President Brezhnev an opportunity to speak to the American people on our television if he will allow me the same opportunity with the Soviet people. We also suggest that panels of our newsmen periodically appear on each other's television to discuss major events.

I do not wish to sound overly optimistic, yet the Soviet Union is not immune from the reality of what is going on in the world. It has happened in the past: a small ruling elite either mistakenly attempts to ease domestic unrest through greater repression and foreign adventure, or it chooses a wiser course—it begins to allow its people a voice in their own destiny.

Even if this latter process is not realized soon, I believe the renewed strength of the democratic movement, complemented by a global campaign for freedom, will strengthen the prospects for arms control and a world at peace.

I have discussed on other occasions, including my address on May 9, the elements of Western policies toward the Soviet Union to safeguard our interests and protect the peace. What I am describing now is a plan and a hope for the long term—the march of freedom and democracy which will leave Marxism-Leninism on the ash heap of history as it has left other tyrannies which stifle the freedom and muzzle the self-expression of the people.

That is why we must continue our efforts to strengthen NATO even as we move forward with our zero-option initiative in the negotiations on intermediate range forces and our proposal for a one-third reduction in strategic ballistic missile warheads.

Our military strength is a prerequisite to peace, but

let it be clear we maintain this strength in the hope it will never be used. For the ultimate determinant in the struggle now going on for the world will not be bombs and rockets, but a test of wills and ideas—a trial of spiritual resolve: the values we hold, the beliefs we cherish, the ideals to which we are dedicated.

The British people know that given strong leadership, time, and a little bit of hope, the forces of good ultimately rally and triumph over evil. Here among you is the cradle of self-government, the mother of parliaments. Here is the enduring greatness of the British contribution to mankind, the great civilized ideas: individual liberty, representative government, and the rule of law under God.

I have often wondered about the shyness of some of us in the West about standing for these ideals that have done so much to ease the plight of man and the hardships of our imperfect world. This reluctance to use those vast resources at our command reminds me of the elderly lady whose home was bombed in the blitz. As the rescuers moved about, they found a bottle of brandy she had stored behind the staircase, which was all that was left standing. Since she was barely conscious, one of the workers pulled the cork to give her a taste of it. She came around immediately and said: "Here now, put it back. That's only for emergencies."

Well, the emergency is upon us.

Let us be shy no longer—let us go to our strength. Let us offer hope. Let us tell the world that a new age is not only possible but probable.

During the dark days of the Second World War, when this island was incandescent with courage, Winston Churchill exclaimed about Britain adversaries, "What kind of a people do they think we are?"

Britain's adversaries found out what extraordinary people the British are. But all the democracies paid a terrible price for allowing the dictators to underestimate us. We dare not make that mistake again. So let us ask ourselves: What kind of people do we think we are? And let us answer: Free people, worthy of freedom and determined not only to remain so, but to help others gain their freedom as well.

Sir Winston led his people to great victory in war and then lost an election just as the fruits of victory were about to be enjoyed. But he left office honorably—and, as it turned out, temporarily—knowing that the liberty of his people was more important than the fate of any single leader.

History recalls his greatness in ways no dictator will ever know. And he left us a message of hope for the future, as timely now as when he first uttered it, as opposition leader in the Commons nearly twenty-seven years ago. "When we look back on all the perils through which we have passed and at the mighty foes we have laid low and all the dark and deadly designs we have frustrated, why should we fear for our future? We have," said Sir Winston, "come safely through the worst."

The task I have set forth will long outlive our own generation. But together, we, too, have come through the worst. Let us now begin a major effort to secure the best—a crusade for freedom that will engage the faith and fortitude of the next generation. For the sake of peace and justice, let us move toward a world in which all people are at last free to determine their own destiny.

1982

THE ATLANTIC ALLIANCE

(Arms Control and the Search for Peace)

Speaking to the West German Parliament, Bonn, West Germany, June 9th

21.

I am very honored to speak to you today and, thus, to all the people of Germany. Next year, we will jointly celebrate the 300th anniversary of the first German settlement in the American colonies. The thirteen families who came to our new land were the forerunners of more than seven million German immigrants to the United States. Today, more Americans claim German ancestry than any other.

These Germans cleared and cultivated our land, built our industries and advanced our arts and sciences. In honor of three hundred years of German contributions in America, President Carstens and I have agreed today that he will pay an official visit to the United States in October of 1983 to celebrate the occasion.

The German people have given us so much; we like to think that we've repaid some of that debt. Our American Revolution was the first revolution in modern history to be fought for the right of self-government and the guarantee of civil liberties. That spirit was contagious. In 1849, the Frankfurt Parliament's statement of basic human rights guaranteed freedom of expression, freedom of religion, and equality before the law. These principles live today in the basic law of the Federal Republic. Many peoples to the east still wait for such rights.

The United States is proud of your democracy, but we cannot take credit for it. Heinrich Heine, in speaking of those who built the awe-inspiring cathedrals of medieval times, said that, "in those days people had convictions. We moderns have only opinions and it requires something more than opinions to build a Gothic cathedral." Over the past thirty years, the convictions of the German people have built a cathedral of democracy—a great and glorious testament to your ideals.

We in America genuinely admire the free society you have built in only a few decades. And we understand all the better what you have accomplished because of our own history. Americans speak with the deepest reverence of those Founding Fathers and first citizens who gave us the freedoms we enjoy today. And even though they lived over two hundred years ago, we carry them in our hearts as well as our history books.

I believe future generations of Germans will look to you here today and to your fellow Germans with the same profound respect and appreciation. You have built a free society with an abiding faith in human dignity—the crowning ideal of Western civilization. This will not be forgotten. You will be saluted and honored by this Republic's descendants over the centuries to come.

Yesterday, before the British Parliament, I spoke of the values of Western civilization and the necessity to help all peoples gain the institutions of freedom. In many ways, in many places, our ideals are being tested today. We are meeting this afternoon between two important summits, the gathering of leading industrial democracies at Versailles and the assembling of the Atlantic Alliance here in Bonn tomorrow. Critical and complex problems face us. But our dilemmas will be made easier if we remember our partnership is based on a common Western heritage and a faith in democracy.

I believe this partnership of the Atlantic Alliance nations is motivated primarily by the search for peace. Inner peace for our citizens and peace among nations.

Why inner peace? Because democracy allows for self-expression. It respects man's dignity and creativity. It operates by rule of law, not by terror or coercion. It is government with the consent of the governed. As a result, citizens of the Atlantic Alliance enjoy an unprecedented level of material and spiritual well-being. And they are free to find their own personal peace.

We also seek peace among nations. The Psalmist said, "Seek peace and pursue it." Our foreign policies are based on this principle and directed toward this end. The noblest objective of our diplomacy is the patient and difficult task of reconciling our adversaries to peace. And I know we all look forward to the day when the only industry of war will be the research of historians.

But the simple hope for peace is not enough. We must remember something Friedrich Schiller said, "The most pious man can't stay in peace if it doesn't please his evil neighbor." So, there must be a method to our search, a method that recognizes the dangers and realities of the world. During Chancellor Schmidt's state visit to Washington last year, I said that your Republic was "perched on a cliff of freedom." I wasn't saying anything the German people do not already know. Living as you do in the heart of a divided Europe, you can see more clearly than others that there are governments at peace neither with their own peoples nor the world.

I don't believe any reasonable observer can deny there is a threat to both peace and freedom today. It is as stark as the gash of a border that separates the German people. We are menaced by a power that openly condemns our values and answers our restraint with a relentless military build-up.

We cannot simply assume every nation wants the peace we so earnestly desire. The Polish people would tell us there are those who would use military force to repress others who want only basic rights. The freedom fighters of Afghanistan would tell us as well that the threat of aggression has not receded from the world.

Without a strengthened Atlantic security, the possibility of military coercion will be very great. We must continue to improve our defenses if we are to preserve peace and freedom. This is not an impossible task; for almost forty years we have succeeded in deterring war. Our method has been to organize our defensive capabilities, both nuclear and conventional, so that an aggressor could have no hope of military victory. The alliance has carried its strength not as a battle flag but as a banner of peace. Deterrence has kept that peace, and we must continue to take the steps necessary to make deterrence credible.

This depends in part on a strong America. A national effort, entailing sacrifices by the American people, is now under way to make long-overdue improvements in our military posture. The American people support this effort because they understand how fundamental it is to keeping the peace they so fervently desire.

We also are resolved to maintain the presence of well-equipped and trained forces in Europe, and our strategic forces will be modernized and remain committed to the alliance. By these actions, the people of the United States are saying: "We are with you Germany. You are not alone." Our adversaries would be foolishly mistaken should they gamble that Americans would abandon their alliance responsibilities, no matter how severe the test.

Alliance security depends on a fully credible conventional defense to which all allies contribute. There is a danger that any conflict could escalate to a nuclear war. Strong conventional forces can make the danger of conventional or nuclear conflict more remote. Reasonable strength in and of itself is not bad; it is honorable when used to maintain peace or defend deeply held beliefs.

One of the first chores is to fulfill our commitments to each other by continuing to strengthen our conventional defenses. This must include improving the readiness of our standing forces and the ability of those forces to operate as one. We must also apply the West's technological genius to improving our conventional deterrence.

There can be no doubt that we as an Alliance have the means to improve our conventional defenses. Our peoples hold values of individual liberty and dignity that time and again they have proven willing to defend. Our economic energy vastly exceeds that of our adversaries. Our free system has produced technological advantages that other systems, with their stifling ideologies, cannot hope to equal. All of these resources are available to our defense.

Yes, many of our nations currently are experiencing economic difficulties. Yet we must nevertheless guarantee that our security does not suffer as a result. We've made strides in conventional defense over the last few years despite our economic problems, and we have disproved the pessimists who contend that our efforts are futile. The more we close the conventional gap, the less the risks of aggression or nuclear conflict.

The soil of Germany, and every other ally, is of vital concern to each member of the Alliance, and this fundamental commitment is embodied in the North Atlantic Treaty. But it will be an empty pledge unless we insure that American forces are ready to reinforce Europe, and Europe is ready to receive them. I am encouraged by the recent agreement on wartime host-nation support. This pact strengthens our ability to deter aggression in Europe and demonstrates our common determination to respond to attack.

Just as each ally shares fully in the security of the Alliance, each is responsible for shouldering a fair share of the burden. Now that, of course, often leads to a difference of opinion, and criticism of our Alliance is as old as the partnership itself.

But voices have now been raised on both sides of the Atlantic that mistake the inevitable process of adjustment within the Alliance for a dramatic divergence of interests. Some Americans think that Europeans are too little concerned for their own secuirty; some would unilaterally reduce the number of American troops deployed in Europe. And in Europe itself we hear the idea that the American presence, rather than contributing to peace, either has no deterrent value or actually increases the risk that our allies may be attacked.

These arguments ignore both the history and the reality of the trans-Atlantic coalition.

Let me assure you that the American commitment to Europe remains steady and strong. Europe's shores are our shores. Europe's borders are our borders. And we will stand with you in defense of our heritage of liberty and dignity. The American people recognize Europe's substantial contributions to our joint security. Nowhere is that contribution more evident than here in the Federal Republic.

German citizens host the forces of six nations. German soldiers and reservists provide the backbone of NATO's conventional deterrent in the heartland of Europe. Your Bundeswehr is a model for the integration of defense needs with a democratic way of life. And you have not shrunk from the heavy responsibility of accepting the nuclear forces necessary for deterrence.

I ask your help in fulfilling another responsibility. Many American citizens don't believe that their counterparts in Europe—especially younger citizens—really understand the U.S. presence there. If you will work toward explaining the U.S. role to people on this side of the Atlantic, I will explain it to those on the other side.

In recent months, both in your country and mine, there has been renewed public concern about the threat of nuclear war and the arms buildup. I know it is not easy, especially for the German people, to live in the gale of intimidation that blows from the East.

If I might quote Heine again, he almost foretold the fears of nuclear war when he wrote, "Wild, dark times are rumbling toward us, and the prophet who wishes to write a new apocalypse will have to invent entirely new beasts, and beasts so terrible that the ancient animal symbols will seem like cooing doves and cupids in comparison." The nuclear threat is a terrible beast. Perhaps the banner carried in one of the nuclear demonstrations here in Germany said it best. The sign read, "I am afraid." I know of no Western leader who doesn't sympathize with that earnest plea. To those who march for peace, my heart is with you. I would be at the head of your parade if I believed marching alone could bring about a more secure world. And to the 2,800 women in Filderstadt who sent a petition for peace to President Brezhnev and myself, let me say I, myself, would sign your petition if I thought it could bring about harmony. I understand your genuine concerns. The women of Filderstadt and I share the same goal. The question is how to proceed. We must think through the consequences of how we reduce the dangers to peace.

Those who advocate that we unilaterally forego the modernization of our forces must prove that this will enhance our security and lead to moderation by the other side—in short, that it will advance, rather than undermine, the preservation of the peace. The weight of recent history does not support this notion.

Those who demand that we renounce the use of a crucial element of our deterrent strategy must show how this would decrease the likelihood of war. It is only by comparison with a nuclear war that the suffering caused by conventional war seems a lesser evil. Our goal must be to deter war of any kind.

And those who decry the failure of arms control efforts to achieve substantial results must consider where the fault lies. I would remind them it is the United States that has proposed to ban land-based intermediate-range nuclear missiles—the missiles most threatening Europe. It is the United States that has proposed and will pursue deep cuts in strategic systems. It is the West that has long sought the detailed exchanges of information on forces and effective verification procedures. And it is dictatorships, not democracies, that need militarism to control their own people and impose their system on others.

We in the West—Germans, Americans, our other allies—are deeply committed to continuing efforts to restrict the arms competition. Common sense demands that we persevere. I invite those who genuinely seek effective and lasting arms control to stand behind the far-reaching proposals that we have put forward. In return, I pledge that we will sustain the closest of consultations with our allies.

On November 18, I outlined a broad and ambitious arms control program. One element calls for reducing land-based intermediate-range nuclear missiles to zero on each side. If carried out, it would eliminate the growing threat to Western Europe posed by the USSR's modern

SS-20 rockets, and it would make unnecessary the NATO decision to deploy American intermediate-range systems. And, by the way, I cannot understand why, among some, there is a greater fear of weapons NATO is to deploy than of weapons the Soviet Union already has deployed. Our proposal is fair because it imposes equal limits and obligations on both sides, and it calls for significant reductions, not merely a capping of an existing high level of destructive power. As you know, we have made this proposal in Geneva, where negotiations have been underway since the end of November last year. We intend to pursue those negotiations intensively. I regard them as a significant test of the Soviet's willingness to enter into meaningful arms control agreements.

On May 9, we proposed to the Soviet Union that Strategic Arms Reductions Talks begin this month in Geneva. The USSR has agreed, and talks will begin on June 29. We in the United States want to focus on the most destabilizing systems, and thus reduce the risk of war. That is why in the first phase we propose to reduce substantially the number of ballistic missile warheads and the missiles themselves. In the second phase, we will seek an equal ceiling on other elements of our strategic forces, including ballistic missile throw weight, at less than current American levels. We will handle cruise missiles and bombers in an equitable fashion. We will negotiate in good faith and undertake these talks with the same seriousness of purpose that has marked our preparations over the last several months.

Another element of the program I outlined was a call for reductions in conventional forces in Europe. From the earliest postwar years, the Western democracies have faced the ominous reality that massive Soviet conventional forces would remain stationed where they do not belong. The muscle of Soviet forces in Central Europe far exceeds legitimate defense needs. Their presence is made more threatening still by a military doctrine that emphasizes mobility and surprise attack. And, as history shows, these troops have built a legacy of intimidation and repression.

In response, the NATO allies must show they have the will and capacity to deter any conventional attack or any attempt to intimidate us. Yet, we also will continue the search for responsible ways to reduce NATO and Warsaw Pact military personnel to equal levels.

In recent weeks, we in the Alliance have consulted on how best to invigorate the Vienna negotiations on Mutual and Balanced Force Reductions. Based on these consultations, Western representatives in the Vienna talks soon will make a proposal by which the two alliances would reduce their respective ground force personnel in verifiable stages to a total of 700,000 men and their combined ground and air force personnel to a level of 900,000 men.

While the agreement would not eliminate the threat nor spare our citizens the task of maintaining a substantial defensive force, it could constitute a major step toward a safer Europe for both East and West. It could lead to military stability at lower levels and lessen the dangers of miscalculation and of surprise attack. And it also would demonstrate the political will of the two alliances to enhance stability by limiting their forces in the central area of their military competition.

The West has established a clear set of goals. We, as an Alliance, will press forward with plans to improve our own conventional forces in Europe. At the same time, we propose an arms control agreement to equalize conventional forces at a significantly lower level.

We will move ahead with our preparations to modernize our nuclear forces in Europe. But, again, we also will work unceasingly to gain acceptance in Geneva of our proposal to ban land-based intermediate-range nuclear missles.

In the United States, we will move forward with the plans I announced last year to modernize our strategic nuclear forces, which play so vital a role in maintaining peace by deterring war. Yet, we also have proposed that Strategic Arms Reductions Talks begin, and we will pursue them determinedly.

In each of these areas, our policies are based on the conviction that a stable military balance at the lowest possible level will help further the cause of peace. The other side will respond in good faith to these initiatives only if it believes we are resolved to provide for our own defense. Unless convinced that we will unite and stay united behind these arms control initiatives and modernization programs, our adversaries will seek to divide us from one another and our peoples from their leaders.

I am optimistic about our relationship with the Soviet Union if the Western nations remain true to their values and true to each other. I believe in Western civilization and in its moral power. I believe deeply in the principles the West esteems. And guided by these ideals, I believe we can find a no-nonsense, workable, and lasting policy that will keep the peace.

Earlier, I said the German people had built a remarkable cathedral of democracy. But we still have other work ahead. We must build a cathedral of peace, where nations are safe from war and where people need not fear for their liberties. I've heard the history of the famous cathedral at Cologne—how those beautiful soaring spires miraculously survived the destruction all around them, including part of the church itself.

Let us build a cathedral as the people of Cologne built theirs—with the deepest commitment and determination. Let us build as they did—not just for ourselves but for the generations beyond. For if we construct our peace properly, it will endure as long as the spires of Cologne.

1982

THE REDUCTION OF NUCLEAR ARMS

(Only Genuine Disarmament Can Serve Mankind)

Speaking to the Second Special Session on Disarmament, United Nations, New York City, New York, June 17th

22.

I speak today as both a citizen of the United States and of the world. I come with the heartfelt wishes of my people for peace, bearing honest proposals and looking for genuine progress.

Dag Hammarskjöld said twenty-four years ago this month, "We meet in a time of peace, which is no peace." His words are as true today as they were then.

More than a hundred disputes have disturbed the peace among nations since World War II, and today the threat of nuclear disaster hangs over the lives of all our people. The Bible tells us there will be a time for peace. But, so far this century, mankind has failed to find it.

The United Nations is dedicated to world peace. And its charter clearly prohibits the international use of force. Yet the tide of belligerence continues to rise. The charter's influence has weakened even in the four years since the first special session on disarmament.

We must not only condemn aggression. We must enforce the dictates of our charter and resume the struggle for peace.

The record of history is clear. Citizens of the United States resort to force reluctantly and only when they must. Our foreign policy, as President Eisenhower once said, is not difficult to state. We are for peace, first, last, and always, for very simple reasons. We know that only in a peaceful atmosphere, a peace with justice, one in which we can be confident, can America prosper as we have known prosperity in the past, he said.

He said to those who challenge the truth of those words: let me point out that at the end of World War II we were the only undamaged industrial power in the world. Our military supremacy was unquestioned. We have harnessed the atom and had the ability to unleash its destructive force anywhere in the world. In short, we could have achieved world domination, but that was contrary to the character of our people.

Instead, we wrote a new chapter in the history of mankind.

We used our power and wealth to rebuild the war-ravaged economies of the world, both East and West, including those nations who had been our enemies.

We took the initiative in creating such international institutions as this United Nations where leaders of good will could come together to build bridges for peace and prosperity.

America has no territorial ambitions.

We occupy no countries and we have built no walls to lock our people in. Our commitment to self determination, freedom, and peace is the very soul of America. That commitment is as strong today as it ever was.

The United States has fought four wars in my lifetime. In each, we struggled to defend freedom and democracy.

We were never the aggressors

America's strength and, yes, her military power, have been a force for peace, not conquest. For democracy, not despotism. For freedom, not tyranny.

Watching, as I have, succeeding generations of

American youth bleed their lives on the farflung battlefields to protect our ideals and secure the rule of law, I have known how important it is to deter conflicts.

But since coming to the Presidency, the enormity of the responsibility of this office has made my commitment even deeper. I believe that responsibility is shared by all of us here today.

On our recent trip to Europe, my wife, Nancy, told me of a bronze statue twenty-two feet high that she saw on a cliff on the coast of France. The beach at the base of that cliff is called St. Laurent. But countless American family Bibles have written it in a flyleaf and know it as Omaha Beach. The pastoral quiet of that French countryside is in marked contrast to the bloody violence that took place there on a June day thirty-eight years ago when the Allies stormed the Continent. At the end of just one day of battle, 10,500 Americans were wounded, missing, or killed in what became known as the Normandy landing. The statue atop that cliff is called "The Spirit of American Youth Rising From the Waves." Its image of sacrifice is almost too powerful to describe.

The pain of war is still vivid in our national memory. It sends me to this special session of the United Nations eager to comply with the plea of Pope Paul VI when he spoke in this chamber nearly seventeen years ago. "If you want to be brothers," His Holiness said, "let the arms fall from your hands."

Well, we Americans yearn to let them go. But we need more than mere words. More than empty promises before we can proceed.

We look around the world and see rampant conflict and aggression.

There are many sources of this conflict—expansionist ambition, local rivalries, the striving to obtain justice and security.

We must all work to resolve such discord by peaceful means and to prevent it from escalation.

In the nuclear era, the major powers bear a special responsibility to ease these sources of conflict and to refrain from aggression.

And that's why we're so deeply concerned by Soviet conduct.

Since World War II, the record of tyranny has included Soviet violation of the Yalta Agreements leading to domination of Eastern Europe, symbolized by the Berlin wall, a grim, gray monument to repression that I visited just a week ago. It includes the takeovers of Czechoslovakia, Hungary, and Afghanistan and the ruthless repression of the proud people of Poland.

Soviet sponsored guerrillas and terrorists are at work in Central and South America, in Africa, the Middle East, in the Caribbean, and in Europe, violating human rights and unnerving the world with violence. Communist atrocities in Southeast Asia, Afghanistan and elsewhere continue to shock the free world as refugees escape to tell of their horror.

The decade of so-called detente witnessed the most massive Soviet buildup of military power in history.

They increased their defense spending by 40 percent while American defense actually declined in the same real terms.

Soviet aggression and support for violence around the world have eroded the confidence needed for arms negotiations.

While we exercise unilateral restraint, they forged

ahead and today possess nuclear and conventional forces far in excess of an adequate deterrent capability. Soviet oppression is not limited to the countries they invade.

At the very time the Soviet Union is trying to manipulate the peace movement in the West, it is stifling a budding peace movement at home. In Moscow, banners are scuttled, buttons are snatched, and demonstrators are arrested when even a few people dare to speak about their fears.

Eleanor Roosevelt, one of our first ambassadors to this body, reminded us that the high-sounding words of tyrants stand in bleak contradiction to their deeds. Their promises, she said, are in deep contrast to their performances.

My country learned a bitter lesson in this century. The scourge of tyranny cannot be stopped with words alone.

So we have embarked on an effort to renew our strength that had fallen dangerously low.

We refuse to become weaker while potential adversaries remain committed to their imperialist adventures.

My people have sent me here today to speak for them as citizens of the world, which they truly are.

For we Americans are drawn from every nationality represented in this chamber today.

We understand that men and women of every race and creed can and must work together for peace.

We stand ready to take the next steps down the road of cooperation through verifiable arms reduction.

Agreements on arms control and disarmament can be useful in reinforcing peace, but they're not magic. We should not confuse the signing of agreements with the solving of problems. Simply collecting agreements will not bring peace. Agreements genuinely reinforce peace only when they are kept. Otherwise we are building a paper castle that will be blown away by the winds of war.

Let me repeat. We need deeds, not words, to convince us of Soviet sincerity should they choose to join us on this path.

Since the end of World War II, the United States has been the leader in serious disarmament and arms control proposals. In 1946, in what became known as the Baruch Plan, the United States submitted a proposal for control of nuclear weapons and nuclear energy by an international authority. The Soviets rejected this plan.

In 1955, President Eisenhower made his open skies proposal, under which the United States and the Soviet Union would have exchanged blueprints of military establishments and provided for aerial reconnaissance. The Soviets rejected this plan.

In 1963, the limited test ban treaty came into force. This treaty ended nuclear weapons testing in the atmosphere, outer space, or under water by participating nations.

In 1970, the treaty on the nonproliferation of nuclear weapons took effect. The United States played a major role in this key effort to prevent the spread of nuclear explosives and to provide for international safeguards on civil nuclear activities.

My country remains deeply committed to those objectives today and to strengthening the nonproliferation framework. This is essential to international security.

In the early 1970s, again at United States' urging, agreements were reached between the United States and the USSR providing for ceilings on some categories of weapons. They could have been more meaningful if

Soviet actions had shown restraint and commitment to stability at lower levels of force.

The United Nations designated the 1970s as the first disarmament decade. But good intentions were not enough. In reality that ten-year period included an unprecedented buildup in military weapons and the flaring of aggression and use of force in almost every region of the world.

We are now in the second disarmament decade. The task at hand is to assure civilized behavior among nations, to unite behind an agenda of peace.

Over the past seven months the United States has put forward a broad-based, comprehensive series of proposals to reduce the risk of war. We have proposed four major points as an agenda for peace:

- Elimination of land-based intermediate-range missiles;
- A one-third reduction in strategic ballistic missile warheads;
- A substantial reduction in NATO and Warsaw Pact ground and air forces;
- And new safeguards to reduce the risk of accidental war.

We urge the Soviet Union today to join with us in this quest. We must act, not for ourselves alone, but for all mankind.

On November 18 of last year, I announced United States objectives in arms control agreements. They must be equitable and militarily significant. They must stabilize forces at lower levels, and they must be verifiable.

The United States and its allies have made specific, reasonable and equitable proposals.

In February, our negotiating team in Geneva offered

the Soviet Union a draft treaty on intermediate-range nuclear forces. We offered to cancel deployment of our Pershing II ballistic missiles and ground-launched cruise missiles in exchange for Soviet elimination of the SS-20, SS-4 and SS-5 missiles. This proposal would eliminate with one stroke those systems about which both sides have expressed the greatest concern.

The United States is also looking forward to beginning negotiations on strategic arms reductions with the Soviet Union in less than two weeks. We will work hard to make these talks an opportunity for real progress in our quest for peace.

On May 9, I announced a phased approach to the reduction of strategic arms. In a first phase, the number of ballistic missile warheads on each side would be reduced to about 5,000. No more than half the remaining warheads would be on land-based missiles. All ballistic missiles would be reduced to an equal level at about one-half the current United States number. In the second phase, we would reduce each side's overall destructive power to equal levels, including a mutual ceiling on ballistic missile throw-weight below the current U.S. level.

We are also prepared to discuss other elements of the strategic balance.

Before I returned from Europe last week I met in Bonn with the leaders of the North Atlantic Treaty Organization. We agreed to introduce a major new Western initiative for the Vienna negotiations on mutual and balanced force reductions. Our approach calls for common collective ceilings for both NATO and the Warsaw Treaty organization. After seven years, there would be a total of 700,000 ground forces and 900,000 ground and air force personnel combined. It also includes a package of associated measures to encourage cooperation and verify compliance. We urge the Soviet Union and members of the Warsaw Pact to view our Western proposal as a means to reach agreement in Vienna after nine long years of inconclusive talks. We also urge them to implement the 1975 Helsinki agreement on security and cooperation in Europe.

Let me stress that for agreements to work, both sides must be able to verify compliance.

The building of mutual confidence in compliance can only be achieved through greater openness.

I encourage the special session on disarmament to endorse the importance of these principles in arms control agreements.

I have instructed our representatives at the forty-nation committee on disarmament to renew emphasis on verification and compliance. Based on a U.S. proposal, a committee has been formed to examine these issues as they relate to restrictions on nuclear testing.

We are also pressing the need for effective verification provisions in agreements banning chemical weapons. The use of chemical and biological weapons has long been viewed with revulsion by civilized nations. No peace-making institution can ignore the use of those dreaded weapons and still live up to its mission.

The need for a truly effective and verifiable chemical weapons agreement has been highlighted by recent events. The Soviet Union and their allies are violating the Geneva protocol of 1925, related rules of international law, and the 1972 biological weapons convention. There is conclusive evidence that the Soviet Government has provided toxins for use in Laos and Kampuchea and are themselves using chemical weapons against freedom fighters in Afghanistan.

We have repeatedly protested to the Soviet Government as well as to the Governments of Laos and Vietnam their use of chemical and toxin weapons.

We call upon them now to grant full and free access to their countries or to territories they control so that United Nations experts can conduct an effective independent investigation to verify cessation of these horrors.

Evidence of noncompliance with existing arms control agreements underscores the need to approach negotiation of any new agreements with care.

The democracies of the West are open societies. Information on our defenses is available to our citizens, our elected officials, and the world. We do not hesitate to inform potential adversaries of our military forces and ask in return for the same information concerning theirs.

The amount and type of military spending by a country is important for the world to know as a measure of its intentions and the threat that country may pose to its neighbors.

The Soviet Union and other closed societies go to extraordinary lengths to hide their true military spending not only from other nations, but from their own people. This practice contributes to distrust and fear about their intentions.

Today the United States proposes an international conference on military expenditures to build on the work of this body in developing a common system for accounting and reporting. We urge the Soviet Union in particular to join this effort in good faith, to revise the universally discredited official figures it publishes, and to join with us in giving the world a true account of the resources we allocate to our armed forces.

Last Friday in Berlin, I said that I would leave no stone unturned in the effort to reinforce peace and lessen the risk of war. It's been clear to me steps should be taken to improve mutual communication, confidence and lessen the likelihood of misinterpretation. I have, therefore, directed the exploration of ways to increase understanding and communication between the United States and the Soviet Union in times of peace and of crisis.

We would approach the Soviet Union with proposals for reciprocal exchanges in such areas as advanced notification of major strategic exercises that otherwise might be misinterpreted, advanced notification of ICBM [Intercontinental Ballistic Missile] launches within, as well as beyond national boundaries, and an expanded exchange of strategic forces data. While substantial information on U.S. activities and forces in these areas already is provided, I believe that jointly and regularly sharing information would represent a qualitative improvement in the strategic nuclear environment and would help reduce the chance of misunderstanding.

I call upon the Soviet Union to join the United States in exploring these possibilities to build confidence and I ask for your support of our efforts.

One of the major items before this conference is the development of a comprehensive program of disarmament. We support the effort to chart a course of realistic and effective measures in the quest for peace.

I have come to this hall to call for international recommitment to the basic tenets of the United Nations charter, that all members practice tolerance and live together in peace as good neighbors under the rule of law forsaking armed force as a means of settling disputes between nations.

America urges you to support the agenda for peace that I have outlined today. We ask you to reinforce the bilateral and multilateral arms-control negotiations between members of NATO and the Warsaw Pact and to rededicate yourselves to maintaining international peace and security and removing threats to peace.

We who have signed the U.N. Charter have pledged to refrain from the threat or use of force against the territory or independence of any state.

In these times when more and more lawless acts are going unpunished, as some members of this very body show a growing disregard for the U.N. Charter, the peace-loving nations of the world must condemn aggression and pledge again to act in a way that is worthy of the ideals that we have endorsed.

Let us finally make the Charter live.

In late spring, thirty-seven years ago, representatives of fifty nations gathered on the other side of this continent in the San Francisco Opera House. The League of Nations had crumbled and World War II still raged. But those men and nations were determined to find peace. The result was this charter for peace that is the framework of the United Nations. President Harry Truman spoke of the revival of an old faith. He said the everlasting moral force of justice, prompting that United Nations conference remains strong in America and in other countries where speech is free and citizens have the right to gather and make their opinions known. And President Truman said if we should pay merely lip service to inspiring ideals and later do violence to simple justice we would draw down upon us the bitter wrath of generations yet unborn.

Those words of Harry Truman have special meaning for us today as we live with the potential to destroy civilization. We must learn to live together in peace, he said. We must build a new world, a far better world.

What a better world it would be if the guns were silenced, if neighbor no longer encroached on neighbor and if all peoples were free to reap the rewards of their toil and determine their own destiny and system of government, whatever their choice.

During my recent audience with his Holiness Pope John Paul II, I gave him the pledge of the American people to do everything possible for peace and arms reduction. The American people believe forging real and lasting peace to be their sacred trust. Let us never forget that such a peace would be a terrible hoax if the world was no longer blessed with freedom and respect for human rights.

The United Nations, Hammarskjöld said, was born out of the cataclysms of war. It should justify the sacrifices of all those who have died for freedom and justice. It is our duty to the past, Hammarskjöld said and it is our duty to the future so to serve both our nations and the world.

As both patriots of our nations and the hope of all the world, let those of us assembled here in the name of peace deepen our understandings, renew our commitment to the rule of law, and take new and bolder steps to calm an uneasy world.

Can any delegate here deny that in so doing he would be doing what the people, the rank and file of his own country or her own country, want him or her to do? Isn't it time for us to really represent the deepest, most heartfelt yearnings of all of our people?

Let no nation abuse this common longing to be free of

fear. We must not manipulate our people by playing upon their nightmares. We must serve mankind through genuine disarmament.

With God's help, we can secure life and freedom for generations to come.

SELECTED BIBLIOGRAPHY

Boyarsky, Bill. *The Rise of Ronald Reagan*. New York: Random House, 1968.

Boyarsky, Bill. *Ronald Reagan, His Life and Rise to the Presidency*. New York: Random House, 1981.

Edwards, Lee. *Ronald Reagan: A Political Biography*. Ottawa, Ill.: Caroline House, 1981.

Evans, Rowland and Novak, Robert. *The Reagan Revolution*. New York: E. P. Dutton, 1981.

Hannaford, Peter. *The Reagans, A Personal Portrait*. New York: Coward, McCann and Geoghegen, Inc., 1983.

Hobbs, Charles D. *Ronald Reagan's Call to Action: Realistic Democracy*. Chicago, Ill.: Nelson-Hall, 1976.

Reagan, Ronald. *The Creative Society*. Old Greenwich, Conn.: Devin-Adair, 1968.

Reagan, Ronald and Hubler, Richard G. *Where's the Rest of Me?* New York: Duell, Sloan, Pearce, 1965.

Smith, Hedrick; Clymer, Adam; Silk, Leonard; Lindsey, Robert; Burt, Richard. *Reagan the Man, the President*. New York: Macmillan, 1980.

Valis, Wayne H., ed. *The Future Under President Reagan*. Westport, Conn.: Arlington House, 1981.

Van der Linden, Frank. *The Real Reagan*. New York: Morrow, 1981.

Von Damm, Helene. *Sincerely Ronald Reagan*. Ottawa, Ill.: Green Hill, 1976.

White, Clifton F. *Why Reagan Won*. Chicago, Ill.: Regnery Gateway, 1981.